LINGUISTICS IN
AMERICA 1769–1924

ROUTLEDGE HISTORY OF LINGUISTIC THOUGHT SERIES

Series Editor: Talbot J. Taylor,
College of William and Mary,
Williamsburg, Virginia

LINGUISTICS IN AMERICA 1769–1924

A Critical History

JULIE TETEL ANDRESEN

ROUTLEDGE

London and New York

First published 1990
by Routledge
11 New Fetter Lane, London EC4P 4EE

Simultaneously published in the USA and Canada
by Routledge
a division of Routledge, Chapman and Hall, Inc.
29 West 35th Street, New York, NY 10001

Set in 10/12pt Baskerville by
Mayhew Typesetting, Bristol
Printed in Great Britain by
T.J. Press, Padstow, Cornwall

British Library Cataloguing in Publication Data

Andresen, Julie Tetel
Linguistics in America, 1769–1924 : a Critical
history. – (Routledge history of linguistic thought
series)
1. United States. Linguistics history
I. Title
410′.973

Library of Congress Cataloging in Publication Data

Andresen, Julie Tetel, 1950–
Linguistics in America, 1769–1924: a critical history / Julie
Tetel Andresen.
p. cm. – (Routledge history of linguistic thought series)
Includes bibliographies and index.
ISBN 0-415-02228-2
1. Linguistics – United States – History. I. Title. II. Series.
P81.U5A64   1990-10385
410′.973–dc20

CONTENTS

PREFACE: AMERICAN LINGUISTICS CIRCA 1925

It is the privilege and, in fact, business of the historian to "cheat": to peek ahead at any given moment in the historical record, to see "what happens next." Exercising this privilege to the limit, I will begin my story at the end, that is, on December 28, 1924, the date of the founding of the Linguistic Society of America. Better yet, I will begin just beyond that end and attempt to evoke "what happens next" in American linguistics in the year 1925.

Given my initial orientation to the founding of the LSA, I will begin my brief survey with the first issue of *Language*. The lead article in this issue is Edward Sapir's "Sound Patterns in Language." Here Sapir argues against the position that phonetic processes can be understood in mechanical terms, as relatively simple sensorimotor habits (i.e. the basic nineteenth-century position), and argues instead for a subtle, psychological interpretation of these processes in terms of phonemes which, according to Sapir, are located in the "inner configuration of the sound system of a language." Sapir's article is followed, in a prophetic way, by Albert P. Weiss's article "Linguistics and Psychology," an essay where the terms "behavior," "stimulus," and "response" figure prominently. Thus, the stage is set for "what happens next" in a significant portion of American linguistics, namely, a theoretical schism between Sapir's mentalism and Leonard Bloomfield's Weissian behaviorism.[1]

Leonard Bloomfield, for his part, in 1925 was engaged in professionalizing the discipline of linguistics from his academic base of operation at Ohio State. Bloomfield was, of course, the major driving force behind the creation of the Linguistic Society of America. His prefatory "Why a Linguistic Society?" to the first

1

issue of *Language* pointedly addresses the need for a "professional consciousness" among American linguists. In addition, Bloomfield had already written "A Set of Postulates for the Science of Language" which he based on Weiss's set of postulates for psychology and which he was to publish in the second issue of *Language* (1926). In "Postulates" Bloomfield cites with approval both Sapir's 1921 *Language* and Saussure's *Cours de linguistique générale* (1922) as helpful steps toward the "delimitation of linguistics" and presages the behaviorist scenario to come.[2]

Whatever divisions were to come later in American linguistics, I consistently detect in 1925 a sense of group effort in progress which was focused toward the twin and intertwined goals of 1) carving out a theoretical space in language that was the particular province of the linguist (e.g. Sapir's "inner configuration of the sound system"); and 2) making linguistics a professionally autonomous academic discipline. Another group effort along this line was the provision made by the Linguistic Society of America soon after its founding for summer linguistic institutes. On the individual level, Sapir left his position as the Chief of the Anthropological Section, Geological Survey of Canada, in 1925 to accept his first academic post (University of Chicago).

Philology was in full swing in America in 1925. The journals *Modern Philology*, *American Journal of Philology*, *Journal of the American Oriental Society*, *Journal of English and Germanic Philology* and the *Transactions and Proceedings of the American Philological Association* all produced healthy volumes for the year in the well-plowed fields of the Classics, be it Horace or Homer, and of Sanskrit and the *Vedas*, and of the language and literature of Old, Middle, and Early Modern English. In 1925, Maurice Bloomfield, a student of William Dwight Whitney and Leonard's uncle, drew the following distinction between history and philology: "History . . . may be compared to a pen and ink drawing, philology lays on the colors. History is engaged with what may be called the more external, pragmatic, secular aspects of the human past; philology deals more with its inner, spiritual aspects" (1925: 5). The sense of "inner feeling"/"outer form" is here reinforced.

It is worth speculating why no existing journal and why no existing American society devoted to language studies (e.g. The Modern Language Association, The American Philological Society, the American Oriental Society) could have been reformed from within to meet the new needs that led to the creation of the Linguistic Society of America. Despite the recognition by the founders of the Society that linguistics was an international discipline, there seems to have been a nascent feeling around 1925 for *American* linguistics.[3] A glance at all the above-mentioned journals and societies of the period confirms that they were devoted to traditional European-style topics and methodologies. I suggest that none of them would have been "home-grown" enough for the founders of the LSA.

On the other hand, a publication such as *Dialect Notes* devoted specifically to the American language would not have been "linguistic" enough for Bloomfield's purposes. Incidentally, volume V, part VIII of *Dialect Notes* for 1925 issued a call for "The Need for an American Dialect Dictionary," thereby indicating fairly accurately "what happens next" in American dialect studies.

A journal already existed in 1925 which was both suitably "linguistic" and devoted to uniquely American language concerns, although it was, perhaps, too specialized to serve exclusively as the official journal of the Linguistic Society of America: *The International Journal of American Linguistics*. In 1925, those linguists who were most active in establishing the Linguistic Society of America were also continuing their work on American Indian languages. The third volume of the journal, which Franz Boas had begun in 1917, appeared in 1924–5, and included articles by Boas, Sapir, Bloomfield, John Swanton, and Truman Michelson. The letters from Bloomfield to Michelson and Sapir have recently been published (Hockett 1987). The Bloomfield–Sapir correspondence clusters particularly between January 1924 and June 1925 and fully confirms Bloomfield's enthusiasm both for the Linguistic Society of America and for American Indian languages. In addition to the exchanges of information on various Algonquin languages (mostly phonemic matters), the letters reveal such disparate information as Bloomfield's painfully inflamed feet and how much to pay an informant (Sapir judged $5 a day to be high).

In October of 1925, another new journal was launched which was devoted to language in a specifically American key. This was *American Speech*. The first issue opens without editorial comment on a worthy, but not ground-breaking, discussion of "Conservatism in American Speech." The most interesting article in the issue, from my point of view, is one by Kemp Malone entitled "A

3

Linguistic Patriot.'' It is devoted to the writings of Noah Webster. When I first came across that article, I was gratified to find that a part (however small) of ''what happens next'' in American language studies after 1924 is a return to ''what came before,'' in this case, to Webster's writings from the 1780s onwards. My historiographic sensibility – or whatever aesthetic sense it is that seeks closure – was initially satisfied that my end (1924) could point, even partially, to my beginning (1769).

Personal and aesthetic gratification aside, however, the more I came to think about Kemp Malone's article, the more I began to realize its anecdotal significance to my entire project. It is this: American linguists of today do not think of Noah Webster as having anything to do with the American linguistic past, and even less with the present. Neither, apparently, did American linguists of 1925. After all, Kemp Malone was a foundation member of the Linguistic Society of America, and he published his article on Webster in *American Speech*, and not in, say, *Language*. Now, any number of reasons come to mind why Malone's article on Webster should appropriately appear in *American Speech*, not the least of those being that Malone was one of the original editors of the journal, along with Louise Pound and Arthur Kennedy. More to the point, however, is the implicit separation made in 1925 between those language concerns and interests of a Webster who viewed language, let us say, *in a radically non-autonomous way* and those of a Bloomfield who was heavily invested in autonomizing both the discipline and the profession of ''the science of language.'' It was tacitly decided, in effect, in 1925 that Webster's and Bloomfield's approaches to language belonged in two different places and to two different traditions: Webster's to some narrowly nationalist (read: non-linguistic, non-scientific) tradition (interpret: of no interest to ''real'' linguists); Bloomfield's to the loftier realms of general (read: enjoying all the rigors of German science) linguistics (interpret: though all the while striving for a ''made in America'' touch). Significantly, however, Bloomfield identified the highest unity of ''that noblest of sciences, philology'' to be ''the study of *national* culture,'' as opposed to, say, *human* culture (L. Bloomfield 1925a: 4, note 1).

Whatever benefits this separation of approaches may have brought to the future growth of linguistics in America after 1925, I maintain that, today, it has outlived its usefulness. Furthermore, if there is among American linguists today a continuing perception of separation between those interests (and perhaps it is an unconscious perception, for I have just said that American linguists do not usually think of Webster at all), this perception is the historically contingent product of the *de facto* separation that occurred in 1925. Over the past sixty years and more, this implicit separation has become part of a received history of what it is to do linguistics in this country, and that history necessarily informs current theories and practices.

This received history – how we view "what came before" – is not cast in stone; and although history is not infinitely plastic, I find a lot of "give" in the possibilities of history-writing and think that history-writing's first purpose is to serve the needs of today. It is now time to rewrite – or, more accurately, to write in the first place – a history of linguistics in America, one that incorporates the interests and concerns of a Noah Webster (to name but one) and that acknowledges them as valid, even central, to what American linguistic theory and practice has always been and continues to be.

What do we gain when we do this? First, I have long noticed a tendency for histories of linguistics to isolate the nineteenth-century American linguist William Dwight Whitney, to make of him a solitary mesa rising out from around a very barren surrounding landscape of nineteenth-century American linguistic activity (L. Bloomfield 1933: 16; Labov 1972: 266–70; Anderson 1985: 194–6; Koerner 1986a). However, a rereading and recontextualization of the impetus and import of Webster's views on the American language and its political consequences in the wake of the American Revolution help to anchor and explain the tradition to which Whitney's sociopolitical linguistic thought belongs. When we put Whitney in line with Webster, we gain a very new history of (non-autonomous, sociopolitico-)linguistics.

Second (and in this context of the traditional academic north-east), the name of a third New England linguist who has also written widely on politics may be invoked. Although a comparison of Chomsky's politics and linguistics to Webster's goes well beyond the bounds of this book, the simple juxtaposition of names (Chomsky–Webster) strikes a new image of linguistic thought and suggests new possibilities in linguistic history; and instead of seeing Chomsky's political writings as something separate from his linguistic writings, one might turn the problem around and ask what the two activities have in common, or even ask how they have come to be separated.[4]

For my part, I will be using the term "political" in this book in a conceptual framework that includes "historical" and "contextual." I maintain, at the outset, that all linguistic theories are political, in that they are elaborated in a specific historical context. When speaking of a particular conception of language, say the "political conception" of language, the term "political" will belong in a conceptual framework that includes "non-autonomous," as well. An examination of the shaping and reshaping of the boundary lines between so-called "autonomous" and "non-autonomous" (i.e. political) linguistics is a central task of *Linguistics in America 1769–1924: A Critical History.*

Thus far, I have insisted that developments post-1924 fall beyond my purview. This periodization is somewhat arbitrary, and in any case, the history of language study in America is too complex to start and top cleanly at either of the edges I have chosen. However, the major periodization of the book is not completely without foundation. Similarly, the periodizations of the five chapters are equally motivated but still problematic. They exist, to a certain extent, for organizational convenience. All of my dates may be thought of as bull's-eyes, that is, centers of large, overlapping, and non-discrete targets.

The rationale behind the various periodizations will be discussed in the Introduction, which is also intended to orient the reader to the goals of linguistic historiography and to expose the challenges, assertions, and thematic boundaries of my study. I have permitted myself an Introduction, in addition to this Preface, because I have repeatedly confronted a number of pre- and misconceptions surrounding my material, like so many prophylactics wrapped around the texts; and it has been borne in on me that it is the very historical understanding of these texts that is the disease (thinking here etymologically of "prophylactic") which these preconceptions are supposed to guard against. That is, I am aware, before even beginning my project, that there exists a strong resistance against interpreting American linguistics in a historical and political context.

From the Introduction, I will focus in Chapter 1, "In the Beginning: The Political Conception of Language," on the years 1769 through 1815. During this period, a distinctly political conception of language prevailed in Colonial and post-Colonial America which shared much in common with the anglo-french tradition of eighteenth-century language studies. The principal figure involved in elaborating this conception is Noah Webster, whose general conception of language is supported by the writings of both Benjamin Franklin, who founded the American Philosophical Society in 1769, and Thomas Jefferson, whose vision of language study included an interest in dialect variation, the recording of American Indian languages, and the institutionalization of Anglo-Saxon.

Chapter 2, "From Philadelphia to the Field," concentrates on the years 1815–42. It is closely intertwined with the first chapter to make one extended movement. Since there is the most groundwork to lay in the period 1769–1842, the first two chapters make up half the book. After describing the various expansions that occurred in the first half of the nineteenth century, the chapter returns to an examination of the complex ideological relationship that existed in the early decades of the nineteenth century between the status of American English and of the American Indian languages. Next is reviewed the image of the American Indian languages that the (Euro-)Americans inherited from the eighteenth century. To the negative European perspective on the American Indian languages, the American response is most articulately outlined by John Heckewelder, Peter Duponceau, and John Pickering, the work of the last two men representing essentially "armchair studies." The move to the field is best exemplified by the work of Henry Schoolcraft and Albert Gallatin, which last founded the American Ethnological Society in 1842, the date marking the end of the second chapter. A first codification of American scholarship is represented by Francis Lieber's *Encyclopedia Americana*, first edition 1830, and his general writings on language represent a high degree of linguistic relativism. However, the general spirit of liberalism and expansion would not last forever, and the study of language in America had to contend with the diffusion of German scholarship "back east," resulting in a return to conservatism.

The formal institutionalization of American linguistics occupies the whole of Chapter 3, spanning the years 1842–94, beginning with the founding of the American Oriental Society (the same year at Gallatin's American Ethnological Society) and ending with William Dwight Whitney's death. In this, the central chapter, Whitney's writings and career are of pivotal importance, along with the practical tensions engendered by the transplanting of German scholarship on American soil. I will argue here that, despite Whitney's sophistication in German erudition, his thought belongs to the distinctly franco-anglophone, non-autonomous, i.e. "political," conception of language, which was incompatible with German approaches. It is the particular interest of this chapter, then, to show how Whitney, the most important American academic of the second half of the nineteenth century, conceived of the "science of language" and what he did to promote its development in the United States. Whitney fundamentally shaped the course of American linguistics for several generations by being actively involved in the organization of the American Philological Association (1869), Spelling Reform Association (1876), Modern Language Association (1883), and the American Dialect Society (1889).

Chapter 4, "The Arcs of Development Separate: 1875–1900," details the separation of the concerns of English studies from those of "the science of language" as well as from those of Powell's and Brinton's approaches to the American Indian languages. Chapters 4 and 5 also make a single, extended movement. Since the topics covered in these chapters have received proportionally more attention from recent historians, I will spend proportionately less space on them in this book. I will focus only on tying these chapters into those themes I have already set out in the first three chapters, with the aim of refreshed readings of such familiar texts as Boas's 1911 "Introduction" to the *Handbook of American Indian languages*.

Chapter 5, then, "The Search for Autonomy: 1900–24," details Bloomfield's early career in the context of existing ways in America for practicing linguistics with the overlay of Germanic scholarship that was to hit high tide in the late nineteenth and early twentieth centuries. Bloomfield's work both links with Whitney's work and breaks with it in ways that have shaped the study of language in America for the whole of the twentieth century. The importance of academic institutions such as Johns Hopkins, whose early development is discussed in Chapter 4, continued on into the early decades of the twentieth century and contrasts with non-institutionalized professional activity, such as

Mencken's and even Sapir's work. Both Boas's and Sapir's life and career are of prime importance here. The chapter will end with a description of the establishment of the LSA in the closing days of 1924.

Thus, we have arrived back at 1925. To complete my little survey of the contemporaneous American linguistic scene circa 1925, I note the inauguration of yet another journal, this one in January of 1924. It is *American Mercury*, and it is bound to the history of American language studies in a variety of ways, beginning with its editor, Henry L. Mencken, who had already published, by this time, the first three editions of his monumental *The American Language* (1919, 1921, 1923). In the first volume of *American Mercury*, those articles pertaining to language reconfirm my sense that a general movement was afoot both to establish some special space inside of language that would be the linguist's privileged territory and to foster a pride in American approaches to scholarship. For instance, under the rubric "Philology," the article by George Krapp on "The Test of English" examines the question of "what sanction must English speech receive before it can be included sympathetically with the circle of the English idiom" (1924: 95). Krapp dispenses with all external factors – etymology, grammar, usage – and argues that the "idiomatic life of the language is not something external . . . but lies within us, a part of every person's living experience" (1924: 97). There is, under the rubric "Anthropology," a contribution by Robert Lowie who balances current American ethnology against the British historical school and the German–Austrian *kulturhistorische* school. Lowie values the American school for its display of "calm commonsense."

Finally, in this first volume of *American Mercury* appears an elegant piece by Sapir entitled "The Grammarian and His Language." Sapir is concerned with the issue of "the very pallid status of linguistics in America" which he attributes to the Americans' general preference for function and their corresponding lack of appreciation for the "inner structure of language," "unconscious psychic processes," and the "world of linguistic forms, held within the framework of a given language." Sapir clinches his arguments with a discussion of *the stone falls*, a particular phrase which echoes with the resonance of Indian glosses involving stones to be found in the literature going all the way back to

Father Le Jeune's *Relations of New France* (1636), at least. I was gratified, once again, that my end could, even so obliquely, evoke my beginnings.

In this same article, Sapir also mentions the then recently published work *The Meaning of Meaning* by the English scholars C.K. Ogden and I.A. Richards. Innocently, I must suppose, Sapir points with this reference to a particular aspect of "what does *not* happen next" in American language studies, namely the notorious (and often notoriously misunderstood) elimination of the study of meaning from the "science of language" (see Bloomfield 1927a, Part II, "The Problem of Meaning"). Nonetheless, by 1925, Sapir had read Ogden and Richards and found it useful.[5] Now, Ogden and Richards orient themselves in a rich tradition of semantics ("the science of symbolism") that includes, among others, the American Charles S. Peirce, a tradition which I do not intend to cover in this study. My symmetry is perfect: I have identified the study of meaning – "what does not happen next" – as part of "what did not come before." However, I am not striving for perfect symmetry. I am rather reminded, in this context, that the identification of "what happens next" and "what came before" (along with their negative counterparts) are mutually determining – and always incomplete.

Happily, the editors of *American Mercury* anticipated my difficulty and wrote for me when they admitted in their first editorial that: "the Editors are not fond enough to believe in their own varieties of truth too violently, or to assume that the truth is ascertainable in all cases, or even in most cases" (Mencken 1924: 27).

INTRODUCTORY ESSAY: THE GOALS OF LINGUISTIC HISTORIOGRAPHY

CHALLENGES

Linguistic historiography is a discipline that has come into its own during the past several decades. It is now possible to cite a large body of literature devoted to linguistic historiography and to identify an international community of scholars dedicated to historiographic research. Although historiography is not yet a standardized part of the linguistic student's training in the United States, historiographic perspectives are appearing more and more in the work of American linguists (see Preface, note 1). The increasing appearance of these perspectives suggests that American linguists perceive an increasing need for the theoretical depth and dimension that historiography provides. However, when it comes to historiographic perspectives on linguistics in the United States, few exist, and almost none at all for the period before the twentieth century. In fact, up to now, the tradition of American linguistics announced in my title has been assumed *not* to exist. This book challenges that negative assumption by providing a history of American linguistics from the founding of the American Philosophical Society in 1769 to the founding of the Linguistic Society of America in 1924.

As a consequence, this book also challenges the assumption that the true study of language in the nineteenth century was Indo-European philology. This book then also necessarily challenges the assumption that the center of linguistic activity in the nineteenth century was Germany. Traditional histories of linguistics – those written by Rudolf von Raumer (1815–76), Theodor Benfey 1809–81), Vilhelm Thomsen (1842–1927), and Holger Pedersen (1867–1953) – established the equation for the nineteenth century whereby *Indo-European studies* plus *Germany* equalled, if not the sum

11

total, at least the *core* or *true center* of language study. This equation of *Indo-European studies* plus *Germany* equals *linguistic center* has proven to be strong and enduring. Many linguists today automatically associate the nineteenth century with historical–comparative Indo-European studies and readily identify their alpha and omega as Franz Bopp (1791–1867) and Karl Brugmann (1849–1919). The absence of any other immediate association reinforces the assumption that Indo-European studies in Germany indeed represent the essence of nineteenth-century linguistics.

Traditional histories of the nineteenth century did sometimes acknowledge other types of linguistic activity. In the United States, Leonard Bloomfield (1887–1949), in his brief history of linguistics in the first chapter of *Language* (1933), identified two types of activities for the nineteenth century: those in the "main stream" and those "not in the main stream." For Bloomfield, who inherited his view of linguistic history primarily from Pedersen (see 1931), the "great stream" of linguistic research was historical, alongside of which ran "a small but accelerating current of general linguistic study" represented by the tradition of Humboldt–Steinthal–Wundt (1933: 17–18). Descriptive studies were also not in "the main stream of historical work" and could be represented by the study of any non-Indo-European language family, e.g. Finno-Ugric or Amerind. Although Bloomfield intends for his history to valorize general linguistics and descriptive studies in the twentieth century, the phrase "main stream" when applied to the nineteenth century is not neutral. In organizing the vision of what it was to do "mainstream" linguistics in the nineteenth century, Bloomfield, at the same time, identifies the "core". The implication results that the research programs and the findings of those researchers "not in the main stream" were not only merely peripheral but also somehow "less": perhaps less numerous, less productive, certainly less central, and then by extension, less scientific, less theoretically important. In other words, those studies "not in the main stream" were, in a word, marginal, and they have been accordingly adjourned to the margins of our received history.

The present study challenges the assumption that the practice of linguistics, and thus its history, falls into the *a priori* divisions of "main" and "not mainstream." It takes issue with the assumption that a predetermined center exists against which other types of study may be measured as marginal.

This deviation from a Germanocentric and Indo-European-oriented view of the nineteenth century does not break new ground. Revisionist histories of the language sciences have been making their marks since the mid-1960s, when there appeared, almost simultaneously, Noam Chomsky's *Cartesian Linguistics* (1966), Michel Foucault's *Les Mots et les choses* (1966), and Hans Aarsleff's *The Study of Language in England, 1780–1860* (1967). Since that time, linguistic historiographers have been critically re-examining the history of linguistics whose sun rises on Bopp and Grimm. In Europe, the *Société d'Histoire et d'Epistémologie des Sciences du Langage* (established 1978) has provided a nucleus around which has gravitated an international group of scholars dedicated to establishing a history of linguistics in the widest possible sense. Studies such as Auroux (1979a) and Swiggers (1984a) have succeeded in reshaping traditional historical boundary lines, with the result that the eighteenth-century French tradition of *grammaire générale* must by now be considered an integral part of our most immediate linguistic past.

In North America, Konrad Koerner has contributed enormously to the theory and practice of linguistic historiography as a whole, founding the journal *Historiographia Linguistica* in 1974 and establishing the triennial International Conference on the History of the Language Sciences in 1978. From a different point of departure and still in North America, Dell Hymes has also incorporated into the scope of his many interests the theory and practice of linguistic historiography. Having focused primarily on American topics, Hymes (1983) has provided many insights into the development of American linguistics on which I will, in part, be building. Thus, as we enter the 1990s, it is not difficult to find multiple histories of linguistics, a unifying theme of which seems to be the basic recognition that the domain of the language sciences, and thus its history, is *not* coextensive with the academic institutionalization of the discipline which occurred in Germany in the second decade of the nineteenth century (cf. Hymes 1974: 8; Aarsleff 1982: 5). Linguistic activity, in the United States and elsewhere, has always been *plural*, and our history should reflect that plurality.

Some readers will recognize in this rewriting of linguistic history a development parallel to the revision of the canon current in literary studies. Other readers will recognize in this rewriting of linguistic history a development parallel to the revision of the nineteenth-century linguistic canon itself. Recent innovations in Indo-European studies and typology have tumbled such stable and treasured orthodoxies from the nineteenth century as Grimm's Law. In the past years, the Soviet linguists Tamaz Gamkrelidze and Vyacheslav Ivanov have succeeded in reversing the direction of change posited by Grimm's Law and in overturning with their glottalic theory the traditional Proto-Indo-European consonantism crystallized in Brugmann (see Gamkrelidze and Ivanov 1980; Cowgill 1986; Lehmann 1986; Vine 1988). The very center of the purported center of nineteenth-century linguistics is under revision. This revision of the nineteenth-century Indo-European canon independently supports the general historiographic revision of the whole of the nineteenth century, of which this book is a part.

ASSERTIONS

So much for the challenges. Now for the assertions. This book asserts that three arcs of development (to borrow an image from Dell Hymes) capture a significant portion of American linguistic activity from 1769 to 1924. The three arcs are defined as:

1 the study of American Indian languages;
2 the study of the distinctive variety of American English, accompanied by its *défense et illustration*;
3 the influence of European theories and practices on American scholarship out of which arose a field of study known as "general linguistics," recognized as an international discipline.

Individually, these three arcs of development do not represent newly discovered territories on the historical landscape. Each arc in isolation has its own self-contained history.

1 Specialists of American Indian languages understand that the impact of American Indian languages on American linguistic consciousness is deeply rooted, stretching back before Franz Boas (1858–1942), J.W. Powell (1834–1902), and well into the seventeenth century with Roger Williams (1603–1683) and his *A Key into the Language of America* (1643), and with John Eliot (1604–90) and his *The Holy Bible; Containing the Old Testament and the New Translated*

into the Indian Language (1663) and *The Indian Grammar Begun* (1666). This rich tradition continues unbroken into the present, the most recent milestone being Joseph Greenberg's *Language in the Americas* (1987).[1]

2 Specialists of American English have known, at least since Henry L. Mencken (1880–1956) and *The American Language* (1963 [1945, 1938, 1923, 1921, 1919]), that the American Colonists were acutely aware both of the divergence of their speech from the standard in England and of the connection between this linguistic self-consciousness and their politics. Here again, scholars have shown renewed interest in this arc of development, evidenced by studies such as Dennis Baron's *Grammar and Good Taste* (1982), David Simpson's *The Politics of American English: 1776–1850* (1986), as well as Shirley Heath's project on the history of the study of American English now in progress.

3 As for the influence of Europe on America over the last several hundred years, scholars have routinely conceded that American thought in all fields in the early years derived considerable energy from Europe. For instance, with regard to the American educational system, Jurgen Herbst states matter-of-factly that:

> In a general way, the influence of European upon American scholars has always been acknowledged. We have spoken of the predominantly British cast of American education during the colonial period, the impact of French science during and after the Revolution, and the model provided by the German states for American secondary and university education during the nineteenth century.
>
> (1965: vii)

The same can be said, again in a general way, of the study of language from the seventeenth century through the early twentieth century. Nineteenth-century Germany was, of course, particularly influential with its exportation of the theoretical thicket surrounding the terminological loads of the various *Wissenschaften: Sprachwissenschaft, Geisteswissenschaft, Naturwissenschaft*. The laying bare of these influences, and the various receptions and reactions to them, is a large part of what my present study is all about. Suffice it to say that a major thrust of the incorporation of German-style *Sprachwissenschaft* into American theory and practice was precisely the carving out of a place, both theoretically and professionally, for "autonomous linguistics." This German-style autonomous linguistics was to be incorporated at the expense of more French-styled non-autonomous approaches to language. The influence of German scholarship was to rise throughout the nineteenth century and to decline only after World War I, its rise and fall thus more or less coinciding with the beginning and end dates of my study.

The interest of my approach should come, then, not from identifying the three separate arcs, but rather from intertwining them and incorporating them into both the linguistic history of the United States and our general history of linguistics. Intertwining these thematic arcs produces a kind of triangulated syncopy in the nineteenth century out of which new historical rhythms can be heard. These new rhythms affect, in turn, our view of what the study of language in this country has been, and continues to be. For instance, when the historical record is read for all three arcs at once, subtle, persistent strains can be heard identifying the theoretical barbarism of the American Indian languages with the reputed barbarism of American English. As a result, the historiographer comes to see that the study of American English and American Indian languages have, at various times, been allied with one another in the pride of their "home-grown" status, or at odds, if one or the other aligns itself with a fancier brand of imported European theory. The alternating affinities and dis-associations that play among these three arcs provide the practical and epistemological tensions that animate linguistic theory and practice in the United States from the founding of the American Philosophical Society to the founding of the Linguistic Society of America.

This book asserts, furthermore, that judgments are historical. That is, the present study attempts to find explanations of present judgments about the nature and study of language in the various ways language has been studied in the past. The view that "judgments are historical," put in its own historical context, seems to derive from a generalized post-structuralist rediscovery of a formerly well-known past. History-writing is indeed a tricky business. While some aura of innovation may cling to the present discovery and rewriting of history, it is a conservative venture and always risks the response "but we knew all of that already." Yet, each period of historical rewriting occurs as a function of the interests of that present which encourages such rewriting, making history-writing the mirror of the present. Thus, "judgments are historical" is not only an observation that present judgments are inescapably inherited from a past we cannot control, but also a claim that history provides a source for recreating a present we can possibly control. As I stated it in the Preface, the identification of "what happens next" and "what came before" are mutually determining.

Which leads me to my last assertion. Since linguistic historiographers are identifying and investigating those texts and practices from the past that fall under some category we are presently calling "language study," it follows that linguistic historiographers approach the history of linguistics with some personal vision (call it a theory) of what language study is. In challenging previous assumptions about the history of linguistics, linguistic historiographers aim at an enriched vision of what language and language study must be by enhancing the sources of our present study. We historiographers have, by and large, carried our investigations into those places which have been previously overlooked. However, the very choice of what comes under historiographic purview is not given in advance, but reflects present concerns and opinions about the nature and study of language. We historiographers think our choices are, nevertheless, somehow obvious: we examine any and all texts or practices where language is either directly confronted, expressed, or discussed. The more explicit and overt the confrontation with language or the discussion of it, the more accessible is the text or practice to historiographic critique. We historiographers aim, then, at reviewing the full range of the various shapes that have been given to language over the centuries. In this idea of "full range," the historiographic approach itself cannot be innocent. It must be another, albeit indirect, way of shaping the study of language, of determining the present view of language by shaping what constitutes the linguistic past.

In this book, then, my own vision of language and its study must be doubly implicated: both as an inherited product of a generalized linguistic past and as my own, individualized historiographic recreation of what that past must be. Given my entire orientation, I am particularly sympathetic to those theories which emphasize language as a human and social-made historical product. Thus, I favor those theories which presuppose a "shallow" level of linguistic specificity in the human biological and genetic program. Always keeping an eye on present trends and future directions, I contend that foregrounding the social-made aspect of language has as many consequences for a theory of the brain as those theories of language with a more essentialist (that is, rationalist, or "hard-wired for language") view of the brain. In foregrounding those theories which emphasize the social nature of language, I hope for my history to demonstrate that a sociopolitical linguistic orientation is neither an after-thought in the history of American thought about language – as the term "sociolinguistics" itself suggests[2] – nor a subdiscipline, but that it has been in the center of the linguistic action from the very beginnings of language study in America.

BOUNDARIES

My individualized recreation of the American linguistic past has distinct boundaries. First are my temporal boundaries, indicated in the title. I have chosen to limit my study – ambitious enough – to one hundred and fifty-five years beginning with the founding of the American Philosophical Society in 1769 and ending with the formation of the Linguistic Society of America in 1924. These temporal boundaries might strike some readers as peculiar. The end-date 1924, for instance, is certainly not the end of anything. This date also creates the disturbing effect in cutting off Leonard Bloomfield and Edward Sapir mid-career. However, all studies need a frame, and I hope that mine will invite a sequel. The book end-dates of 1769 and 1924 are not, however, arbitrary and do reflect a theoretical bias: with them I am calling attention to the fact that the language sciences – or any science – are primarily a group activity. Traditional histories of linguistics have been accustomed to summarizing rather extensive group-efforts eponymously. Thus, it was, and still often is, customary to use such labels as "Grimm's Law," "Verner's Law," "Grassmann's Law," "Saussurean linguistics," "Bloomfieldian linguistics," "Chomskyean linguistics," and the like. I do not deny the importance of any of the individuals in this list to the group or group-effort they define; surely, if the moving-forward of linguistics has proceeded by the transmission of knowledge, this transmission has been effected by key individuals. However, with this periodization, as well as the periodization of the individual chapters, I have chosen to de-emphasize the importance of the individual in order to stress the transmission of knowledge that has been effected by libraries, journals, professional societies, and academic institutions.

My overt goal, then, is to understand the dynamics of American linguistic activity up to 1924. The explicit connection between "what came before" 1924 and "what happens next" after 1925 must be left, for now, to other studies and to the reader's imagination. Still, I am writing from the perspective of present concerns, and so current interests (historiography among them) have implicit value for those readers also interested in developments after 1924, the broad outlines of which I will make explicit in my Conclusion.

Here, and in passing, I refer the reader to an intriguing observation made by Paul Friedrich in his recent book *The Language Parallax* (1986). There he writes that he sees in Benjamin Lee Whorf (1897–1941) "a continuation of the New England philosophy that originates as transcendentalism, particularly in his vision of language and his idea that language itself is a sort of vision – hence the often passionate acceptance of his works in [the United States]" (1986: 13). Friedrich puts Whorf's thought in touch with Ralph Waldo Emerson (1803–82) – that quintessential American – and, in so doing, explains the particular American reception of Whorf's thought in the present. Ideally, I would like for my history to be able to suggest to the reader such evocative possibilities as an Emerson–Whorf tradition (in addition to the Webster–Chomsky dynamic, mentioned in the Preface). Or even, embroidering further on the alliance of the linguistic and the literary, one could incorporate the poetry of Sapir (which appeared in *The Dial* and *The Freeman*, among other places during the nineteen 'teens and 'twenties) into his general vision of language, perhaps, to his concept of "Drift." In any case, an improved and enlarged tradition of American thought about language includes approaches to poetry, and to this tradition the linguistics/poetics of Paul Friedrich's work today certainly belongs (see Andresen 1988b).

Second are the boundaries described by my chosen arcs of development. Although I am advocating a strongly plural approach to American linguistic activity before 1924, I cannot possibly do justice to all the topics that have presented themselves to me in my readings. Thus, my focus in the present book will, for the most part, exclude the development of American Sign Language, whose signers so recently proclaimed their linguistic "declaration of independence" in political acts worthy of Webster.[3] It will also exclude, as indicated in the Preface, the writings of Charles S. Peirce (1839–1914), that icon of the peculiarly American school of pragmatism. My rationale for this decision is based almost entirely on the fact that Peirce's real impact on American linguistics has been a rather delayed one, not coming until the mid-1960s and the "rediscovery" of his work by Roman Jakobson (1896–1982).[4]

My boundaries will also exclude, for the most part, the rise of the consciousness and the recording of Black English – surely an important chapter in dialect study and language variation, and in the formation of American English itself – and this omission exists for the simple reason that researchers in the history of Black English, for example Guy Bailey, are just now in the process of unearthing these historical materials.[5]

My temporal boundaries will also exclude current feminist lexicographic revisions of the type exemplified by *A Feminist Dictionary* (1985), edited by Cheris Kramarae and Paula Triechler, another unfortunate omission, since lexicography has long played a vital role in that second arc of development which is the study of American English. These are my limitations. Time and space do not allow me to exhaust the riches of the historical record.

Third, I am bounded by the English language. My historiographic account of American linguistic activity from 1769 to 1924 will include a study of the distinctive configurations that exist in English for speaking about language. That is, I am interested in discovering the "folk-linguistic" attitudes and ways of speaking about language that have been in the (American) English language for the past several centuries. With the thoughts on folk linguistics of Hoenigswald (1966) in mind, I became curious to know how many unformulated – or at least unconscious and English-language-based – preconceptions about language went into linguistic theory as it became codified and institutionalized in the United States during the course of the nineteenth century. The relationship between language and money, for instance, extends back well into the eighteenth century and is intimately related both to the non-autonomous conception of language and the franco-anglophone tradition. This tradition has experienced a distinctive resurgence today, in the wake of the work of, say, Pierre Bourdieu (1982) which has excited interest in certain current (pragmatics-oriented) schools of thought in the United States (see Conclusion).

This last boundary, then, serves as my point of departure. Hymes (1974) characterizes linguistic thought as proceeding according to a tripartite movement from *folk linguistics* to *national philologies* to *general linguistics*. That the development of these three divisions should be so temporally compressed and so thematically intertwined in the United States can only add texture and shape to my recreation of the formation of American linguistics.

1

IN THE BEGINNING
(1769–1815): THE POLITICAL
CONCEPTION OF LANGUAGE

LANGUAGE STUDIES IN AMERICA IN THE EARLY YEARS

Taking 1769 and the founding of the American Philosophical Society as a point of departure, the level of linguistic activity in the American Colonies, when measured against the state of European language studies, might be said to begin at point zero.

In the American Colonies, no individual existed to rival the stature in language studies of, say, Etienne Bonnot de Condillac (1714–80) in France. No work was produced of the theoretical importance of Condillac's *Essai sur l'origine des connaissances humaines* (1746). Nor did a formal or informal group of individuals exist at that time in the American Colonies to compare to the *grammairiens philosophes* and with no pre-eminent *grammairien* of the order of Nicolas Beauzée (1717–89). Thus, there was no identifiable intellectual tradition similar to *grammaire générale* which would develop into what was to become after the French Revolution, *idéologie*, and no group to correspond to the *Idéologues* who were to dominate French intellectual life from about 1790 to 1815. Nor, even, does an immediately promising terminology surface in language discussions in the American Colonies – for example disparate references to signs or sign theory – that might serve as evidence for some kind of heretofore unassembled theoretical orientation in American language studies. Nor, again, then, would there have been any reason, after the turn of the nineteenth century, for Americans to want to summarize the preceding period with the kinds of linguistic histories that packaged the French tradition for posterity, such as François Thurot's *Tableau des progrès des sciences grammaticales* (1796) or Dieudonné Thiébault's "Lettre à

Pinglin sur l'histoire de la science grammaticale" of his *Grammaire Philosophique* (1802).

Shifting across the Rhine to continue this negative comparison, the American Colonies had not produced, as had the German states, a Leibniz or a Kant. They were gestating no Bopp, no Grimm, no Humboldt. That is, no subtle critiques were being elaborated against any previous philosophical positions, nor were institutional frameworks in place in which to discuss them. In America of 1769, no prize essay contest can be found equivalent to the one launched that very same year by the *Preussische Akademie der Wissenschaft* with the question: "Could human beings, if left to their own natural capacities, have invented language? and by what means would they have most suitably acquired it?"[1] This essay contest was won by J.G. Herder for his *Ueber den Ursprung der Sprache* of 1770.

Furthermore, Americans did not work off French thought as profitably as did the Germans. Benjamin Franklin (1706–90) and Thomas Jefferson (1743–1826) frequented the same Parisian *salons* of the 1780s and 1790s as did Wilhelm von Humboldt (1767–1835), and there they all three met with the rising group of French intellectuals who were to be known as the Ideologues. From these encounters, Franklin and Jefferson brought *idéologie* back to the New World, where it was congenially received. However, only Humboldt envisioned the static limitations of *signe* and *système* and *usage* that the Ideologues inherited from the French Enlightenment tradition of Condillac and the *grammaires générales*; only Humboldt recast linguistic philosophy in the dynamic terminology of *individuelle Taetigkeit* and *innere Sprachform* which was to reshape linguistic philosophy in the nineteenth century.

On the score of having access to sheer quantities of data, Americans were lagging behind Europeans at the close of the eighteenth century. Although, and as stated in the Introduction, the American Colonists such as Roger Williams and Jonathan Edwards had begun in the mid-seventeenth century an active interest in American Indian languages, the Colonists were far from the libraries of Europe rich in data on the world's "exotic" languages that had been accumulating since the Renaissance. At the close of the eighteenth century, there had clustered into the marketplace of linguistic ideas such inventories of the world's languages as: Antoine Court de Gébelin's *Monde Primitif* (1773–82); Abbé

23

Lorenzo Hervàs y Panduro's *Catalogo delle lingue conosciute et notizia della loro affinità e diversità* (1784); and Peter Pallas's *Linguarum totius orbis vocabularia comparativa* (1787–9), produced under the direction of Catherine the Great.

American researchers, however, were fully alive to these inventorying efforts. The naturalist/doctor Benjamin Smith Barton (1766–1815) was thoroughly familiar with Pallas's work and published an impressive comparative wordlist of American Indian languages entitled *New Views on the Origin of the Tribes and Nations of America* in 1797. Drawing on the language studies of Roger Williams, David Zeisberger, and John Heckewelder, Barton claims that his "collection of original manuscripts respecting the Indians of North-America is . . . already more extensive than that of any other individual in the country" (1797: xii). At the head of the wordlist columns, Barton uniformly places the Delawares, or *Lenni-Lennape*, because "we are better acquainted with the language of this tribe, that with that of any other in North-America" (xxv). In stating that he "will endeavour to show, that the language of the Cheerake is not radically different from that of the Six-Nations" (xlv), Barton is one of the first in writing to posit a genetic relationship of Cherokee to Iroquois (but see King 1977 for the oral tradition of the understanding of this relationship). Barton is aware of the contribution he and other Americans stood to make to the European inventories. In a letter of 1803 entitled "Hints on the Etymology of certain English words, and on their affinity to words in the languages of different European, Asiatic, and American (Indian) nations," Barton reproaches Pallas's vocabulary for its lack of American Indian data and sets out to fill the gap.

This general omission of American Indian data was soon repaired in the German-speaking world. Through the intermediary of Alexander von Humboldt (1769–1859, Wilhelm's brother) who met in 1804 with Barton and Duponceau in Philadelphia and Thomas Jefferson, James Madison, and Albert Gallatin in Washington, the German researchers Friedrich von Adelung and J.S. Vater were able to include American Indian data in their *Mithridates oder allegemeine Sprachenkunde* (1806–17). An improved version appeared in 1822 as Adelung's *Uebersicht aller bekannten Sprachen und ihrer Dialekte*, followed soon thereafter in Paris by Adrien Balbi and his *Atlas ethnographique du globe, ou classification des peuples anciens et modernes d'après leurs langues* (1826). Although Barton participated in the European compilations and produced his own important work (*New Views, 1797*), and although Americans took great interest in these studies (as evidenced by John Pickering's review of Adelung, 1822), neither Barton nor Pickering nor any other American produced a global inventory to rival the European *vocabularia comparativa*.[2]

Finally, and in comparison with the tradition of language studies in Great Britain, nothing appeared on the American horizon to equal John Locke's *Essay Concerning Human Understanding* (1690) which gave shape to eighteenth-century sign theory both in England and in France where it strongly influenced Condillac. Nor was there anything close to James Harris's *Hermes* (1750), or even John Horne Tooke's *Epea Pteronta* or *The Diversions of Purley* (1784–1805), this last influencing both anglophone sides of the Atlantic in its attempt to improve on the perceived deficiencies in Locke's and Condillac's views of language. From Scotland came the frequently quoted *Of the Origin and Progress of Language* (6 vols, 1774–1809) by James Burnet (Lord Monboddo) as well as the work of the linguist/economist Adam Smith, particularly his "Considerations Concerning the Formation of Languages" (1761).

The American Colonists were not, for all of that, unaware of European language-science trends. In fact, they were as well versed and eager to dialogue with Europeans on language matters as they were on every other subject. Thomas Jefferson's lifelong interest in languages is well known. He received a classical education in Greek and Latin, and was proficient in Italian, Spanish, and French. He corresponded on linguistic and other subjects with the most important Ideologues of the day (Condorcet, Destutt de Tracy, Volney, de Sacy). Although he only visited Germany once (1788) and did not, apparently, ever acquire a reading knowledge of modern German, he corresponded (in French) with leading German intellectuals such as Alexander von Humboldt, and J.S. Vater.

Jefferson's second, or "great," library contained (by Jefferson's own count) 602 titles under the category "literature and language." Since the entire collection was sold to the United States government in 1815 to replace the Library of Congress which the British had burned in 1812, its contents give a fair indication of available resources in the post-Colonial period. In addition to three polyglot dictionaries that included German, as well as a grammar of that language, Jefferson possessed studies of "exotic" languages such as Arabic, Persian, Bengali, Syriac, Turkish. Over a period of thirty years, Jefferson had collected some forty different American Indian vocabularies. The manuscript was damaged as a result of being thrown into the James River during an incident in 1809, but was presented to the American Philosophical Society Library in 1817. A rapid overview of the European-oriented studies in Jefferson's library catalogue reveals the titles of: Destutt de Tracy's five-volume *Idéologie* (1803–18); Volney's *Ruines* (1791); Adelung's *Pamphlet's* [sic] *on Languages*; and John Jamieson's *Hermes Scythicus, or radical affinities of the Greek, Latin and Gothic Languages* (1814). In addition to works by Aelfric and Bede, Jefferson possessed, as well, *Grammatica Anglo-Saxonica ex Hickesiana Linguarum septentrionalium thesauro excerpta* (1711); Elizabeth Elstob's *Rudiments of Grammar for the English Saxon Tongue* (1715); Bosworth's *Elements of Anglo Saxon Grammar* (1823); Benson's Saxon vocabulary; and Francis Grose's *Provincial Glossary* (1787). Jefferson himself wrote an *Essay on the Anglo-Saxon Language* and has scattered references to language throughout all his writings.[3]

Although less is known about the contents of Benjamin Franklin's library, it is certain that he possessed a copy of the first volume of Horne Tooke's enormously popular *Diversions of Purley* (1784; as did Jefferson) and lent it out to Noah Webster in 1787. As a result, Webster took his *Grammatical Institute* of 1783 and rewrote it into his *Dissertations on the English Language* in 1789, a work that might well figure as the first home-grown American treatise on language. In Dissertation IV on the "Formation of Language," Webster notes his familiarity with writers of great ingenuity and profound learning, such as "Harris, Smith, Beatie, Blair, Condillac and others" (1951 [1789]: 181), but Webster argues that the discovery of the true theory of the construction of language "seems to have been reserved for Mr. Horne Tooke" (182). This "true theory" was Horne Tooke's dual discovery that 1) nouns and verbs – but, above all, nouns – were the essential parts of speech and gave rise to all the others; and that 2) Anglo-Saxon is the original element and perdurable core of the English language.

So taken was Webster with Horne Tooke's system, that the *Diversions of Purley* was to influence him for the rest of his life (Laird 1946, 1966). To the organizational meetings of the New

York Philological Society in 1788, Webster carried the *Diversions* "as a mark of respect for the book which contains a new discovery and as a mark of respect for the author" (Read 1934: 133). This society was, however, short-lived (1788–90), perhaps owing to the very shaky philology of Webster's "Dissertation concerning the Influence of Language on Opinions and of Opinions on Language" delivered to the society wherein is found his now infamous assertion that "the word *devil*, in English, is merely a corruption of *the evil*, occasioned by a rapid pronunciation" (quoted in Read 1934: 132).

Not only were general ideas about language for the most part imported, the standard of language itself in the American Colonies of 1769 was also imported, in the form of prescriptive grammar rules and lexical items authorized in English-made grammars and dictionaries. Again, Jefferson's library included Robert Lowth's *English Grammar* (1762), often considered today as the archetypal eighteenth-century prescriptive grammarian, as well as the dictionaries of Bailey, Walker, Perry, Sheridan, and Johnson. There is nothing unexpected in this. In 1769, the United States itself was not yet in existence, and most social institutions, from laws to fashion to money, came from England as well.

Nor did the Glorious Revolution of 1776 bring immediate change. A quarter-century elapsed before there appeared the first dictionary of American origin, *The Columbian Dictionary of the English Language* by Caleb Alexander (that is, in 1800). Webster's own first dictionary attempt (*Compendious Dictionary*) dates from 1806. While attacks and satires against Americanisms may have begun as early as 1737, the term "Americanism" was not coined until 1781 with the Reverend John Witherspoon's attacks on American "corruptions" and "barbarisms." At issue was the use of words particular to the American landscape such as *bison*, or *bluff*, words particular to the new American system of government such as *caucus, congress*, and *congressional*, and finally words used in America but not (supposedly) in England which were either archaisms or neologisms, such as *lengthy* (every commentator's favorite).

In the early years of the nineteenth century and in such public forums as the *Monthly Magazine and American Review* and the *New-England Palladium*, numerous articles appeared ridiculing the dictionary attempts of Alexander and Webster. Debate on the vices and virtues of Americanisms continued well into the fourth decade of the nineteenth century, and even appeared in the early issues of the *North American Review*, where, to name but one, the verb *to locate* was denounced (Mencken 1963: 135). The so-called vices were exposed in wordlists such as those prepared by David Humphrey (1815), John Pickering (1816), Adiel Sherwood (1827; 1837), and Jonathan Boucher (1832). The virtues, or rather the celebration of the national idiom, were spiritedly displayed in Webster's 1828 *American Dictionary of the English Language* (where appears, incidentally, the correct etymology for *devil*). Everyone advanced an opinion on Americanisms. Jefferson, for instance, was a linguistic innovator, coining the noun *breadstuffs* and the verb *to belittle* and used *lengthy* (Mencken 1963: 130, 5, 135). He made his position clear when he wrote in 1813 that "I am no friend . . . to what is called *Purism*, but a zealous one to the *Neology* which has introduced these two words without the authority of any dictionary" (quoted in Baugh 1940: 102). Franklin was generally against Americanisms (but coined the use of *currency* applied to paper money, see below p. 47).

In addition, despite Webster's *Dissertations* of 1789 and much to his dismay, the most popular language text in America before 1800 proved to be the traditional British speller *New Guide to the English Tongue* by Thomas Dilworth, while the most popular grammar of the early 1800s was that of Lindley Murray, an American-born merchant who moved to England and who modeled his *English Grammar* (1795) on that of Lowth (see Baron 1982: 130, 140). Murray is generally regarded as the father of American prescriptive grammar (Drake 1977: 10). Of the general language situation in the United States for many decades after 1776, it has been said that: "it was to prove more difficult to declare independence from Samuel Johnson than it had been to reject George III" (Simpson 1986: 33).

This general state of point zero of language studies and of the American language itself – or of *any* cultural form whatsoever – was not necessarily perceived negatively by the Americans, even after independence; and, conversely, having a history or traditions to work off of was not necessarily considered an advantage. In fact, in the beginning, many Americans perceived Europe to be weighted down by its ponderous history and clearly on the decline, but "not so America," writes David Simpson:

The United States had the unique advantage of seeming to superimpose one part of the cycle on another, thus defeating the principle of repetition. It *begins* in a state of perfection, or incipient perfection, and because it has no *history*, it need not be assumed to be on the point of decline.

(1986: 65)

In language studies, this sense of fresh start, of America as the clean, eighteenth-century-style *tabula rasa*, was most forcefully expressed by Noah Webster. In his *Dissertations*, Webster was furthermore among the first to announce a kind of Manifest Destiny *avant la lettre* for the English language as spoken in America:

The English is the common root or stock from which our national language will be derived. All others will gradually waste away – and within a century and a half, North America will be peopled with a hundred millions of men, *all speaking the same language*.

(1951 [1789]: 21)

This vision of the (linguistic) glories to come, coupled with the sense of America as *tabula rasa*, went hand-in-hand with the need to remain independent of European example in all fields of endeavor, for "to copy foreign manners implicitly," Webster writes, "is to reverse the order of things, and begin our political existence with the corruptions and vices which have marked the declining glories of other republics" (179; also quoted in Simpson 1986: 65).

However, now two hundred years later, the absence of any history of the beginnings of American linguistics certainly suggests that those beginnings were a void. This void can be easily explained. For instance, it is not difficult to believe that Americans of the Colonial and early post-Colonial period were too busy getting a new nation off the ground to devote much time to linguistics as such.[4] These early Americans could not have had the luxury to think and write about language in an elevated or "high" manner, that is, to meditate on language as a kind of abstracted entity, as language *itself*. Language studies in early post-Colonial America could then be portrayed to be in a kind of "rough and ready" state, preparatory to a more mature, more sophisticated period of linguistic reflection to come later – much later, if one wanted to begin the story of linguistics in America with Bloomfield.

Taking this speculation a provocative step further, one might say that language studies in early post-Colonial America were in their infancy, in a kind of "prelinguistic" period, a period of "learning to speak linguistically." One could then draw a parallel between this "pre-linguistic" state and the language situation of the West African slaves in Colonial America who were identified by the extent of their English: "Ran away . . . a new Negro Fellow named Prince, he can't scarce speak a Word of English" (New York *Evening Post*, December 17, 1744; quoted in Read 1939a: 250). In both cases, the (Euro-)Americans and the (Afro-)Americans could be seen to operate in a parallel kind of linguistic void.

This transition of perception from Webster's sense of positive fresh start to the present-day sense of negative lack has been the very product of our received history of linguistics, or, rather, the perceived lack of one for the United States; and it is presumably the above-mentioned catalogue of negative comparisons that has diverted attention from the possibility of writing that history. Put another way: not having a history has so far been part of the history of American linguistics.

THE POLITICAL CONCEPTION OF LANGUAGE

Now, language studies in America were no more at a point-zero state of grace or of void at the end of the eighteenth century than was English spoken in America "rawer" and more "barbarous" than it is today. That either could still be conceived as having been at point zero would be merely a continuing projection of that time-period's presuppositions into the present. We cannot accept those time-period's presuppositions today any more than we would accept the idea that the runaway prince who knew no English was linguistically deficient.

In the period 1769–1815, a distinct conception of language existed in American thought, but if there is no evidence of medita-tion on "language itself," this lack is completely consistent with the idea that such an entity did not exist, or at least, did not have any kind of independent existence. This conception of language was, thus, not an autonomous theory, but rather an *approach* to language, a way of using and speaking about language which I will call – following Auroux and his analysis of the French Ideologues (1986a) – the *political* conception of language. An understanding of this political conception of language gives consistency and shape to discussions and attitudes about language in pre- and early post-Colonial America. The political conception of language finds expression in much of American thought about language well into the second half of the nineteenth century, that is, it still figures in the foundation of William Dwight Whitney's writings (see Chapter 3).

The political conception of language, furthermore, contrasts starkly with the competing conception of language that was elaborated from the beginning of the nineteenth century onward, namely the *mechanical* conception of language (see again Auroux 1986a), or what Frederick Newmeyer in his recent book *The Politics of Linguistics* calls "autonomous linguistics" (1986). The mechanical conception of language underlies that tradition of language study that has been so well represented in traditional histories of linguistics. As a first approximation, the mechanical conception of language may be defined, again following Auroux, as one which recognizes "kinds of laws, come from who-knows-where, which transcend individual speaking acts [*actes de parole*] to impose their norms or to automatically change the language [*langue*]" (1986a: 262).[5] Newmeyer's definition of "autonomous linguistics" points to the same conception of language from another perspective in his statement that "all autonomous linguists share the belief that a language can be analyzed successfully without taking into consideration the society or beliefs of its speakers" (1986: 6). However, Newmeyer does not describe or refer to any alternative conception of language, namely one which *does* take into consideration the society or beliefs of its speakers, as having any historical presence or theoretical coherence, and that absence reinforces the impression that such an alternative does not exist.

The political conception of language *is* such an alternative. However, in order to understand the political conception of language in America in the early years, it is necessary to appeal to the French tradition of *grammaire générale*, and this for two reasons: 1) although Americans such as Webster were drawing on the confluent French and English traditions mingling, for instance, in Horne Tooke, it was generally the case that, after 1776, the newly independent Americans embraced French thought whole-heartedly and this meant, then, embracing *idéologie* (see Introduction p. 13) although *idéologie* or *la science des idées* was consciously building on the theoretical language framework of Condillac and *grammaire générale*, no specifically identifiable *grammaire idéologique* was elaborated. That is, language theory was not so much topicalized by the Ideologues as used to argue other ends which were pedagogic and political. In this instrumentalization of inherited eighteenth-century language theory, French and American thinkers of both post-revolutionary periods stood on common ground.

For a definition of the political conception of language, then, we cast back to the time and the tradition where language theory was very much topicalized. As Auroux (1986a) sees it, in France, from the establishment of the *Académie Française* (1647) through the *Révolution*, there prevailed a consistent and coherent conception of language, *langue*. During this period, which is coextensive with the entire movement of *grammaire générale* from Port-Royal (1660) through the Ideologues, language (*langue*) "is conceived neither as the result of immanent and mysterious agents, nor as an abstraction produced by the scientific approach, but as a reality constructed by specific human agents" (Auroux 1986a: 262).[6] The identification of *langue* was straightforward, Beauzée's 1757 *Encyclopédie* definition functioning canonically: it is "the sum total of usages specific to a nation in order to express its thoughts orally."[7] Now, the *grammairiens* distinguished the subject matter of *langue* from that of *grammaire générale*, which latter concerned itself with the universal conditions of the construction of utterances. This distinction prompts Auroux to write, for eighteenth-century France: "the subject of *grammaire générale* is the human mind, reason equally distributed in each human being," while "*the subject of language* [langue] *is the nation*" (1986a: 261; emphasis mine).[8]

Similarly, in America from Webster to Whitney, there was an inalienable association of language and the nation, both of which qualified as a *res-publica*, that is, "thing of the people," and very much at the disposal (conscious and otherwise) of the beliefs of the of the members of the society. When arguing for the reasons why America should have a language of its own, Webster establishes a transitive relationship among customs, habits, language, and government by juxtaposition when he writes:

> Customs, habits, and *language*, as well as government should be national. America should have her *own* distinct from all the world. Such is the policy of other nations, and such must be *our* policy, before the states can be either independent or respectable.

(1951 [1789]: 179; quoted also in Simpson 1986: 65)

What is presupposed in the political conception of language is the conventionalist thesis of language, where words only become signs of ideas by *tacit and free convention* among the speakers in a given community, say, a nation. For speakers in a community, Webster declares, "the practice of a nation . . . has, in most cases, the force and authority of law; it implies mutual and general consent, and becomes a rule of propriety" (1951 [1789]: 92). For Webster with his terminology of *practice, force, authority*, and *general consent*, language is precisely the sum total of the society and beliefs of its speakers.

This political conception of language with its presupposed conventionalist thesis is by no means exclusive to the American and French traditions. It is part and parcel of the English tradition as well. Prescriptive grammarians, for their part, share the same conception of language as a "thing of the people." For instance, the English prescriptivist, Thomas Sheridan, mentioned above, wrote treatises on pronunciation and wished to fix the language based on a prescriptive model. In 1756, Sheridan writes of language reform that:

> The result of the researches of rational enquirers, must be rules founded upon rational principles; and *a general agreement amongst the most judicious*, must occasion those rules to be generally known, and established, and give them the force of laws.

The new note struck in this mid-eighteenth-century passage is Sheridan's interpretation of "general agreement." He continues:

> Nor would these laws meet with opposition, or be obeyed with reluctance, inasmuch as they would not be established by the hand of power, but by *common suffrage*, in which *every one has a right to give his vote*: nor would they fail, in time, of obtaining

33

general authority, and permanence, from the sanction of custom, founded on good sense.

(*British Education*, quoted in Baugh and Cable 1978: 269–70; emphasis mine)

That is, the new prescriptive model would be introduced not by force but by general consent, *common suffrage* or "voting" – with the understanding that only "the most judicious," i.e. the speaking elite, got a vote.

What, then, is indissoluble from the political conception of language is the concept of the nation. In France, the concept of nation certainly changed throughout the course of the eighteenth century from the monarchial authority of *l'état, c'est moi* to royalist tyranny and then on to republican democracy, with at all times an identification of *langue* and *nation*. Likewise, throughout a good part of the American nineteenth century, the political conception of language consistently intersects with the American conception of nation: a social and political democracy driven by a private-enterprise, laissez-faire economy.

This language–nation intersection manifests itself not only in the metalinguistic metaphors of "voting" (see above, and below, Chapter 3, p. 146) and "economy" (language and money, see below, and Chapter 3), but also and most fundamentally in the confrontation with the problem of (linguistic) authority. Although the English, the French, and the Americans might have belonged to one confluent intellectual tradition in the eighteenth century, the three nations variously worked out their responses to authority (linguistic and otherwise). The French, long accustomed to centralized government, had established their *Académie* in 1647. The English attempted throughout the eighteenth century to follow suit with an English Academy, but eventually gave up on it (Read 1938). Similarly, between the years 1780 and 1820, the Americans debated the establishment of a national academy of language. Although leaning during those years to French thought, and at war with England, the Americans followed their transatlantic anglophone counterparts and repeatedly voted against establishing such an academy. The history of the debate in the new nation over the language academy are ably discussed in Heath (1977) and Baron (1982: 99–118).

The reasons *for* the academy might be best summed up as being

34

dictated by the needs of the developing foreign policy. John Adams, for one, envisioned future American power, and he recognized that nations of power had languages of power. Adams wanted a codification of language *and* government for presentation and expansion to other nations. As early as 1780, that is, before Webster, Adams prophesied that:

> English will be the most respectable language in the world and the most universally read and spoken in the next century . . . American population will in the next age produce a greater number of persons who will speak English than any other language.
>
> (quoted in Heath 1977: 20)

Although Adams never got his language academy, he did succeed in organizing the American Academy of Arts and Sciences in Boston in 1780.

Similarly, Benjamin Rush followed Adams's prediction that English "will probably be spoken by more people, in the course of two or three centuries, than ever spoke any one language, at one time, since the creation of the world" (quoted in Heath 1977: 18). Since for Rush the scientific community was universal, he felt an academy would help regulate the language to promote the new American science. In the process, it would help extend news of the new American political system which was also believed to have universal appeal.

The reasons *against* the academy were primarily domestic: it was the case that the young United States negatively viewed any national polity-sponsored manipulation of language and self-consciously avoided prescribing national cultural modes or models. Thomas Jefferson, decidedly a linguistic liberal, was against the academy. Language choice was an individual matter, and individuals were collectively free to follow whatever guidance was available in the standardization of language according to their special interests, be they literary, scientific, religious, or business (Heath 1977: 11). Thus, the domestic, national need for insuring individual (linguistic) freedom took precedence over perceived foreign, international interests and the desire to "spread the good news" abroad.

For Webster, the predicted numerical superiority of speakers of American English over British English was all the initial authority he needed to argue for the abandonment of British precept and example in language matters. Webster anticipated "the period when the people of one quarter of the world, will be able to associate and converse together [in English] like children of the same family" and compared this prospect, "which is not visionary," to the state of the English language in Europe which is "almost confined to an Island and to a few millions of people" (1951 [1789]: 21). Webster's is a "might makes right" argument, a kind of majority rule in linguistic matters, consonant with the prevailing political ideology.

Through his reading of Horne Tooke, Webster was aware that language was an ever-changing product of ever-changing human endeavors. To fix language permanently (to "ascertain" it Thomas Sheridan-style, or to construct the *langue bien faite à la* Condillac) was impossible. Authority in language change, Webster argued, would come from the language-internal rule of *analogy*, "the great leading principle that should regulate the construction of all languages." However, Webster sees language-making as an on-going process and denies a *strongly* language-internal system which could ever regulate change: "languages are not formed at once by system, and are ever exposed to changes." He concludes that "it must necessarily happen that there will be in all languages, some exceptions from any general rule; some departures from the principle of uniformity" (1951 [1789]: 92). Thus, there will always be need for language-external regulation. The authority for this regulation will come – to repeat – from "the common consent of a nation [which] is sufficient to stamp [deviations from analogy] with propriety" (1951 [1789]: 93). For the young Webster, at least, "a *national language* is a band of *national union*" (1951 [1789]: 397). Thus, linguistic authority equals "common consent."

In light of the above discussion, the political conception of language can be seen as distinctly discontinuous from the mechanical ("autonomous") conception of language. The latter was institutionalized first in Germany in the early decades of the nineteenth century where a very different political, linguistic, and academic history was shaping language studies. The mechanical conception of language culminated in Germany with the *Junggrammatiker*, in which school the two most influential linguists of the first half of the twentieth century, Saussure and Leonard

Bloomfield, were trained. Bloomfield successfully transmitted his version of a mechanical conception of language to twentieth-century American linguistics, and it still underlies a distinctive portion of American academic linguistic activity today, namely that portion with which Newmeyer (1986), for instance, is occupied in describing.

Now, I cannot write my version of American linguistics in the late eighteenth century from any other perspective than that of the late twentieth century. If historiography does nothing else, it allows me, at least, to reflect on those presuppositions about language and linguistics that have been uncritically inherited from previous eras. For instance, it would be part of the late twentieth-century structuralist ("autonomous") inheritance, either from Saussure or from Bloomfield, to affirm:

1 that speech and writing are separate phenomena; for the linguist, speech is primary, writing is secondary;
2 that the linguist, being a scientist, is prohibited from intervening in the mode of existence of his/her object of study (see Auroux 1986a: 260); and
3 that language, being a social fact (*fait social* for Saussure; "social habit" for Bloomfield) whose subject is the speaking masses, cannot be the object of conscious action, that is, of deliberate change (see Auroux 1986a: 260).

"Change" and "conscious action" are the key words here. It is part of the Neogrammarian, mechanical conception of language that language change is an unconscious, regular occurrence. That is, historical–comparative linguists presuppose that regularity is immanent to language, that change is internally regulated within the (somewhat mysterious) mechanism of language. If one shifts the burden of regulation to a language-internal system, then the need to appeal to external, political authority evaporates. Linguistic authority then becomes equivalent to something abstract and transcendent, like Nature, and the laws that are spoken of in language studies cease to be society's laws but (linguist-discovered) laws such as Grimm's Law, Verner's Law.

It is, however, the case that none of the three above-mentioned dogmas of modern linguistics had any weight in the eighteenth-century political conception of language (see Auroux 1986a: 260). Consciousness, enlightened consciousness, was the very goal of

Condillac's linguistic theory (see Andresen 1983). Consciousness, that is, the manipulation of consciousness, played the central role in prescriptive grammar as well, for prescriptive grammarians presuppose the idea that speaking norms are available to consciousness change. They believe, furthermore, that 1) irregularity in the speaking community is the undesirable norm and 2) their role is to introduce regularity in the speaking community, to level all the idiosyncratic differences that prevail among the various speaking agents. It is, however, the idea that speaking norms can and *should* be consciously manipulated that has been particularly scorned by (mechanical) linguists.

Although Webster was also against prescriptive grammars, he was committed to the notion of standard language, whereby all irregularities would be eliminated in the cause of achieving a unified nation. This standard would be democratically available to everyone in the classroom. An initial difference between prescriptive grammar and the notion of standard language hinges on the question of authority: to a Thomas Sheridan, for instance, the speech of the aristocratic elite – "the most judicious" – had more weight. Their "votes," i.e. usages, counted more. For Webster, standard language was the common man's propriety, a "power to the people" language in a linguistic democracy of "one citizen, one vote."

A second difference between a prescriptive grammar and a standard language derives from the source of their authority. In the former, prescriptive authority operates in an essentialist view of the world: "the most judicious" make their grammatical choices on the basis of "what is right," "what is logical." In the latter, a standard is, quite literally, a place to stand, in the etymological sense of Old French *estandard*, a flag to mark a rallying place (see Webster's Third).[9] One *place* might be just as good as the next, as long as everyone agrees to stand there. A case in point is the double negative. For Lowth *et al.*, the double negative was "illogical," with the rule "two negatives in English destroy one another, or are equivalent to an affirmative." For Webster, the double negative is entirely acceptable, even preferable. He questions Lowth and his "innovation," i.e. the single negative, in democratic, not aristocratic, terms. Webster argues that the single negative has not reached the great mass of the people, "and probably never will reach them; it being nearly impossible, in my opinion, ever to change a usage which enters into the language of every cottage, every hour and almost every moment" (quoted in Baron 1982: 139). However, Webster is not interested here in *descriptive* linguistics as the twentieth century knows it; he is rather more concerned with establishing a "politically correct" standard language.

As a coherent approach to language, this political conception of language has not survived the vagaries of the historical record of the nineteenth century. That is, it does not figure in the histories written by Benfey, Thomsen, and von Raumer, and it has not been passed on to the present. Given that I stated in the Preface that all theories of language are political in that they are elaborated in a specific historical context (p. 6), it might well be argued that the deeply embedded language–nation intersection of the political conception of language is a contingent by-product of the politically heightened atmosphere of the pre- and post-1776 era. It might then be argued that one needed to let that political excitement die down before one could get on with the business of studying language in and of itself, without the distorting effects of political revolution.

No. Rather, to write the political conception of language into the history of linguistics is precisely to challenge that mechanical or autonomous conception of language that has become historically and academically and, thus, practically, equivalent to the notion *true center* or *core* of linguistics. To rewrite linguistic history becomes equivalent to redefining what is meant by the term *linguistics*, the study, or science, of language.

THE CRUCIAL HINGE PERIOD IN LINGUISTICS

As was stated in the Introduction (p. 18) with regard to motivating the larger periodization of my study (1769–1924), so it is with the subdivisions: the choice of 1815 as my end-date to the first chapter has the peculiar effect of cutting off Webster and Jefferson mid-career. However, the date very well reflects my premise of linguistics as the group activity, and coincides nicely with other American and European intellectual trends; and, in any case, Webster and Jefferson express throughout their entire lives the eighteenth-century political conception of language.

With respect to the periodization in other American fields of endeavor, the date 1815 has often been chosen to mark a milestone. In American literature, for instance, Spiller uses 1815 in his *The American Literary Revolution* (1967) to cap the period he calls "The Aftermath of Independence." With the war of 1812 over, Spiller notes that American nationalism surged and became more complex. This new turn in the development of American cultural consciousness found concrete expression in the establishment of the *North American Review* (1815), which was, according to Spiller, to have consequences for the new literary nationalism (1967: viii–ix).

The founding of the *North American Review* was to have consequences for the new linguistic nationalism as well. Along with the *Transactions of the American Philosophical Society*, the *North American Review* was one of the most important American forums for linguistic ideas until the founding of the *Journal of the American Oriental Society* in 1849. Even after that, *The North American Review* continued to be an important outlet for, for example, the early outline of Peirce's pragmatic position ([1871] vol. 113: 449–72), as well as a variety of Whitney's writings, for instance, his critique of Max Mueller's *Lectures on the Science of Language* ([1865] 100: 565–81) and his critique of Steinthal's *Abriss der Sprachenwissenschaft* ([1872] 114: 272–308). An examination of the editorial policies towards language articles and a composite overview of those articles in the *North American Review* deserves a study in itself but will not be undertaken here.

Furthermore, in 1815, the American Philosophical Society recognized linguistics by creating the Historical and Literary Committee. This committee chose two objectives: 1) the collection of historic documents; and 2) manuscripts recording Indian languages (see Wissler 1942: 192). After this date, the two most important linguists of the first half of the nineteenth century, Peter S. Duponceau and John Pickering, became particularly active.

The date 1815 has also been traditionally invoked as a watershed in the development of American English or, rather, a consciousness of a distinct variety of American English. It was after this time that such influential educators and statesmen as Joseph Cogswell (1786–1871), George Ticknor (1791–1871), Edward Everett (1794–1865; first editor of the *North American Review*, first American to be awarded the PhD degree, Goettingen, 1817, among other things), and George Bancroft (1800–91) would return from their Grand Tours of Europe no longer awed by British English. It was after this time that the westward expansion began and that Americans, facing west, quit looking over their shoulders to the British model for approval. In his *American Language*, Mencken chose Andrew Jackson to symbolize the new American who appeared after 1814: "ignorant, pushful, impatient of restraint and precedent, an iconoclast, a Philistine, an Anglophobe in every fiber" (1963: 144). In this way, then, the date 1815 serves my purposes as well as it does, say, Spiller's and Mencken's.

In another, and equally important way, the date 1815 serves to tie American linguistic activity into European trends. Koerner has spoken of "linguistics after Waterloo," which marks the period after which historical and comparative linguistics really began to take off, particularly in Germany. Koerner notes that the year 1816, for instance, "witnessed the publication of Raynouard's Grammar of Old Provençal and Grimm's discovery of the causes of umlaut in Middle High German" (1986b: i). Similarly, in France, 1816 saw the re-edition of Court de Gébelin's *Histoire naturelle de la parole*, in whose introduction the Comte Lanjuinais opened language investigation into *"la science générale du langage"* (Désirat and Hordé 1982: 15). And at about this same time, significantly, the French Ideologues – those proponents of the political conception of language – were crumbling under the weight of their own failed terminology and of the unanswerable historical–comparative challenge from Germany (see Andresen 1988a).

On the subject of this historical–comparative challenge from Germany does the interesting theoretical issue surrounding the term *linguistics* emerge. Today, we are accustomed to identify the "true" beginnings of linguistics as those first studies of Bopp and Grimm. However, this application of the term *linguistics* is more an artifact of received history than a reflection of how linguistics was conceived in the early nineteenth century. It has been somehow forgotten, for instance, that neither Grimm nor Bopp refer to their own works with the words *Sprachwissenschaft* or *Linguistik*. Bopp's first work, published in 1816, bears the title *Ueber das Conjugationssystem der Sanskritsprache in Vergleichung mit jenem der griechischen, lateinischen, persischen und germanischen Sprachen*; while Grimm's first work, published in 1819, is entitled *Deutsche Grammatik*. Although Bopp and Grimm might have realized that they were moving away from the literary orientation of traditional philology, they made no attempt to divorce themselves from it openly and, indeed, regarded themselves as "philologists." Although the term *Sprachwissenschaft* existed at the time, they did not make use of it (Koerner 1982: 406).

In a recent study, Auroux (1987) has discovered that, beginning as early as 1812, the term *linguistique* was not used in France to refer specially to the methodological rigor for which Bopp and Grimm received "revolutionary" credit in retrospect. The term, was, indeed, connected with the idea that a new development of language studies had been initiated, but what was most novel to the mind of the early nineteenth-century scholar was the quantitative rise of the knowledge about the different languages of the world (Auroux 1987: 451). From the seventeenth century onward, the word *linguist* had been uniformly equivalent to *polyglot*. At the beginning of the nineteenth century, the main references of the use of the French term *linguistique* are to the works of Adelung and Vater, Balbi and Klaproth, that is, to those grand compilations of data on the world's languages, mentioned above (pp. 23–4).[10]

By 1867 and his *Geschichte der Sprachwissenschaft*, Benfey himself uses the adjective *linguistisch* to refer to the interest in the languages of the newly discovered parts of the globe. Of the eighteenth century, Benfey writes: "Rich was this century in geographical discoveries [which] produced an already very marked *linguistic interest*, in that [researchers] devoted right from the start a not insignificant attention to the languages of these newly-discovered territories" (1867: 263; emphasis mine).[11]

In America, in the first half of the nineteenth century, the terms *universal* or *philosophical grammar* – so resonant of the French tradition – were used to designate this new and exciting confrontation with the world's languages. John Pickering, one of the first Americans to wish "to study human speech as a science," considered a knowledge of American Indian languages indispensable to that science. In an 1820 article in the *North American Review*, Pickering makes a clear bid for the up-and-coming "science of language." In this article, it is Pickering's intention to draw the attention of "our philologists to the . . . structure of [the American Indian] languages," for Pickering is: "strongly inclined to believe . . . that we have yet much to learn upon the subject of *universal or philosophical grammar*." Pickering anticipates the philologists' objections, when he queries in the very next sentence: "Will it be asked of what use is it to examine the structure of languages in which there is no literature to compensate us for our labour?" And he replies: "If, indeed, our only motive in the study of languages were to repay ourselves by the stores of learning locked up in them, we should be but poorly rewarded for the labour of investigating the Indian dialects." He then makes his programmatic statement for the science of language:

> but if we wish *to study human speech as a science*, just as we do other sciences, by ascertaining all the facts or phenomena, and then proceeding to generalize and class those facts for the purpose of advancing human knowledge; in short, if what is called *philosophical grammar* is of any use whatever, then it is indispensable to the *philologist of comprehensive views*, to possess a knowledge of as many facts or phenomena of language as possible; and these *neglected dialects of our own continent* certainly do offer to the *philosophical inquirer* some of the most curious and interesting facts of any languages with which we are acquainted.
>
> (1820a: 113, misprinted in original as 213;
> emphasis mine throughout)

Pickering is attempting here to carve out a place for the study of the *facts and phenomena of language*, independent of a study of the language's literature. This study, then, is to be the basis on which the science of human speech is built and which must necessarily depend on a universal database, amply enriched by American Indian language data. We are at a delicate point here, however, for Pickering, as we shall see in Chapter 2, was deeply influenced by the new German science and eventually replaced the French-flavored "philosophical" or "universal grammar" as designations for the new science with "general philology". Even in 1820, though, Pickering is still very close to proposing a study of the *facts and phenomena of language* in and of themselves, that is, of orienting American language studies towards the mechanical conception of language, of drawing the philologist's attention to "the curious structure" (in and of itself) of the native American languages. Whether or not this "curious structure" exists apart from "the society and the beliefs of its speakers" is not yet at issue. What is at issue here is Pickering's attempt to dislodge the written from the spoken and making a place for the study of unwritten languages in the new science of language – however that science is to be named.

The immediate point to make here is the idea that what was felt as new around 1815, on both sides of the Atlantic, was the enlarged database on which the new science of language – linguistics – was to build. It was certainly not a given in 1815 that the Indo-European languages were predestined to be the center of the nineteenth-century linguistic universe, as Pickering's quote shows, nor that their study was going to become equivalent with the science of language or linguistics. That has happened only in retrospect, as a result of the unprecedented success of the German university in the nineteenth century and the packaging of German scholarship in such histories as Benfey's (see Chapters 2 and 3).

So important has this entire period of gestation leading up to 1815 been in the development of all subsequent attitudes and practices toward language in both Europe and America that it has been dubbed the *période charnière*, the "hinge period," in the history of linguistic theories (Auroux, Désirat, and Hordé 1982: 73). Strictly speaking, this crucial "hinge period" spans the thirty-year period on either side of the turn of the nineteenth century. In addition to the collapse of *idéologie*, the production of the grand, global inventories of the world's languages, the institutionalization in Germany of historical and comparative schools, and the shakedown of the use of the term *linguistics*, this hinge period encompasses the rise of the interest in Sanskrit, i.e. Indianism.

Or, it might be said (and has often been said) that Indianism provided the impetus for the whole linguistic enterprise of the nineteenth century. The first professional society devoted exclusively to language was the Asiatic Society of Calcutta (founded in 1783), and the first professional journal was *Asiatic Researches* (founded in 1788). Researchers in the United States saw fit to follow suit. The first professional linguistic society was the American Society of Oriental Studies, founded in 1842, and the first linguistic journal, the *Journal of the American Oriental Society* (1849). Indianism, furthermore, was to play a profound role in William Dwight Whitney's thought and reputation, both at home and abroad (Chapter 3).

The very subject of Indianism is, furthermore, a pivotal one in a discussion of the importance of history-writing. Sir William Jones (1746–94) is regularly credited with having gotten the

historical–comparative ball rolling with his 1786 discourse concerning the suspected relationship between the various European
languages with Sanskrit and Persian. It has been pointed out on
more than one occasion (most notably by Hoenigswald 1963;
1974) that Jones's observation in his famous Third Anniversary
Discourse to the Asiatic Society of Calcutta would not have had
the impact it did, had it not been for Friedrich Schlegel (1772–
1829) and others who buttressed the suspected relationship with
comparative evidence. Jones then later had his work acknowledged
in the histories of Benfey, Thomsen, and von Raumer, and then
reaffirmed by most subsequent historians, right down to the
present with Newmeyer's chronology of modern linguistics (i.e.
"autonomous linguistics") as beginning with Jones's 1786
discourse (1986: 17–18).

Recently, historiographers have drawn attention to an equally
provocative observation about possible language relationships
among the *other* Indians (Wolfart 1982; Koerner 1986b; see also
Wissler 1942: 190). One year after Jones's discourse (1786) but
one year before its publication (Calcutta, 1788), that is, in 1787,
the American Jonathan Edwards (1745–1801) addressed the
Connecticut Society of Arts and Sciences. In this lecture, Edwards
states from his "own knowledge" that "the language of the several
tribes in New England, of the Delawares, and of Mr. Eliot's Bible,
are radically the same with Mohegan" (see also Wolfart 1982:
403). Edwards goes on to provide parallel data from Mohegan and
Chippiwan (i.e. Ojibwa) – a move which Jones did *not* make in
his discourse – and concludes:

> It is not to be supposed, that the like coincidence is extended to
> all the words of those languages. Very many words are totally
> different. Still the analogy is such as is sufficient to show, that
> they are mere dialects of the same original language.
>
> (quoted in Koerner 1986b: iii)

In the United States, Edwards's paper was certainly regarded as
an important statement concerning the affiliation of various North
American languages, given the fact that several editions were
made of it in America, the last appearing in 1823 and provided
by John Pickering (Koerner 1986b: ii). Now, in parallel fashion to
the German-oriented Indo-Europeanists, Pickering and Duponceau
and Gallatin and Schoolcraft and other American linguists of the

first half of the nineteenth century, building on Edwards, forged ahead in their studies of the American Indian languages. However, in the absence of any subsequent affirmation of Edwards's contribution to historical and comparative linguistics in a history of the nineteenth century, it must be said that Edwards has remained, until recently, a marginal figure, at best, in the history of linguistics, however deserving he may be of receiving some special status in the historical record.

Yet there was another circumstance, from my group-effort perspective, to hinder the proper appreciation of Edwards's contribution to linguistics: Edwards, who died in 1801, was never elected into the American Philosophical Society. Neither was David Zeisberger, a specialist in the Delaware language. The only specialist in Indian languages elected to the society before 1800 was a friend of Zeisberger's, namely John Heckewelder in 1797. Of course, Duponceau had been elected before Heckewelder in 1791. However, Duponceau was not actively engaged in Indian languages until after 1815. Added to which was the fact that neither Duponceau nor Pickering nor any other Indianist of the early nineteenth century ever held academic positions. In the absence of 1) any group affiliation, such as Jones enjoyed in the Asiatic Society, 2) subsequent academic institutionalization, as in Germany, and 3) historical "packagings" such as Benfey's, it must be said that Edwards, Zeisberger, Heckewelder, as well as, for the most part, Duponceau and Pickering have been doomed to historical oblivion. Any sense of American Indian language studies belonging to any integrated tradition of American language studies in general has been lacking.

Neither was Noah Webster, a prominent expositor of the political conception of language, elected to the American Philosophical Society until very late in his career. Although a friend to Benjamin Franklin and his linguistic protégé as early as 1787 – for instance, Webster dedicated his *Dissertations* to Franklin – Webster was not granted membership in the American Philosophical Society until 1827, just before the publication of his life's work *The American Dictionary of the English Language*. Like Edwards, Webster has seemed an isolated, lonely figure in the formation of American linguistics. When we glance back at American language studies before 1815, we have a reinforced impression of general lack. This sense of isolation in American language studies is, however, easily dispelled by an investigation of the American Philosophical Society.

THE AMERICAN PHILOSOPHICAL SOCIETY

Benjamin Franklin (1706–90)

Before turning to an examination of the important and influential American Philosophical Society, let us consider Benjamin Franklin and his general impact on American language studies in the early years, for he begins the story of American linguistics in more ways than one. In addition to having helped Webster along, Franklin opened up four other paths for American language studies.

1   Franklin is the first in the historical record to forge an English-language relationship between language and money. Franklin coined the term *currency* in the sense of "money intended for circulation" and used it, according to the *Oxford English Dictionary*, as early as 1729. On the other side of the Atlantic, Samuel Johnson stigmatized Franklin's sense of the term in his *Dictionary* of 1755 in the sixth and last entry under *currency*: "the papers stamped in the English colonies by authority and passing for money." It is noteworthy that Johnson included the term at all. He had made well known his aversion for the socially inferior linguistic imports from the American Colonies, and his dictionary specifically excludes the majority of new colonial terms and usages. For instance, entries for *America* and *American* are conspicuous by their absence.

Despite Johnson's censure, the Scottish economist/linguist Adam Smith took up Franklin's use of *currency* in his *Wealth of Nations* (first published in the year of the American Revolution), and the term *currency* passed into currency in the English language. The intersection of the linguistic and the economic over the last several hundred years, and in particular the Saussurean sources of *valeur*, has been the subject of several recent studies (Swiggers 1982; Auroux 1985).

The most notable effort to re-intersect the two realms of discourse – the linguistic and the economic – is Bourdieu's "The Economics of Linguistic Exchanges," where he boldly effects a three-fold displacement in the concepts of contemporary linguistics:

i) in place of *grammaticalness*, he puts *acceptability* and *legitimacy*;

ii) in place of *relations of communication*, he puts *relations of symbolic power*;

iii) and in place of *linguistic competence*, he puts *symbolic capital* (1977: 646).

Bourdieu then defines *philologism* as "a particular form of the intellectualism and objectivism which pervade the social sciences" and which is "the theory of language which foists itself on people who have nothing to do with language except study it" (1977: 646). Bourdieu then asks: "What did [anthropologists, sociologists] have to concede to linguistics in order to be able to carry out their mechanical transcriptions of the principles of linguistics?" The answer will hinge precisely on the question of authority – for Bourdieu, "symbolic capital", what I will call "linguistic capital" – which was so pivotal in the political conception of language (see above pp. 30ff.). For Bourdieu, the most visible manifestation of philologism is the primacy linguistics gives to *competence* over the *market* (1977: 647), a move that was *not* made within the terms of the political conception of language. In fact, the political conception of language gives primacy precisely to the *market* and to *legitimacy* and to *power*. In this light, we can now identify, for instance, Thomas Sheridan's "most judicious rational enquirers" as those speakers possessing the most linguistic capital.

The general American English-language association of the two realms of discourse, language and money, was complete by the early decades of the nineteenth century. So was the perception of the political dimension of that association. What began as a social skirmish between England and America with Franklin's coinage in 1729 had become political warfare by 1812. In the midst of both British military attacks on American soil and British linguistic attacks on American English, John Adams declared patriotically that "the United States had the right to coin words as well as money" (quoted in Heath 1977: 28). The dollar had already replaced the pound as the standard of American currency, suggested by Thomas Jefferson, and along with it Jefferson's other coinages of mill, cent, disme, and eagle, made official by the Act Establishing a Mint in 1792 (Mencken 1938: 116). Still, the issue of American linguistic coinages, "Americanisms," was not so easily settled by any governmental act or reform. In all events, the folk-linguistic association of language and money was firmly established by 1815, so that today an expression such as *money talks* hardly has metaphoric force anymore and is entirely platitudinous.

2   Franklin might also be said to be the first to have conceived of "English" as a subject matter fit to be taught in schools. In his *Idea of an English School* (1750), Franklin attempted to shake off the ties binding New World educational practices to the Old by suggesting the wholly new idea of providing a "utilitarian education for citizenship conducted entirely in the English language" (Parker 1967: 342). Though apparently too radical at the time to be fully implemented, this idea did provide a precedent for later American educators who advocated the study of modern subjects over the "unaccountable prejudice in favor of ancient customs and beliefs" (see Applebee 1974: 19, note 42). Franklin's new idea was also not without immediate influence in his own times. Franklin's friend, Ebenezer Kinnersley, was America's first professor of any aspect of English (specifically: Professor of the English Tongue and Oratory) at an academy which opened in Philadelphia in 1751 and which included an "English School." That academy, incidentally, became a college in 1755 and was later to be called the University of Pennsylvania (Parker 1967: 342). Since English as a major school subject did not emerge until the 1890s, Franklin's idea was truly far-reaching.

3   Franklin was a printer, among other things, and as such, he was concerned with the written representation of the spoken word. In 1768 he proposed a scheme for a new alphabet and a reformed mode of spelling. This concern would tie him into the various spelling-reform movements so characteristic of American English studies from Webster to Whitney, one of the most widely known proposals being William Thornton's, which was first put before the American Philosophical Society in 1788.

The concern for the written representation of language is, once again, a concern of those who operate within a political conception of language, which does not recognize a schism between the spoken and the written word. Or, rather, until Saussure's pronouncement to the contrary, the spoken word was considered to have every bit as material (that is, *substantial* as opposed to merely *formal*) an existence as the written. In a letter from Franklin to Webster of December 26, 1789, Franklin first thanks Webster for having been chosen as the dedicatee to the latter's *Dissertations*. Franklin praises Webster for the work and makes the following analogy: "A book, for example, ill printed, or a pronunciation in speaking not well articulated, would render a sentence unintelligible, which from a clear print or a distinct speaker would have been immediately comprehended" (1848 [1789]: 204). Franklin's analogy is not chosen at random: the spoken and the written were considered equally material. In lamenting the disuse of the long *s*, Franklin observes, in the same letter to Webster: "Certainly the omitting the prominent letter makes a line appear more even, but renders it less immediately legible; as the paring off all men's noses might smooth their features, but would render their physiognomies less distinguishable" (1848 [1789]: 205). Here, Franklin views language and its written form as something substantial, "as plain as the nose on your face."

Webster, too, envisioned both the spoken and the written language as equally material, and, in fact, quite literally material, like clothing. Webster was fond of issuing declarations of independence against England in the matter of orthography as well as coat buttons and was given to statements "We shall wear our clothes as we please" which had as much linguistic force as sartorial (see Malone 1925: 26). At the turn of the nineteenth century, the intersection of language and clothing was as commonplace as that of language and money. John Adams would write to Webster on the occasion of the latter's *Compendious Dictionary*: "we *can* manufacture words as we can manufacture broadcloth for ourselves" (quoted in Malone 1925: 28), although in this particular passage Adams was a lot more censorious of Webster in 1806 than he was to become as a result of the war of 1812, evidenced by his rather Websterian statement quoted on the page before. It would take the whole of the nineteenth century to make of language something incorporial, to "divest" it of its "dress."[12]

Webster's concern for spelling reform is, of course, that the spoken and the written match, and that both are uniform. His concern derives primarily from recognition of the domestic need for a literate citizenry. Franklin has the same concern that there be no gap between the spoken and the written, but in the above passage his concern springs from a foreign-policy desire to see the English language more generally known among mankind, the same desire that impelled the various designs for the American

Language Academy (see above pp. 34–5). After commenting on the relationship between poor printing and poor pronunciation, Franklin continues, in the same letter as quoted above: "If, therefore, we would have the benefit of seeing our language more generally known among mankind, we should endeavor to remove all the difficulties, however small, that discourage the learning of it" (1848 [1789]: 204–5). Franklin sees that French possesses most of the intellectual and linguistic capital of the day, for a few lines above in the letter to Webster, he writes: "It is, perhaps, owing to its being written in French, that Voltaire's Treatise on Toleration has had so sudden and so great an effect on the bigotry of Europe, as almost entirely to disarm it." Franklin understands the frank economic benefits of acquiring some of this intellectual and linguistic capital for English and continues:

> The general use of the French language has likewise a very advantageous effect on the profits of the bookselling branch of commerce; it being well known, that the more copies can be sold that are struck off from one composition of types, the profits increase in a much greater proportion than they do in making a greater number of pieces in any other kind of manufacture.
>
> (1848 [1789]: 204)

In thinking that "English bids fair to obtain the second place" after French, Franklin wishes a uniform spelling and a clear and distinct printing to facilitate the spread of English in the world marketplace. We have here an early American example of "Avis Tries Harder."

4   Franklin was the first American to visit Goettingen in 1766. Toward the end of the eighteenth century, the German universities of Halle and Goettingen were rising in importance in America, while the prestige of the French intellectual community was waning. Following in Franklin's footsteps in the early decades of the nineteenth century, Ticknor, Everett, Cogswell, and Bancroft would also visit these universities and would return to extol the critical methods of Germany's historical and social sciences. After 1815, the new German scholarship would be welcomed, stateside, with the same enthusiasm that Americans were greeting everything fresh and promising. In language studies, this meant an enthusiastic embrace

of German philology as conceived in 1777 by Frederich Wolf at the University of Goettingen. Although Wolf's interest focused on the culture of Greece and Rome, he defined his task broadly as providing the "biography of a nation," which would eventually allow philology to encompass modern language study (see Applebee 1974: 25).

Of course, Franklin's most far-reaching contribution to the study of language in the United States endures in the American Philosophical Society, "held at Philadelphia for promoting useful knowledge." The American Philosophical Society was the most prestigious and influential intellectual society in any field of inquiry in the early years of the republic. After a false start in 1743, Franklin succeeded in creating the American Society in 1769, modeling it more or less on the Royal Society in London, which was chartered in 1662. Franklin was the society's first president from 1769 to his death in 1790. The focus of the society, as written in the charter of 1780 by John Bayard, speaker, and signed by Thomas Paine, clerk, was simply:

> this country of North America, which the goodness of Providence hath given to us to inherit, from the vastness of its extent, the variety of its climate, the fertility of its soil, the yet unexplored treasures of its bowels . . . offers to these United States one of the richest subjects of cultivation, ever presented to any people upon earth.
>
> (Bayard 1910 [1780]: 3–4)

Among the "unexplored treasures of its bowels" were recognized to be the native American languages, and the society promoted the gathering of any and all materials concerning the indigenous languages, particularly after 1815, such that the record of native American texts and vocabularies gathered by the American Philosophical Society doubles as a history of American Indian studies up to the Civil War. In fact, the Library of the American Philosophical Society was so closely allied with the native American languages that it seemed only natural to house the impressive Boas Collection there in 1945.

In its original charter, the society identified six committees or sections to be established: i) Geography, Mathematics, Natural Philosophy, and Astronomy; ii) Medicine and Anatomy; iii) Natural

History and Chemistry; iv) Trade and Commerce; v) Mechanics and Architecture; vi) Husbandry and American Improvements. A seventh Committee, on History, Moral Science, and General Literature, was added in 1815, and this was the committee that would so firmly establish American Indian languages as one of the priorities of the Society.

The list of resident members of the American Philosophical Society with an interest in language represents the widest possible conception of linguistic theory and practice. In the two-hundred-year register of its resident membership appear the names (with the date of their election to the society in parentheses) of: John Witherspoon (1769); John Walker (1769); John Adams (1780); Thomas Jefferson (1780; president of the society from 1797 to 1814); Peter S. Duponceau (1791; president of the society from 1828 to 1844); John Heckewelder (1797); Benjamin S. Barton (1789); George Gibbs (1810); John Pickering (1820); Noah Webster (1827); Edward Everett (1831); Henry Schoolcraft (1833); Joseph Story (1844); George Marsh (1849); William Dwight Whitney (1863); Ralph W. Emerson (1867); Daniel Brinton (1869); Albert Gatschet (1884); J.W. Powell (1889); Albert Gallatin (1891); Herman Collitz (1902); Basil Gildersleeve (1903); Franz Boas (1903); Maurice Bloomfield (1904); Edward Sapir (1937); Alfred Kroeber (1941); and Leonard Bloomfield (1942).

The society was eager to promote and maintain contact with the Old World intellectuals. Among the prominent foreign linguists who were elected to membership in the American Philosophical Society figure: M.J. Condorcet (France, 1775); Antoine Court de Gébelin (France, 1783); Christian Michaelis (Germany, 1785); Pierre J.G. Cabanis (France, 1786); James Beattie (Scotland, 1786); Peter S. Pallas (Russia, 1791); Dugald Steward (Scotland, 1791); Constantin Volney (France, 1797); William Jones (England, 1801); Antoine Destutt de Tracy (France, 1806); Johann Vater (Germany, 1817); Friedrich von Adelung (Germany, 1818); Jean Lanjuinais (France, 1819); Wilhelm von Humboldt (Germany, 1822); Heinrich Klaproth (Germany, 1824); Rasmus Rask (Denmark, 1829); Karl Lepsius (Germany, 1845); Jacob Grimm (Germany, 1863); Franz Bopp (Germany, 1863); Friedrich Max Mueller (England, 1863; note: the same year as Whitney's election); Horatio Hale (Canada, 1872), Paul Broca (France, 1872); Ferdinand de Saussure (Switzerland, 1873); Lucien Adam

(France, 1886); Hyacinthe de Charencey (France, 1886); Wilhelm Wundt (Germany, 1895); and Benedetto Croce (Italy, 1944).

As with the resident membership, this list of foreign members represents a wide range of linguistic activity. Among the French names, a slight emphasis on linguists interested in American Indian languages, from Court de Gébelin to Charency, may be discerned. Among the German linguists, an anthropological orientation, from Michaelis to Wundt, weights the lists. These emphases arise from the society's orientation toward investigating the native American languages and the need for interpreting that data in a larger, anthropological framework.

These emphases also coincide with the initial sense of "linguistics," mentioned above, where the newness of the enterprise, both in Europe and America, was focused on the quantitative rise in data. The anthropological orientation of the society is also reflected in Bopp's and Grimm's rather late invitation to join in 1863, suggesting that their work was of less immediate importance to the Americans in the nineteen- 'teens and -'twenties than was that of their compatriots, namely Vater, Adelung, and Klaproth.

Notably absent in this list are English names, save for that of William Jones. Horne Tooke's, for instance, does not appear (which, given Webster's avowed admiration for him, may also account for Webster's long-term marginalization from the society). The reasons for this absence are not hard to find. Although English members were elected into the society between 1776 and 1812, a period of Anglo-American tension, American feelings toward the English were anything but cordial. Then, too, Thomas Jefferson, the society's third president from 1797 to 1814, was very much taken up with French Ideology, and it so happened that the French, in contradistinction to the English and the Germans, were devoted to Amerindian studies in the nineteenth century.

French Ideology and the American Philosophical Society

The first names on the foreign members' list, especially those from France, i.e. Condorcet, Court de Gébelin, Cabanis, Volney, Destutt de Tracy, had a particular importance in shaping language studies in France during and after the French Revolution. These names represent the most prominent Ideologues, a group which included the chemist Lavoisier, who was among the very first foreign members elected to the American Philosophical Society, in 1775. Ideology was to play a prominent role not only in the political writings of Thomas Jefferson, which cannot be investigated here, but also it was to later surface in the linguistic writings of Peter Stephen Duponceau (see Chapter 2). In order to understand the change of orientation that was to occur in language studies in the United States after the turn of the nineteenth century, it is worth developing a context for French Ideology which issues out of eighteenth-century French language philosophy and which comes to an end during the crucial "hinge period" in linguistics.

The most important names in the list, in terms of the development of language studies, are Antoine Destutt de Tracy (1754–1836) and Constantin Volney (1757–1820). Of all the Ideologues, Destutt de Tracy is the most representative. His name, more than any other, is historically linked to Ideology in that he published his monumental five-volume *Eléments d'idéologie* (1803–15); and earlier, he published *Mémoire sur la faculté de penser* (1796), wherein he coined the term *idéologie*. There he proposed Ideology to be the *science des idées*, the science which would supplant metaphysics, a unifying kind of superscience of "theory of theories." He had a total vision for Ideology which would eventually be seen as undesirably totalitarian and which he defined as "la science qui résulte de l'analyse des sensations." With the words *analyse* and *sensations*, he identified his Condillacian heritage.

However, Tracy went beyond Condillac and the eighteenth century. No longer content with approaching the human sciences in the style of the eighteenth-century *as if* human beings might not have a divine origin, Tracy made it official by announcing in the Preface to his *Eléments* that Ideology was part of zoology. With this move, Tracy not only made a radical theological break, he also separated man from the possibility of permanent enlightened consciousness, from the possibility of fixing the mind in its flux, which was to have been attainable through the construction of the *langue bien faite*. Tracy, of course, is writing at the turn of the nineteenth century, *after* the French Revolution had shaken philosophical thought out of its static, self-satisfied abstractions and language theory out of its claims at universalism. Tracy is thus tottering on the edges of linguistic relativism. Whereas

Condillac had wished to make of language something ultimately transparent, Tracy stumbled across the object in his way and begins to recognize the idea of "language barrier."

The recognition of "language barrier" is not only a consequence of the unsettling climate produced by the French Revolution, it also follows from within Condillac's theory of language. Pushing Condillac's sensualism to the limit, Tracy's "ideationism" recognizes only that reality which is mediated by the perception of a subject who establishes her/his existence with the same movement that s/he establishes that of exterior objects. For Tracy, the individual can never completely rise above the physical, cultural, and linguistic forces which determine individuality. The individual can never be completely other than the product of conditions over which s/he might not have control. That is, the individual is now immersed in a predominantly social, or more correctly, *political* (and not rational) dynamic. Even though Tracy arrives at the point of trying to understand the *individual*, he is not at a point of affirming *linguistic* individualism. He is interested, rather, in the genetic development of the formation of the system of signs that determines this individuality; and meditation on the sign always presupposes the fundamentally *social* nature of language, where signs represent social contracts in miniature. Each word exists to the degree that it is *conventionally* agreed upon by the speaking community, however large or small. In relativizing the results of each society's process of language-making, Tracy does not remove language from its social arena; thus he does not make of language an individual possession. Tracy, we might say, following Auroux (1986a), is concerned here with the subject of *langue*.

Volney, for his part, also travelled down the path of linguistic relativism: "It is no longer sufficient," he wrote in 1819, "to know Greek and Latin in order to pursue the philosophy of language, in order to construct these theories which one calls 'universal grammar'" (quoted in Auroux, Désirat, and Hordé 1982: 76).[13] By appealing to the tradition of "universal grammar," Volney is allying himself to that other subject, the subject of *grammaire générale*, namely: the human mind, "reason equally distributed in each human being." In this distribution of reason, the problem then became to account for global linguistic diversity. The problem was, furthermore, dynamized on an historic axis. Volney opted for a polygenetic explanation for the world's languages. He wished to group them according to their *constitutions différentes*, these constitutions or *plans* being recognized as historical social products. Volney's general project, then, was to discover "the history of peoples on the basis of the history of their language" ("l'histoire des peuples à partir de celle de leur langue") – a project that is empirical and *a posteriori* and which, above all, places the accent on the differences. Volney clearly recognized a version of linguistic relativism, with the built-in problem that would vex the whole of the nineteenth century on both sides of the Atlantic: namely, the epistemological tension between that relativistic study soon to be called ethnography (i.e. "l'histoire des peuples à partir de celle de leur langue") and the universalism of Ideology (as one outgrowth of *grammaire générale*, whose job it was to elaborate a theory of mind inherent in all languages; see Auroux, Désirat, and Hordé 1982).

Although Tracy and the Ideologues in general affirmed (to varying degrees) the importance of the study of signs and, more generally, the *plan* of ideas formed by each particular system of signs, they did not write about sign theory so much as use it to serve political ends. Ideology was, furthermore, by its very nature, interdisciplinary, a true child of the Encyclopedic spirit. The *Décade*, the major publication for the expression of this spirit, did not, for instance, publish much on language. Rather, this journal accorded most of its space to inventions, applied sciences, economic problems, and medicine. The *Décade* was received in Philadelphia during the years of its existence from 1794 to 1807, and a brief comparison between it and the *Transactions of the American Philosophical Society* shows that both publications displayed a similar Voltairian spirit of utility and common sense.

Although sign theory and French Ideology were to receive strong competition from German thought, particularly from Wilhelm von Humboldt (see Chapters 2, 3, and 4), the first two decades of the American nineteenth century were still invested in reacting and responding to French thought, as can be seen in the work of Thomas Jefferson.

Thomas Jefferson (1743–1826)

As the third president of the American Philosophical Society, after Benjamin Franklin and David Rittenhouse, Thomas Jefferson is an integral part of the early history of American language studies. Jefferson's interest in the study of language has been described above (pp. 25–6).

In true eighteenth-century style, Jefferson believed, first, that nation and speech thoroughly intersected, the usual formulation of this idea being that "the character of a nation is most fully reflected in its speech." Second, in the style of the turn of the nineteenth century, Jefferson, like Volney, understood the nation–speech intersection to have a third dimension, that of historical embeddedness. Jefferson was interested in the genetic reconstruction of language, be it of the European languages in general (and English, in particular) or of the American Indian languages. In a letter to that great compiler J.S. Vater, Jefferson wrote in 1812: "I have long considered the filiation of languages as the best proof we can ever obtain of the filiation of nations" (quoted in Hauer 1983: 880).

At the same time, it would be a distortion to overemphasize Jefferson's involvement with the study of language. He was just as likely to write that the theoretical study of grammar had "never been a favorite with me," or that "I acknowledge myself . . . not an adept in the metaphysical speculations of Grammar" (quoted in Hauer 1983: 892); and his *Essay on the Anglo-Saxon Language* has been finely criticized by Hauer (1983). Furthermore, for instance, Jefferson's lack of understanding of the phonetic process of metathesis strikes the contemporary reader as rather quaint when he writes that Old English letters were not always arranged in the "correct" order, thus *birds* was "wrongly" spelled *brides*, *grass* as *gaers*, and so on (Baugh 1940: 95). These weak points aside, what emerges from Jefferson's work on language is a sense of the consequences of the eighteenth-century political conception of language, those directions in language study that he sketched out and that others were to develop in the course of the nineteenth century. I have identified five of Jefferson's interrelated pursuits.

1 *Language history*. Jefferson was not a Romantic, and his conception of language history remains non-mechanical. That is to say, then, that the introduction of an historical perspective into language study does not necessarily lead to comparative grammar.

Just as Horne Tooke thought Saxon the authentic core of modern English, so Jefferson saw Saxon laws as the authentic core of democracy. For Jefferson, the study of Old English, which he began as early as 1762, served particular legal ends, in that he felt its study valuable for determining the "true" laws of the English-speaking peoples (cf. Sir William Jones and his need to study Sanskrit in order to understand Hindu Law). During Jefferson's time, the "Saxon myth," as legal historians have termed the movement, was a prevalent interpretation of the English constitution and common law as essentially Anglo-Saxon legacies, reflecting the primitive democracy portrayed as early as Tacitus' *Germania* (first century AD). The elective monarchy, the folk-moot, trial by jury, and common law were all traced to the fifth-century invaders of Britain and the codes of law devised by their descendants. According to this view, feudalism was a Norman-imposed deformation of these rights, which were not restored until the Magna Carta and ultimately the American Revolution. Jefferson believed that a reading knowledge of Anglo-Saxon was essential for a complete understanding and appreciation of both the letter and the spirit of the law.

2   With such a view of the nature of the importance of language history, Jefferson had a rather modern awareness of *dialectology*. Jefferson recognized the importance of the study of provincial English dialects and – always a linguistic liberal – advocated the resuscitation of archaisms that such dialects preserved. He displayed a lifelong interest in the non-standard branches of English and what they could teach about the native tongue. He understood fully the concept of dialect conservatism when, in a letter of 1825, he wrote of the benefits of dialect study that: "It is probable we shall find that there is not a word in Shakespeare which is not now in use in some of the counties in England" (quoted in Hauer 1983: 892–3).

3   The historical study of English led Jefferson to recognize, like Webster and Franklin, the need for *spelling reform*. Through working with the Anglo-Saxon manuscripts, Jefferson found the characters of the insular minuscule "rugged, uncouth, and appalling." Jefferson deplored the spelling variations and lack of standardization of Old English, apparently *not* recognizing here the possibility of dialect variations. He also saw that many English spellings were products of historical accident and, thus, supported spelling reform. He even had the charming idea to reform Old English spelling.

4   Again, in concert with Franklin and Webster, Jefferson tied his concern for spelling reform into his deep belief in *the importance of pedagogy*. When the University of Virginia opened its doors in 1825, Jefferson made sure to include Anglo-Saxon as a part of the Department of Modern Languages, and wished to see a national policy for its instruction to *all* American undergraduates (a desire, we all know, which was not fulfilled), along with Latin and Greek. Although Jefferson was not an active promoter of the new German science, he was aware of the coming trends, and the professor he engaged for the subject was the German-trained Dr Georg Blaettermann of Leipzig (see Bruce 1920: 89–95 for an account of Blaettermann's teaching duties). In a real sense, then, Jefferson was instrumental in integrating the new German science into American academic life. He laid heavy emphasis on the learning of modern languages: number one was French, of course, then came Spanish, because of its importance in the New World, followed by Italian, then German.

5   Finally, Jefferson actively promoted *the study of American Indians and American Indian languages*, sounding many of the themes that would dominate the nineteenth century. In addition to his Indian-vocabulary collection, Jefferson was also interested in archaeology, having excavated in 1784 "a barrow," or burial mound, in Virginia. He reported his techniques in detail, anticipating some of the modern archaeological methods, and making some valid inferences, which are discussed in his *Notes on the State of Virginia* written between 1781–5 (1950: 116–18). He also encouraged others in ethnographic research. In his instructions to Lewis and Clark, just before their expedition of 1803–6, Jefferson suggested that the explorers particularly investigate Indian religious customs. Since Jefferson made the suggestion so that Lewis and Clark could search for affinities between Indian ceremonies and those of the ancient Jews, Jefferson must have had in mind the theory, then in vogue, that the Indians were descendants from the Lost Tribes of Israel.

Many of Jefferson's most influential remarks on the Indians and language occur in his *Notes on Virginia*. In this work, he first asks the question: "whence came those aboriginals of America?" and then attempts to answer by suggesting a passage from Europe to America by way of Norway to Iceland, from Iceland to Greenland, from Greenland to Labrador (1950: 119). He recognizes that to fully support this answer, one needs to be "skilled in the languages of the old world [and] to compare with these [languages spoken in North and South America], now, or at any future time, and hence to construct the best evidence of the derivation of this part of the human race" (1950: 119).

Jefferson also offers an opinion on the probable vast quantity of stocks of the American Indian languages. He admits that "imperfect as is our knowledge of the tongues spoken in America," he nevertheless observes the "following remarkable fact" that by arranging the languages of the new world:

> under the radical ones to which they may be palpably traced, and doing the same by those of the red men of Asia, there will be found probably twenty in America, for one in Asia, of those radical languages, so called because if they were ever the same they have lost all resemblance to one another. A separation into dialects may be the work of a few ages only, but for two dialects to recede from one another till they have lost all vestiges of their common origin, must require an immense course of time; perhaps not less than many people give to the age of the earth.
> (1950: 119–21).

This passage synthesizes several of Jefferson's sensitivities to language, both his anthropological and philological bent, and shows how deeply embedded in American linguistics is the single, unified effort of "linguistic anthropology," though it is signalled by a dual term. For Jefferson, at least, the effort toward "linguistic anthropology" springs from within his political conception of language. The passage also contains an implicit question that will be explicitly asked by scientific inquiries after Jefferson's death: what *is* the age of the earth?

Benjamin Smith Barton honored Jefferson's contribution to the study of Indian language by dedicating his *New View on the Origins of the Tribes and Nations of America* of 1797 to Jefferson, then vice-president of the United States. Barton's one-hundred-page Preface is devoted, in large measure, to investigating the implications of Jefferson's assertions in the passages quoted above. Quite respectfully disagreeing with Jefferson, Barton notes that since, "when the Europeans took possession of the countries of North-America, they found the western parts of the continent much more thickly settled than the eastern'', he is led to the conclusion that ''all the earlier visitors of America . . . are of Asiatic origin'' (1797: xcv). Secondly, Barton's classifications of the Indian languages ''do not favour the opinion of Mr Jefferson, that the number of radical languages in American is so great.'' Barton offers a palliative:

> It is true that hitherto we have discovered but very little resemblance between several of these languages. But then it should be remembered, that our collections of words are very small and imperfect, and of course, that as yet we have not had opportunities of pointing out all the resemblances which may exist.
>
> (1797: lxii–lxiii)

To decide these issues, Barton points to ''the labour of future inquirers.''

Still in his *Notes on Virginia*, Jefferson predicts a major trend in American language studies, namely the refuting of European views of the American Indian (see Chapter 2). In particular, Jefferson took issue with Georges de Buffon (1707–88) by quoting at length the ''afflicting picture'' Buffon paints of the ''savage of the new world'' in his *Histoire naturelle* (1749), which ''for the honor of human nature'' Jefferson is ''glad to believe has no original.'' Jefferson then continues, on the strength of his own knowledge and better informed sources than Buffon's, that the Indian of North America:

> is neither more defective in ardor, nor more impotent with his female, than the white reduced to the same diet and exercise; that he is brave, when an enterprise depends on bravery . . . that he will defend himself against a host of enemies, always choosing to be killed, rather than to surrender . . . that he is affectionate with his children . . . that his friendships are strong and faithful to the utmost extremity; that his sensibility is keen.
>
> (1950: 89–90)

It was, however, as we shall see, to take more than Jefferson's words to convince the Europeans, and many Americans, of the Indians' worth, and with limited success.

Although some of Jefferson's approaches to the study of the Indians did not stand the test of even his own time, his overall approach to the Indians was neither that of the ''Enlightened'' nor the "Romantic" European speculative philosopher. Rather, he, like many other Colonists, was a practical man who found himself cohabiting a continent with other ordinary human beings whose co-operation was necessary for survival. Jefferson held to the "self-evident" truth that all men are created equal, and it was apparently upon Jefferson's insistence that the Lockean phrase be included in the Declaration of Independence (Malefijt 1977: 216). While Jefferson might have had some reservations about the equal status of Negroes, he harbored no such doubts about the Indians, and similar to Franklin, Jefferson remained a defender of Indians – in his writings, at least – throughout his life.[14]

Noah Webster (1758–1843)

Noah Webster was not elected into the American Philosophical Society until 1827, making him something of a "left-over" problem in this overview of the trends in language studies within the context of the American Philosophical Society.

Webster's long-time marginalization from the society is not difficult to motivate. When Franklin died in 1790, Webster lost his strongest sponsor. Although Jefferson did, for example, possess a copy of Webster's *Compendious Dictionary* (1806), it is well documented that Jefferson did not like Webster. In a letter to James Madison, for instance, Jefferson stigmatized Webster as a "mere pedagogue, of very limited understanding" (August 12, 1801). Earlier, in a personal letter from Jefferson to Webster of 1790, Jefferson had politely disagreed with Webster on a point of Webster's overzealously expressed federalism. The impression conveyed by Webster's recent biographers confirms Jefferson's negative opinion. It seems that Webster was a crank. He had no close friends and was obsessed with the idea that nobody liked him. Lest Webster be further branded as paranoid, his biographers suggest that Webster was probably right (Rollins 1980; Moss 1984).

More than any other American devoted to the study of language, Webster has symbolized the solitary effort of the early American: dedicated despite little praise and much opposition and without institutional support (Heath 1977). Webster was not the "gentleman scholar" of Jefferson and was in debt most of his life. It is reported that he even had to mortgage his home to bring out a second edition of his *American Dictionary*, the first having sold only 2,500 copies (Warfel 1936).

There is something of the pre-Romantic Rousseauian *promeneur solitaire* in this image of the rather noble (though cranky) solitary scholar. The image certainly jibes well with the received image of the lack of early American efforts in the study of language. However, I hope to have drawn in this chapter a less bleak picture for the early years, a picture which includes a high degree of communication among Americans and between Americans and Europeans on issues of language. I hope, as well, that a clear and consistent political conception of language has emerged, a conception of language as a political tool, as a pragmatic instrument of the people, whose existence is not at all autonomous but fully integrated into all other social institutions and whose study is fully integrated, as well, into other aspects of social life. If the image of Noah Webster that has been handed down to us is one of solitude and isolation, it might well have been his own fault, for he seems to have invited attack his entire life. As for that life, Webster underwent a series of changes, but none of them seemed to endear him to the world in which he lived.

A central issue in the elaboration of the political conception of language is that of authority. Webster sought it at all times, and during the course of his life, he passed through three phases in identifying the locus of linguistic authority: he began with a belief in the authority of the common person; he passed to a belief in the authority of an elite ruling segment; and he ended with a belief in the "ultimate" authority, namely God.

The young Webster believed universal liberty was of ultimate importance, and had great faith in the will of the people. It was not long, however, before he lost his faith in the capacity of the masses to rule themselves. Deeply disturbed by domestic incidents like the Shay's Rebellion (Massachusetts 1786–7) and terrified by the outcome of the French Revolution, Webster, roughly around 1800, abandoned his beliefs in the goodness of humankind and in the plurality of truths, and began his life-long search for other kinds of authority. In the second stage, he set the laws and supreme will of the state above individual authority and set forth to establish federal English. Later in life, his revolutionary ideals shattered, fearing the common man, thoroughly skeptical of political endeavors, having seen his brand of federalism defeated, and mistrusting the nation's leaders, Webster devoted much of his energies to an extremely authoritarian-minded group of evangelical Protestants. In 1780 he had thought the answer to everything was the school. By 1823 it was God. He dedicated his *The American Dictionary* of 1828 "To the great and benevolent Being, who during the preparation of this work, has sustained a feeble constitution" (see Rollins 1980: 45). It is entirely apposite that Webster's sole contribution to the language, his sole surviving "Americanism," should be the verb *to demoralize* (Mencken 1963: 134; Pyles 1952: 123; Paine 1987).

For the young Webster, there was Horne Tooke's authority and the theory of the historical emergence of the parts of speech. To Webster's ever-lasting infamy is his statement that Horne Tooke's theory derives great strength from analyzing the words called conjunctions, with the following example:

> It will perhaps surprise those who have not attended to this subject, to hear it asserted, that the little conjunction *if*, is a *verb* in the Imperative Mode. That this is the fact can no more be controverted than any point of history, or any truth that our senses present to the mind. *If* is radically the same word as *give*; it was in the Saxon Infinitive, *gifan*, and in the Imperative, like other Saxon verbs, lost the *an*; being written *gif*. This is the word in its purity.
>
> (1951 [1789]: 186–7)

However wrong-headed in points of fact Webster may have been, he did identify etymology and definition as the twin foundations of lexicography and of his dictionary. With regard to the incorporation of historical perspective into Webster's work, it becomes clear, once again, that the incorporation of historical perspective in language studies does not inevitably lead to comparative grammar. That is, Webster's conception of language remains political and not mechanical. History – for Webster, etymology – would come to his aid to justify usage which, for Webster, was losing its "synchronic" determination, in that his first-stage belief in the pluralism of the common man was giving way to his second-stage belief that this pluralism was really chaos. As for his third stage, Webster's driving interest in etymology was not differently motivated than many other scholars' before and after him: to reconstruct the *original*, God-given language, the one True Standard.

With each stage, Webster became less tolerant and less plural-
istic about "the truth." It is understandable how a life-long,
plural-minded, (linguistic) liberal like the republican Jefferson
would not have taken to the federalist Webster. Jefferson also had
a better acquaintance with foreign languages than did Webster.
Although neither of them commanded Anglo-Saxon, Jefferson
actually fared better than Webster, by some accounts (Laird 1946:
11; but cf. Hauer 1983). In addition, Jefferson had a broader
involvement in American Indian languages. Webster, of course, is
aware of the Indian languages, but his comments are confined to
one reference, as far as I have been able to discover. Following
Horne Tooke, Webster notes that nouns and verbs are the only
absolutely necessary parts of speech for communication among
rude nations. Webster cites, in fact, Dr Edwards on the Mohegan
tongue (1788), in his observation that "some tribes of savages in
America use no adjectives at all" (1951 [1789]: 185).

Despite the fact that Jefferson's outlook on language, like
Webster's, was fully the product of the eighteenth century, Jefferson's rather unique place in American history has buffered him
from more severe criticism of his language studies. Furthermore,
Webster suffered more, historically, from the prestige of German
learning, by virtue of the fact that he lived and produced longer
into the nineteenth century than Jefferson. Webster was, after all,
61 years old in 1819 when Grimm first published *Deutsche Grammatik*, and he was in his seventies when *The American Dictionary* at
last appeared. Webster was not receptive to Grimm's, or anyone
else's, work either, when advances in historical methods were
recommended to him. Webster was roundly attacked in a Boston
newspaper of 1837 for his lack of German learning (see Chapter
2, pp. 106–7), and it is the case that his etymologies of the
American Dictionary were not enthusiastically received by the
American intellectual public. Although he had engaged James
Percival (1795–1856), a student of German linguistic science, as a
proofreader, Webster convinced few people with his etymology of
the American *woodchuck* as coming from the Zend word for "pig,"
or his speculation that *Minerva* might be derived either from
English *man* or from German *Arbeit*. Webster's etymologies were
ridiculed as late as 1860 in George Marsh's *Lectures on the English
Language*, citing Webster's etymology for *issue* as coinciding with
the Ethiopic *watsa* (1860: 63). A formally German-trained linguist,

C.A.F. Mahn, was eventually brought in to overhaul the entire etymology of the Webster dictionaries in time for the celebrated edition of 1864 (Friend 1967: 79).

By 1837, however, it must be said that Webster was wholly accustomed to public attack. He had already been ridiculed in 1801 for having merely proposed an American or "Columbian" dictionary. In 1801, at issue was not Webster's scholarship (or lack of it), but the problem of Americanisms, as well as that of spelling reforms. On the front page of the *Port Folio*, a pro-British organ, of November 28, 1801 was an anonymous attack on Webster signed only "Aristarcus." The attack, equating "barbarisms" with "Americanisms," ran as follows:

> Now, in what can a Columbian dictionary differ from an English one, but in these barbarisms? Who are the Columbian authors, who do not write in the English language, and spell in the English manner, except Noah Webster, junior, Esq.? The embryo dictionary, then, must either be a dictionary of pure English words, and, in that case, superfluous, as we already possess the admirable lexicon of Johnson, or else must contain vulgar, provincial words, unauthorized by good writers, and, in this case, must surely be the just object of ridicule and censure.

"Aristarcus" then continues, in the tradition of all eighteenth-century "Aristarcuses," with his sardonic critique: "If the Connecticut lexicographer considers the retaining of the English language as a badge of slavery, let him not give us a *Babylonish dialect* in its stead, but adopt, at once, the language of the *aborigines*" (quoted in Howard 1930: 302). "Aristarcus" could not have found a more damaging comparison than the one between *American* English and the language of the *aborigines*.

Whatever doubts about Webster's ideas during his lifetime, there have remained few after his death; and whatever the poverty he endured during his life, time was to prove that he did in fact write a "best-seller." *The American Spelling Book*, the "blue-backed speller," had sold in its millions in the nineteenth century and continued to sell into the twentieth century (Mencken 1963: 482). As for his personal isolation and his never-ending quest for authority, Americans have chosen to canonize the name of Webster as the prime American linguistic authority, well-entrenched in the folk-linguistic phrase "according to Webster."

2

FROM PHILADELPHIA
TO THE FIELD: 1815–42

EXPANSIONS

After the war of 1812, Americans headed west, past the Alleghenies, to the Mississippi, and beyond. During the course of this westward expansion, it was inevitable that the pioneers, settlers, merchants, and military would encounter, and encounter again, the Indians.

Mention of the military is not gratuitous. From its creation in 1816 until 1849, the Bureau of Indian Affairs was part of the War Department. In the first half of the nineteenth century, it can be said that the Indians represented the expanding nation's biggest foreign-policy problem. Government policy toward the Indians created domestic unrest, as well. Andrew Jackson, the man Mencken extolled as the "new American," who appeared after 1814, "pushful" and "Anglophobic," was also the man who signed the Cherokee Removal Bill in 1829, triggering years of legal manoeuvering that culminated with the Circuit Court of Georgia's decision to expel the Cherokee from the State of Georgia in 1832. This ruling roused negative public sentiment in certain quarters. In far-away Boston, John Pickering presided over a series of meetings to protest "the threatened flagrant wrong," and he helped draft appeals to Congress on behalf of the "oppressed and suffering Cherokees" to support the Cherokee's right to their own territory (M.O. Pickering 1887: 387–8). Despite these protests and although the Circuit Court's decision was initially overturned by the Supreme Court, some 14,000 Cherokee were eventually "removed" from Georgia to Oklahoma in 1838. Along this "trail of tears" to Oklahoma, about 4,000 Cherokee died of exhaustion.[1]

While the Cherokee (and other Indian populations) were

suffering decimation, if not outright extermination, speakers of English were expanding apace. In 1790, the (Euro-)American population hovered at 4 million, 90 per cent of which lived east of the Alleghenies. By the 1840s, the United States population had soared to about 20 million, all (or most) speaking English. America was on its way to fulfilling the "Manifest Destiny" of American English prophesied by Adams, Rush, and Webster.

Awareness and interest in this expanding American English increased accordingly. In the early 1830s Americans had become tired of English-based Lindley Murray-style prescriptivism and were seeking descriptive norms as the basis of the educational standard (Drake 1977: 11). As evidence of the interest in descriptive variety, an unusual collection of papers was published in 1829–30 and signed by an anonymous "Wy." The author is believed to have been none other than Georg Blaettermann, America's first professionally (i.e. German) trained linguist and the man Jefferson hired to teach modern languages at the University of Virginia. The papers are remarkable in that they represent the earliest American dialect studies, thereby actively continuing Jefferson's interest in the subject. "Wy" correctly identified the social sources of American English as being derived from a mixture of lower-class London speech and various provincial dialects, particularly those of East Anglia and the North. "Wy" also gives some insight into the grammar and pronunciation of what is now called "Black English," which cannot be taken up here (see Miller 1983).

While American English spread over the continent, the prolonged, and genocidal encounter with the Indians, which had begun already in the eighteenth century, took the study of the American Indian languages from the armchair into the field. Like Jefferson and "Wy", both of whom relied for their studies almost entirely on published lists, Duponceau and Pickering were engaged primarily in "armchair" studies. Yet they recognized the importance of first-hand linguistic and ethnographic observation. Pickering, for one, pursued his philological investigations of Cherokee in 1823 with the aid of a native informant, David Brown (M.O. Pickering 1887: 331–3).

The third decade of the nineteenth century also saw a significant move to the field. In 1820, Lewis Cass (1782–1866), Governor of Michigan Territory, who, like Jefferson and Gallatin, was concerned with the plight of the Indians, but held a very poor opinion of their language, and consequently, their culture (see Cass 1826), nevertheless appointed Henry Schoolcraft (1793–1864) an Indian agent at a site authorized by the War Department at Sault Ste Marie. From there Schoolcraft plunged into his "algic researches." Two of his articles on the Algonquin language were translated by Duponceau into French and won him, in 1831, a gold medal from the Institut de France. It was not long before what had been mere word lists – Benjamin Smith Barton's eighteenth-century-style armchair *vocabularia comparativa* – had become solid genetic classifications of the kind Jefferson had envisioned and Albert Gallatin first consolidated in *A Synopsis of the Indian Tribes of North America* of 1836. Gallatin, who had been the Secretary of the Treasury under Jefferson, co-founded the American Ethnological Society in 1842, and that date marks the end of this second chapter.

In addition to the spatial, i.e. *geographical*, and the concomitant database expansions, the first half of the nineteenth century was generating two other expansions, both temporal: 1) the new and ever-expanding realms of *geological* time onto which could then be superimposed 2) the equally new dimensions of *evolutionary* time. Both of these new temporal spaces were carved out in England: the first, in *Principles of Geology* (1830–3) by Charles Lyell (1797–1875), who was elected to the American Philosophical Society in 1842; the second (and here taking liberties with the periodization of this second chapter), in *The Origin of the Species* (1859) of Charles Darwin (1809–82) who was elected to the American Philosophical Society in 1869.

Charles Lyell occupies an unusual place in the history of American linguistics. First, it was he, in his *Travel in North America in the Years 1841–42* (London 1845; New York 1852), who credits Webster with having claimed the invention of *to demoralize* (Mencken 1963: 134). Second, Lyell gave the Lowell lectures in Boston in October and November of 1841, and these were attended by Josiah Dwight Whitney (1819–96), an eminent geologist. From this early contact with Lyell's "uniformitarianism," Josiah Dwight passed the geological principle on to his linguist brother, William Dwight, who would work it into a linguistic principle.

These new temporalities would take time to be assimilated into language studies. In the first edition of the *Encyclopedia Americana*

(1830), for instance, in the article "Language" (vol. VII), the author grapples with the problem of how to account for the "organic differences" in grammatical structure among the world's languages. Although the author states that "it is not our business to reconcile [our] theory with the Mosaic records," the author nevertheless builds an argument around a time-depth of 6,000 years which was "the generally received chronology" for the age of the world. The author, furthermore, refers to the "confusion of tongues" (i.e. Babel) as an historical event that must be taken into account (VII: 413). Gallatin shared this foreshortened Biblical time-scale of human prehistory (1836: 5). It was another three decades before William Dwight Whitney would declare, in a passage discussing the Egyptian monuments, that "a period of three thousand years is coming to be regarded as not including a very large part of man's existence on the earth" (1867: 377; see Chapter 3).

During the course of the nineteenth century and in a variety of natural, physical, and human sciences, linguistics included, the new, geological chronology would begin to expand the Biblical, "received chronology." These competing chronologies would come to be known by the labels "uniformitarianism" and "catastrophism," terms coined in 1832, in a review by the British polymath William Whewell (1794–1866) of Lyell's *Principles* (Christy 1983: 5). Whewell also coined the term "scientist" in 1840 as a substitute for "savant" or "philosopher" (see R. Bruce 1987: 80). Earlier geologists, the "catastrophists," had believed in a past of abrupt, cataclysmic, God-ordained changes. The linguistic version of "catastrophism" would claim that language begins with the Adamic language, unified, God-given, and all-at-once which is followed by the catastrophic break-up of human language in the wake of the Tower of Babel. After Lyell, however, "uniformitarianism" would make its way into language studies, first, not through the Germans, but through the American William Dwight Whitney (Christy 1983: 78; see also Chapter 3). Through Whitney, the history of language came to be understood as the ceaseless repetition of still-continuing processes. The question, then, became: if languages were not formed all at once, what are those language-formation processes? Webster had earlier anticipated the question by asserting that: 'Languages are not formed at once by system, and are ever exposed to changes" (quoted above on p. 36). In any case, these new views of time would have in language studies (as in other sciences) the effect of the "Big Bang": once the temporal universe began expanding, it has not stopped, even down to the present. Before 1842, the rumblings of the coming explosion can be fully felt.

If the English were the "creators" of the new temporal dimensions, the Germans were the theoreticians and the institutionalizers of the new historical consciousness. Nineteenth-century German Romanticism was a response – and in Wilhelm von Humboldt's case, a *direct* response – to eighteenth-century French Enlightenment thought. In language philosophy, that meant that Condillac was out, and Humboldt was in.

Condillac's concept of history, so characteristic of much of the eighteenth century, sought to find the common ground which constituted a thing's universality and which had the consequence of also eliminating the thing's individuality. Condillac intended, by the method of genetic analysis, to reduce all understanding to the least common denominator that would be both logically and temporally prior to the rest. This goal was consistent with the goal of *grammaire générale* which sought to determine the universal conditions of the construction of utterances (see above p. 32). *Grammaire générale*, the study of "the human mind, reason equally distributed among mankind" (*l'esprit humain, la raison pareillement distribuée en chaque homme*), was a distinctly *a*temporal pursuit. Language was, first and foremost, a social product (an *organon* or *ergon*), each linguistic sign functioning as a "tile" that represented some little piece of the society's collective reality. The Romantics, who revolted against convention and Classicism, desired escape from this balance and reason and restraint of the imagination.

By contrast, the historical explanation, characteristic of Humboldt and the nineteenth century, sought to explain how something develops in its uniqueness and individuality. Destutt de Tracy had arrived at the point of considering the individual enmeshed in the complex of social forces that determined existence (see pp. 55-6), but there he stopped. And where Tracy stopped, Humboldt began. Humboldt replaced the cool, passive abstractions of French rationalism with fire: active, individual fire (*organ, energeia*). Language would no longer be a social product but a personal possession. The individual, and not the society, was in the center of the (linguistic philosophic) action. In yet another kind of nineteenth-century expansion, Humboldt also replaced a discussion of *Zeichen* – those little "tiles" of prepackaged significations which, when pieced together, would make a static mosaic of the world – with a meditation on language as a whole, *ein organisches Ganze*, making the expanded whole of language more important than the sum of its parts. Attention would focus now on the inner, spontaneous, and unreflexive dynamic of the organic structure of language – not just of language as a dynamic possession of the individual (as opposed to a static, received and reflexive product of society), but language *as such* with *its own* individual and internal form, by which it is identifiable and with which through history it perdures.

The French Volney's project for finding the *plan* of language, an essentially spatial, two-dimensional construct, would thus have a different philosophical point of departure from the German Humboldt's notion of *innere Sprachform* which added a third, temporal dimension. Both influences – the French and the German – would be felt in America, the French influence from Volney through Duponceau, the German influence from Humboldt coming in through Pickering, who argued against Humboldt's position before it surfaced in full force in Daniel Brinton (see Chapter 4).

Then, too, there was language history as practiced by Grimm and his *Deutsche Grammatik* of 1819. By 1822 and the second edition, which brought out the formulations that have since come to be known as Grimm's Law, the fame of Grimm and Goettingen was assured, hardly to be marred by his dismissal therefrom in 1837. As for the impact of the German *Philologen*, Bopp and Grimm, let us rely, for the moment, on Benfey's assessment:

> With the year 1819 came into the realm of Germanic philology– above all the linguistic [*sprachwissenschaftlichen*] branch of it – a turning point, which not merely brought about a complete transformation, but also for linguistics [*die Sprachwissenschaft*] as a whole was of the deepest meaning.
>
> (1869: 427)[2]

By the early decades of the nineteenth century, Americans had become aware that the German states were producing the most intellectual capital and at the fastest rate. In Germany, the great vehicle of science was the university, which was dedicated, above all, to research. The effect on the American intellectual community was marked: the prestige of German science and the learning of the German language grew steadily until World War I. Historical assessments such as Benfey's operated powerfully on the American intellectual community, and it is certainly part of the history of American linguistics – or rather lack of it – that Benfey does not find either Pickering or Duponceau or any other American worthy of mention.

Nevertheless, Americans in the 1820s, '30s, and '40s were enthusiastically assimilating these European changes in perspectives and responding to them, eagerly and confidently, in a liberal, nationalist spirit. These first decades were, thus, in America, a period of expansion on all fronts, a pressing forward in many directions at once. The expansive spirit would not, however, last indefinitely. There would come in the fourth decade a move for consolidation – and a return, in language matters, at least, to prescriptivism and to the importance of the academic north-east where Americans came to terms with "the hard advances" of German scholarship. The more the academic institution rose to meet the challenge of German scholarship, the less room there would be for the talented, independent, i.e. non-institutionalized amateur, e.g. Pickering or Duponceau, or the backwoods linguist, e.g. Schoolcraft. After 1842 would come a significant eclipse of the independent amateur.

With these expansions, or, rather, because of these expansions, Americans were still attempting to settle a net of fundamental questions, peculiarly American questions, and inter-relatedly linguistic ones at that. The first question was one of reference: what people were the proper referents of the designation "American"? The next, one of semantics: what did it mean to be American? Finally, given the nation–language intersection inherent in the prevailing political conception of language of the time: what was the political status of the(se) "American" language(s)?

ON THE STATUS OF THE AMERICAN LANGUAGE(S)

The 1801 quote from "Aristarcus" at the end of Chapter 1 is not merely an ironic attack aimed at a pompous lexicographer; it is also the expression of a complex ideological relationship that existed at one time between *those Babylonish dialects* of the native Americans and the status of American English.

Although the histories of the study of American Indian languages and of American English have traditionally been written separately, these two arcs of development were more closely intertwined in the first half of the nineteenth century than has been previously acknowledged. A brief scan of the work of John Pickering and Peter S. Duponceau confirms that they did not separate the various fields. Duponceau was as likely to write on English phonology (1818) as on the polysynthetism of the American Indian languages (1819). Similarly, John Pickering was as likely to compose a *Vocabulary* of Americanisms (1816) as he was to write on "the *American* plural," that is on the "inclusive" and "exclusive" plurals he found in Cherokee (1830–1).[3] So, too, did Bloomfield write on a wide variety of topics a century later, but by then, he himself had redistributed the subject matters into separate theoretical compartments.

These two arcs of development are, furthermore, cross-cut by the third arc of development, namely the assimilation – or the rejection – of European approaches to language. In simplistic terms, nineteenth-century America may be seen as a battleground between French-style ethnolinguistics and German-style Indo-European studies. By World War I, Germany and its particular brand of *Sprachwissenschaft* had won handily.

The phrase "arc of development" suggests the very idea that the domains now considered to be separate realms of language study developed over time from some common source, from a kind of nucleus of thoughts and attitudes about language. By the term "nucleus" I do not mean some (nineteenth-century) germ of thought. I do not mean to imply some embryonic state of thinking about language which has subsequently been elaborated in different directions, i.e. from which the arcs of development – the study of American Indian languages, the study of American English, or the assimilation or rejection of European perspectives – developed, as if the identification and separation of the arcs were natural, inevitable, organically predetermined. I use "nucleus" "merely" to refer to a grouping of ideas in a certain historical time and place which I, the historiographer, have identified as the antecedent to present ways of thinking about those same ideas. Clearly, every moment or era is the nucleus of what is yet to come, but what is yet to come is at every moment multiply determined. The points to be made here are that the status of English spoken in America in the early decades of the nineteenth century was in a complex rivalry with both the American Indian languages and with British English and that the outcomes of the rivalries were not given in advance.

A brief excursion into a bit of old-fashioned lexicography on the word *American* gives insight into the rivalries and underscores the value of reading the historical record for all three arcs of development at once. In 1798, Benjamin Smith Barton could use "American" in his *New Views* to refer unambiguously to the red-skinned natives of North America. In 1801, "Aristarcus" ridiculed the need for a *Columbian* dictionary, different from an English dictionary, a further indication that "American" had not yet come to settle on the (Euro-)American. Webster hedged on the point in his *Compendious Dictionary* of 1806 with the definition of "American" as "a native of America" and "pertaining to America." It was not until 1828 that Webster could define "American" as "a native of America; originally applied to the aboriginals, or copper-colored races, found here by the Europeans; but now applied to the descendants of Europeans born in America."

In 1801, "American" was still distinct from "post-Revolutionary Colonial," and "Aristarcus," in effect, sums up the real fear felt by many (Euro-)Americans that linguistic (and otherwise) distance from the English of the Mother Country entailed an uncomfortable and highly undesirable proximity to the American aborigines; and conversely, that proximity to the English of England assured distance from *those Babylonish dialects*. However, after the war of 1812, when (Euro-)Americans headed resolutely west, American linguists such as Duponceau and Pickering enthusiastically embraced the study of American Indian languages and passed the torch on, so to speak, to men in the field such as Schoolcraft and Trumbull. In the early decades of the nineteenth century, then, it might have been the case that a successful stereoscopy of the term "American" might have been achieved. That is, it was still possible for a peaceful mingling of the two "Americans," posited theoretically, at least, by Franklin and Jefferson, to have succeeded.

Schoolcraft indicates as much. If for "Aristarcus" proximity to the Indians meant uncomfortable distance from civilization, Schoolcraft gives us the opposite view: in 1827, he states that "there is nothing in the geography of America, which impresses the observer more than the Indian names" and then goes on to rhapsodize on the mystic sonority of Indian place-names such as "Canada," "Connecticut," "Chicago," and "Massachusetts" (1962 [1826–7]: 124–5). Later, in a letter addressed to the Mayor of New York written in 1844, Schoolcraft observes that Indian place-names have become so integrated into the American vocabulary that they no longer distinguish themselves as being blatantly "Indian." He continues that it was too late to change the name "New York" to "one more appropriate, or better suited to inspire sentiments of nationality." He proposes that all names of streets and squares of the city be derived from aboriginal vocabulary. These terms, he argues, would be more meaningful than a "foreign" one such as "York" which, having been adopted as a basis and used for one hundred and eighty years, is "barren of all national association" (1860, V: 621–2). For Schoolcraft, then, distance from England meant nationality and a welcome proximity to the Indians. Here is envisioned the possibility of a stereoscopic American nationality, a nationality blending the two Americans, red and white, and their two languages.

However, by the time this letter was printed in Schoolcraft's monumental *Archives of Aboriginal Knowledge* of 1860, the wish can only be retrospective and nostalgic, for by then the Indians' fate had been well determined, and we know that the Indians today are not part of mainstream American life. We know that the arcs of development did indeed separate and that the study of American Indian languages is not currently flourishing in American academic institutions. Thus, the question that forms the focal point of Chapter 2 may now be asked: how did the attitude expressed by "Aristarcus" prevail?

To answer the question, let us return briefly to the problem of the historical reception of Jonathan Edwards's 1787 address before the Connecticut Society of Arts and Sciences on the filiation of the Algonquian languages. It is an uncontroversial fact, pointed out above (pp. 45–6), that Edwards's address has lacked the impact on historical–comparative studies enjoyed by William Jones's 1786 address on the proposed relationship between Sanskrit, Latin, and Greek. I suggested that Edwards's lack of historical impact was due to 1) a lack of institutionalization on the American side of the Atlantic, as opposed to Europe and in particular, Germany; and 2) a concomitant lack of interest in (or, indeed, perceived need for) inscribing Edwards's and other similar works into a written history of American linguistic activity.

While this account of Edwards's relative oblivion in terms of institutional "lacks" is certainly valid, it still only skims the surface and fails to explain why those lacks existed and continue to exist. That is, these institutional lacks are merely symptomatic of other, more profound lacks with regard to the status of the American language(s) at the beginning of the nineteenth century.

Returning to the problem of "Americanisms," nowhere was the debate more hotly contested than in the exchange between Pickering with his 1816 *Vocabulary*, first addressed to the American Academy of Arts and Science (vol. 3, 1809), and Webster with his 1816 reply to Pickering. Pickering, who had begun an interest in the subject during his stay in England from 1799–1801, displays his conservatism and his linguistic purism under the entry "Americanize," which alone tells the story: '"To render American.' *Webst. Dict.* I have never met with this verb in any American work, nor in conversation." Pickering's denial of the very verb "to americanize" is not dissimilar to Samuel Johnson's denial of an entry for "America/n" in his 1755 *Dictionary*. Referring in his Preface to "thirsty reformers" and "presumptuous sciolists" (i.e. Webster and his 1806 dictionary), Pickering intended to include in his vocabulary "*all* words, the *legitimacy of which has been questioned*; in order, that their claim to a place in the language might be discussed and settled" (1816: vi), i.e. those words not in use in English, obsolete in England, or with different significations in England. In his Introductory Essay, Pickering is concerned with the deviations between American English and British English, but he reassures his audience that he does not mean

that so great a deviation has taken place, as to have rendered any considerable part of our language unintelligible to Englishmen; but merely, that so many corruptions have crept into *our English*, as to have become the subject of much animadversion and regret with the learned of Great Britain.

(1816: 11)

Pickering then quotes at length various opinions expressed in British reviews and newspapers condemning *"that torrent of barbarous phraseology*, with which the *American* writers threaten to destroy the purity of the English language" (1816: 13).

Webster himself was responsible, to a certain extent, for the fear expressed on both sides of the Atlantic of the two Englishes drifting apart. He had declared in his first "Dissertation" that a variety of causes – distance from England, local conditions, new associations of people, new combinations of ideas, and some intercourse with tribes wholly unknown in Europe – would "produce, in a course of time, a language in North America, as different from the future language of England, as the modern Dutch, Danish and Swedish are from the German, or from one another" (1951 [1789]: 22–3). This would have displeased Franklin, for instance, who envisioned selling many books abroad on the condition that only one English language existed, and Franklin became, accordingly, a linguistic conservative who, toward the end of his life, censured, in strong language, "the popular errors several of our states were continually falling into." In any case, after Pickering's *Vocabulary*, Webster rattled back with a letter, strongly attacking Pickering and agreeing "sciolists we have in magnitude." In the letter, Webster takes nearly everyone to task, including Franklin, who, Webster writes, "never pretended to be a man of erudition – he was self-taught" (1951 [1789]: 32). Going so far as to differ in opinion from Horne Tooke, Webster writes that:

for is from a word signifying *cause, motive* – that *from* signifies *beginning* – and *to* signifies *act, effect*, and I find, by resorting to higher sources, that this is a mistake, [and] I shall differ from the author, whatever risk I may encounter.

(1817: 35)

Although Webster waxes eloquent with his closing arguments that "there is nothing which, in my opinion, so debases the genius and character of my countrymen, as the implicit confidence they place in English authors, and their unhesitating submission to their *opinions*, their *derision*, and their *frowns*" (1817: 51), he was hardly likely to have convinced a man as learned as John Pickering that under the entry *Pappoose* "it is worthy of remark that *babosa* is the Syraic word for a little boy" (1817: 19) or that – upon the authority of Sir William Jones, no less – "a great many Ethiopic words are in European languages – indeed there are words in English which can hardly be understood without the aid of the Ethiopic'' (1817: 40).

For this cantankerous letter, Webster received a less-than-favorable response in the *North American Review* written by Sidney Willard, Hancock Professor of Hebrew at Harvard, and a good friend of Pickering. Willard's attitude against Webster can be summed up in his declaration that ''we can see no reason for adopting what many consider a vulgar word'' (1817: 86), namely *lengthy*.[4]

The debate over Americanisms took a turn in Webster's favor after the European Grand Tour of the influential educator and statesman Edward Everett. In a letter to Pickering, of 1818, Everett expressed his disgust that, in England, ''American Innovations on the English language are ipso facto corruptions, the British, improvements; & in this, as every other case, I have found a resolute spirit of decrying every thing American to be pretty universal'' (quoted in Read 1939b: 120). Everett took a public stand on the issue a year later when he wrote in a section entitled ''Americanisms'' to a statistical compilation about America that the language spoken in America was far more desirably homogeneous than that in England because of ''the more general diffusion of education, the superior condition of all classes, and especially the non-existence of paupers, and persons extremely illiterate.'' Everett concludes:

> Where two countries . . . are separated by such a distance as England and America, and differ so much in manners and institutions, it is not to be expected that the standard of propriety in speech, a thing somewhat capricious in its nature, will remain precisely identical.
>
> (quoted in Read 1939b: 121)

It is of particular interest to note that in this same article, Everett observes wryly that: ''An American, on arriving in England, is not unfrequently requested, by intelligent persons, to give a specimen of his native tongue, in the supposition that this is either a distinct dialect of English, or even an Indian language.'' This statement confirms the stereoscopy of the two Americans (Euro- and aboriginal) and their languages, at the very least in the minds of ''intelligent'' Europeans.

The final word on the topic of Americanisms seems to have been reserved for Pickering in the first edition of the *Encyclopedia Americana* (1830). Identified as the author of the entry "Americanism" (see M.O. Pickering 1887: 370, note 2), Pickering runs through the history of the various denunciations of Americanisms, alludes to his own vocabulary with restraint, and seems to have mellowed in his position in stating that "no language is so settled as not to undergo continual changes, if spoken by a nation in the full vigor of social and political life" (1830, I: 211). In a phrase ripe with the political conception of language, Pickering concludes: "Authority, in regard to language, will go far, but never can withstand for a long time the energies and wants of a free, industrious and thinking people" (1830, I: 211).

While the acceptance of "Americanisms" was hard-won, there were many advocates – Webster, Everett, finally Pickering – to plead the cause. Similar defenders of the American Indian languages existed, e.g. Heckewelder, Duponceau, and Schoolcraft, but their work did not gain such wide public attention. The Indians, furthermore, had other "lacks" to overcome in order to gain the attention of (Euro-)American or European students of language. Let us take, for example, the issue of how American Indian studies might have been affected by the European shift in perspective from Enlightenment to Romanticism. With regard to language studies in general, Jacob Grimm with his brother Wilhelm might have best expressed the new European sentiments in the Introduction to their *Deutsches Woerterbuch*. Although this *magnum opus* appeared first in 1854, Grimm's words have the effect of a Romantic Manifesto for the early decades of the century, identifying the *Romantiker*, who,

> the farther back in time he can climb, the more beautiful and perfect he finds the form of language, [while] the closer he comes to its present form, the more painful it is to him to find the power and agility of the language in decline and decay.
>
> (1854: iii)[5]

This passage articulates the well-known change from the forward-looking belief in the ever-perfectable future of Enlightenment thought, so allied with the French eighteenth-century, to the backward-looking nostalgia for the previously perfect past of

Romanticism, so ardently articulated in Germany. We can now be reminded that the pursuit of (East) Indianism in the nineteenth century was richly supported by the existence of ancient texts, the *Vedas*, which dated to 1500 BC.

Those *other* Indians, those speaking Babylonish dialects, by way of contrast, were devoid of written records – yet another lack which was to have serious theoretical and methodological consequences in the unfolding of nineteenth-century language studies. First, in the absence of written records, there was nothing to indicate the "former beauties and perfections" of Ur-Amerindian, so to speak, which would attract admiration and inspire study and which was the case for Sanskrit. Second, in the absence of written records, the possibility of time-depth was actually denied American Indian cultural studies until Sapir's *Time Perspective in Aboriginal American Culture, a Study in Method* of 1916 (see Chapter 5). American Indian languages served as vehicles, then, not for the "serious" historical science of the nineteenth century, but as a matter of psychological generalization. The unexplored space of the New World with their languages served as the space where the Old World could unravel general laws operating regardless of specific time, in a Volney-style ethnography.

The New World, in fact, represented an *empty* space to the Old World. It did not take the Romantics with their glorification of the past to marginalize the study of American Indian languages. The marginalization, that liminalization, had already taken place in the Enlightenment. As a *pre*liminary, then, to understanding American Indian studies throughout the nineteenth century, it is necessary to describe first how the American Indian languages were, in effect, eliminated by Enlightenment theories of language. It is in that context that we can better understand how eminently unimportant was Edwards's address to the Connecticut Society. We can then understand where the charmed circle around language was drawn, defining that which fell within as "acceptable" and "civilized" and that which fell without as "exotic" and "barbaric." We can then understand why "Aristarcus"'s charge of the barbarism of *American* English, why Pickering's denial of the existence of the verb *to americanize*, or why his quote about *"that torrent of barbarous phraseology"* could have acted so powerfully on the mind of the early nineteenth-century American.

THE ANTI-IMAGE OF THE AMERICAN INDIAN
LANGUAGES IN THE EIGHTEENTH CENTURY.
THE EUROPEAN PERSPECTIVE

The image of the American Indian languages in eighteenth-century Europe was, above all, an anti-image. That is not to say that eighteenth-century European scholars were ignorant of the New World languages or that a database was lacking. Mentioned several times above is European interest at the turn of the nineteenth century in global inventories of the world's languages and the European interest in the exotic data from American Indian languages. Still, it must be acknowledged that the study of non-European languages was not at the center of language reflection in the Enlightenment; the question of non-European languages was in fact so marginal that one must piece together – or *bricoler* – the image of the American Indian languages from very little material. However, if the subject of American Indian languages was, for example, absent from the grand current of *grammaire générale*, it was precisely that the theory of language in the Enlightenment succeeded indirectly in reducing the American Indian to zero, from a cultural and psychological as well as a linguistic point of view. That is to say the Enlightenment – the Age of Reason – effectively *de-rationalized* the American Indian languages.

Thus, a disjunction symptomatic of the zero value of the American Indian languages is revealed here: the *grammairiens philosophes* did not occupy themselves with data from the American Indian languages and the ''anthropologists'' concerned with the New World did not yet have an ethnolinguistic orientation. Onto this list of the various disjunctions in the study of the New World languages can be added the arbitrary geographic fault lines drawn as a result of the territories particular nationalities of Europeans tended to colonize. It is generally the case that, in intellectual circles, the French, the Germans, and the British (that is, Scottish, in the case of James Burnet) dialogued with one another, but were not in great contact with the Spanish. Thus the data on the American languages coming from what is now Mexico was, to a certain extent, further marginalized.

When first discovered, the great geographical expanse from New France (Quebec) to New Spain (Mexico) was unknown and considered to be essentially empty. Among Enlightenment thinkers from Buffon to Voltaire to Kant to Burnet, two basic strategies were devised to account for the essential nothingness of this space and the zero state of the Indians occupying it. It is worth "deconstructing" these two strategies along with their variations, for it was against them and the theory of language inscribed into them that the (Euro-)American linguists of the early nineteenth century reacted so strongly – and, ultimately, so ineffectively.

The Case of Huron

From Shakespeare's *Tempest* through James Fennimore Cooper and beyond, the American Indian has held a particular place in anglophone literature. Alongside that tradition has run the French literary version of the American Indian. Given the French Enlightenment's influence on American language studies, it is to the French literary tradition that we turn first for insights into the image of the American Indian inherited by the nineteenth century. The *Ingénu* of Voltaire's 1767 *conte* is perhaps the most famous literary Indian of the eighteenth century. He was a Huron. Over six decades earlier, that is in 1703, a first Huron, named Adario, appears as the interlocutor of the Baron de Lahontan's *Dialogues curieux* (1703). In the vast travel literature of the period, the stories which represent the aborigines of North America do not necessarily have a Huron as a protagonist. Abbé Prévost chose a fictive *Abaquais* named "Igloo" as the slave in *Monsieur Cleveland* (1734), and J.-H. Maubert de Gouvest creates the Iroquois "Igli" in his *Lettres Iroquoises* (1752). However, despite the enormous diversity of the indigenous Americans (or perhaps because of this diversity), the Huron tribe was singled out and generalized as the example of all Indians, without anyone paying too much attention to the particular details of Huron society. The Hurons are, for instance, one of the few Indian peoples to merit mention in D'Alembert and Diderot's *Encyclopédie* (1751–65), and the Huron language happens to be the only one which gets a description. However, the *Encyclopédie* devotes but one sentence to them, namely: "The language of these savages is guttural and very impoverished, because they have knowledge of only a very few number of things."[6]

It is important to identify the sources of this generalized eighteenth-century conception of the Hurons and their language, for these now forgotten sources were the very descriptions that

American linguists from Heckewelder to Boas had to confront. The primary source responsible for the negative image of the American Indian in the eighteenth century proves to be the work of the French missionary Gabriel Sagard-Théodat. In the seventeenth century he wrote a series of cultural descriptions and grammatical studies, the *Grand voyage au pays des Hurons . . . avec un Dictionnaire*, which included a commentary "De la langue des Hurons" composed by Jean de Bréboeuf in 1636 and finally a *Grammaire* prepared in the 1640s by P.J.M. Chaumonot. Sagard-Théodat informs the reader that he is describing "a savage language, almost without rules . . . very imperfect" (*une langue sauvage, presque sans regle . . . tellement inparfaicte*) (1865 [1636]: 10), and with "a great instability of speech." Instability for Sagard-Théodat was the mark of imperfection:

> Our Hurons, and generally all the other nations, have the same instability of speech, and change so much their words that in the course of time, ancient Huron is almost entirely different than at present, and changes still, according to what I can determine and learn in speaking with them: for the mind becomes more subtle as it grows old and corrects things and puts them in their perfection.
>
> (1865 [1636]: 9)[7]

Although it is not specifically mentioned in Sagard-Théodat's text, one reason often given for the instability of "savage" languages was their lack of writing to fix the language. The "ascertainment" of the language was the goal of most eighteenth-century language studies, in France as in England, the *philosophes* like Condillac and the prescriptivists such as Thomas Sheridan in England.

Sagard-Théodat often repeats the phrases "these poor Huron savages," "the poor people." This cultural poverty coincided, for Sagard-Théodat, with linguistic poverty. Bréboeuf reinforces his ideas in terms of that which the language and the culture lack:

> They lack all the labial letters; it is doubtless because they all hold their lips open so gracelessly, and hardly can one understand them when they "whistle" or speak low. Just as they have almost no virtue, no religion, no science at all, or police, they also do not have any simple words available to signify all that truly exists.
>
> (quoted in Thwaites 1897 [1636]: 116)[8]

This description of the Huron pronunciation seized the attention of the Europeans who worked with these French missionary texts. Certainly, once again, if a language is not written, the "real live" pronunciation of the language by native speakers is the first point of contact. Huron is "gutturale", according to the *Encyclopédie*; "hardly can one understand them," writes Bréboeuf; even Herder, who, in his prize essay *Ueber den Ursprung der Sprache*, touches on many exotic languages, quotes Chaumonot, who complained of the Hurons and their "guttural letters and their unpronouncable accents" (*Kehlbuchstaben und ihre unaussprechlichen Accente*). In the same passage, Herder quotes another Frenchman who travelled to South America:

> De la Condamine says of a small nation on the Amazon River, that a part of their words cannot be written, not even once very incompletely. One needs to use at least nine or ten syllables where they, in their pronunciation, seem to use hardly three.
>
> (1959 [1770]: 9)[9]

Finally, in the English-speaking world, the Scot James Burnet (Lord Monboddo) was thoroughly familiar with Sagard-Théodat's work and used it to build a theory of language progress in *Of the Origin and Progress of Language*. In this work, Burnet proposes that the most primitive languages were guttural and composed of cries. With regard to the labials of Huron, Burnet remarks that: "La Hontan says the same thing, and he adds, what indeed is a necessary consequence, that they never shut their lips in speaking; which is the case of every animal that utters only natural cries" (1970 [1774]: 479–89). In the United States, Lewis Cass did no better in his review of Heckewelder's and Duponceau's description of Huron, "spoken by the Wyandots, the Iroquois, and their kindred tribes." Cass writes:

> Mr. Duponceau's opinion of the harmony and music of the Wyandot language struck us as remarkable. Of all the languages spoken by man, since the confusion of tongues at the tower of Babel, it least deserves this character. It is harsh, guttural, and undistinguishable; filled with intonations, that seem to start from the speaker with great pain and effort.
>
> (1826: 74)

According to Cass, not only is Huron difficult to listen to, it is also difficult for the Hurons to speak, "starting" from the speaker "with great pain and effort." The Huron language, as soon as the Huron opens his or her mouth, is unintelligible, that is to say, bestial.

As far as the phonetic inventory of Huron goes, let us note that Bréboeuf is technically correct. His work, for instance, was used as a valuable source for a recent study of seventeenth-century Mohawk (Michelson 1981). Also, Bréboeuf describes two grammatical phenomena which were to capture the imagination of both American and European "anthropological" linguists of the nineteenth century, beginning with Duponceau and Humboldt, namely: (1) the expression of inalienable possession; and (2) the expression of close structural unity, which was to be given the name "polysynthetism" by Duponceau, or "incorporation" or *Einverleibung* by Humboldt. However, for Bréboeuf and his contemporaries in the seventeenth century, grammar was something imposed from outside the language. Bréboeuf helped establish the very seductive idea that various linguistic structures – that is grammatical ("without rules"), phonetic (lack of "labials"), and semantic ("no simple words") – reflected the level of culture of the speaking community. Bréboeuf saw everywhere the void that so well fits the already established vision of the New World: "no virtue, no religion, no science at all, or police."

The idea of *absence* and *lack* prevailed over the possibility of equality with any European language. Absence and lack prevailed even over the possibility of *superiority* and *richness* in the category of the verb, for instance. In his examination of all *wilde Sprachen*, Herder explains that, while they are all poor and miserable, a language like Huron displays a certain abundance:

> The Hurons have a double verb for inanimate and animate objects: so that "to see" as in "to see a stone" and "to see a man" has two different expressions – if one follows that principle through the entire realm of Nature – what richness!
>
> (1959 [1770]: 63)[10]

However, Herder interprets that richness as wasteful, extravagant. A further interest in this passage appears in the particular example Herder chooses from Huron of the gloss with "stone": the difference between "to see a stone" and "to see a man" which (as far as I have been able to discover) may be attributed to Father

LeJeune's *The Relations of New France* of 1636, who first observed a difference in the Huron verbs according to whether the object is animate or inanimate, and it is, I presume, from LeJeune that Herder establishes the rather minor leitmotif in Indian studies of "romancing the stone."

Although there were many Lewis Casses and "Aristarcuses," Americans, generally, did better at describing and understanding the Indian languages, as one would expect. Some even achieved a high level of descriptive subtlety, for instance Experience Mayhew (1673–1758), who realized that Eliot's *Indian Grammar Begun* (1666) had missed a generalization in that it contained more letters than were required for writing Natick. Mayhew understood, in effect, that voicing of consonants is not distinctive in Algonquian and, as a result, regarded the letters *b*, *d*, and *g* as unnecessary (see Miner 1974: 174). As for another early Indianist, Roger Williams, he pointed out as early as 1643 that there was variation in regard to the use of *n*, *l*, and *r* in several of the languages that he had observed. Two hundred years later, Pickering picked up on Williams's observation but failed, in Mary Haas's opinion, to make the proper use of the sound correspondences, so that "it seems scarcely credible that nearly a century more would pass before a systematic comparison of all the sounds in a particular set of Algonkian languages would be undertaken" (1967: 817). It must be remarked at this point that if early work in Indian languages was lacking anything, it was phonetic finesse.

In any case, the work of Williams, Eliot, and Mayhew did not travel well across the Atlantic. Sagard-Théodat's did, and eighteenth-century European grammarian philosophers were happy to accept the negative interpretation of the Huron language and culture, and they used it to derationalize the American Indian languages as a whole. It is well known that the eighteenth century, believing in an objective reality the proper description of which would be rendered by *la langue bien faite*, did not conceive of the concept of linguistic relativity. It is equally well known that the eighteenth-century idea of progress had a quantitative value: the degree of progress attained by a culture was measurable in terms of the number of ideas expressed in the language (Huron had "a very small number") and the number of rules which "policed" the society.

The descriptions of Indian life left no doubt that the Indians were less "policed," that is, less "evolved," than the Europeans. The particular description of the Indians given by Georges de Buffon (1707–88) in his *Histoire naturelle* (1749) and quoted directly by Jefferson in his refutation (see above p. 62) reveals the following composite of Indians and Indian life: he was weak and small in his reproductive organs; he had neither hair nor beard, and no passion for his female; love between parent and child was weak, at best; no relationships between families existed at all; as a result, *no* unity, *no* republic, *no* social state. Supporting Buffon was the *Encyclopédie* entry under "Caraibe" which focused on anthropophagy (i.e. *no* civilized eating customs), nudity (i.e. *no* clothes), and sexual promiscuity (i.e. *no* sexual organization). This last observation ignored the contradiction that the Indians could not be both sexually deficient and sexually over-active. Herder seems to have done the same with the description of the Huron verbs.[11]

When one adds linguistic unintelligibility to the general picture of the American Indian, one has the full force of the first strategy for derationalizing the Indians: the Indian–beast strategy. Here is the description of the Freudian Id, the level of the personality *without* language. The derationalization is complete: the Indians belong to a subhuman race. The equivalence *homo loquens* = *homo sapiens*, which has existed since the Greeks, excluded the Indians from the human domain. In the face of all evidence of the existence of the American Indian languages, of the descriptions which might have been used accurately, and even of the recognition of different language families (Sagard-Théodat correctly distinguished the Iroquois from the Algonquian), the eighteenth-century European concluded that the American Indian and the American Indian languages did not really exist within the realm of the human and the rational.

There remained, then, the problem, of where to situate the Indians on the "evolutionary" scale. In *Of the Origin and Progress of Language*, James Burnet was generous. He admits the humanity of the Indians, however low their position might have been. "I think the Pope, by his bull [of 1537]", he writes, "decided the controversy well, when he gave it in favour of the humanity of the poor Americans." However, Burnet, carried away by his generosity, also includes the orang-outangs on the scale: "And, indeed," he continues, "it appears to me, that [the Orang Outangs] are not so much inferior to the Americans in civility and cultivation, as some nations of America were to us, when we first discovered that country'' (1970 [1774]: 347–8). Here, Burnet operates in a pre-Darwinian framework, so that what the *Origin of the Species* was to dynamize on a temporal axis, Burnet was viewing in a "spatial" domain. That is, all the evolutionary possibilities existed for Burnet (and his contemporaries) on the earth at the same time. The problem, was, thus, one of establishing the chain or scale of evolution of existing peoples and cultures (and higher primates).

In situating the American Indian on the chain, Europeans varied the Indian–beast strategy by associating the Indian with the ancient Europeans viewed as children. J.F. Lafitau, for instance, announces already in his title *Moeurs des sauvages amériquains comparées aux moeurs des premiers temps* (1724) that he is comparing the Indian to the ancient European, and he bases his study primarily on religious criteria. In this way, he reduces the Indian to a credulous child, and if one renders the Indian infantile enough, one is able to place the Indian at a prelinguistic state, indicated by the etymological force of *infantus*, the "non-speaker." The Indian–infant contrasts, of course, with the European, that is, the adult who possesses the power and authority to speak. This attitude, contrasting the Indian–infant to the European–adult, is very widespread in European anthropological texts and endures until the end of the nineteenth century, and even beyond, in such studies as Lévy-Bruhl's *La Mentalité primitive* (1922).

Out of the rather more positive theme of the Noble Savage arises the second strategy for eliminating the American Indian languages: the Noble Savage strategy. Voltaire's Ingénu and Lahontan's Adario speak a *different* language from their native language, and with good reason: the Huron is unintelligible and without knowledge. The fact that both Indian protagonists express themselves very beautifully in French is not only proof of their intelligence, it also suggests a sort of cultural transparency, or at least, the denial of a language barrier. The essence of this strategy for derationalizing the American Indian languages in the eighteenth century is located in the refusal of the least possibility of linguistic relativity. To speak French, the Ingénu and Adario are not perceived as foreigners (except physically), that is, they are not struggling to express themselves "properly" in French with interference from their native language. It is rather as if these

Indians, in speaking French, are passing from a world of silence into the world of dialogue. When an Indian speaks in any of the travel literatures, he is shown dialoguing with a European. Even when presented in his natural habitat, the "savage" dialogues only with a "civilized." The "savages" are never portrayed speaking with each other.

In this context, even (or especially) Jean-Jacques Rousseau contributes to the derationalization of the Indian in a variation of the Noble Savage strategy. In valorizing the silence of his "promeneur solitaire idéal," Rousseau adopts a position similar to that of Voltaire or Lahontan, but for very different reasons. The European is nervous and needs to talk. However, "the savages of America," Rousseau claims in his *Essai sur l'origine des langues*, "rarely speaks outside of the home; each maintains silence in his hut, he speaks by signs to his family, and these signs are not very frequent" (1968 [1781]: 91).[12] As a consequence, the two sides of this second, "Noble Savage," strategy for derationalizing the American Indian languages eliminate the need for these languages. In the case of Voltaire, the native language is supplanted without linguistic difficulties and replaced by French, indicating that the Savage is Noble to the extent that he retains the nobility and good of the state of Nature and assimilates and speaks the reasonable and reasoning language of civilization. For Rousseau, it is simply that the Noble Savage is "above" civilization and does not *need* to speak, but his dignity is acquired at the high price of silence.

Given such a thorough dismantling of the American Indian languages and given the prevailing eighteenth-century language–nation intersection (no language, no nation; no nation, no language), it is difficult to interpret positively David Simpson's treatment of J.F. Cooper and the latter's portrayal of the Indian languages. In *The Politics of American English, 1776–1850*, in particular the chapter "Silence and Poetry: The Language of the Native American," Simpson interprets the language of the Indian in James Fennimore Cooper's novels as

the cult of silence, or minimal articulation . . . valorized in particular ways, as it is in the language of the sailor and the tracker. It is a sign of inscrutable stoicism, and also of the subservience of expression to function, of word to deed. As for the sailor on the sea, survival in the forest depends on such priorities; while others talk of performing, and miss their chance, the Indian performs in silence.

(1986: 206)

I take no issue with Simpson's portrayal of the language in Cooper's novels. Cooper may, indeed, have made of the Indians the ultimate "performers" – but we know since Austin and Searle that words "do" things, too. In the speaking *political* world, the Indians – having had their language effectively taken away from them – were competing in their "noble" silence and losing. Seen in the context I have outlined above, this Indian silence was to prove a distinct, even fatal, disadvantage.

At the other extreme, Simpson identifies the over-eloquence of the Indians, with a "propensity to high poetry." According to Simpson, John Heckewelder's missionary mind saw

a barbarism in the approval of ornament, of which metaphor is the linguistic corollary. The very suspicion of trinkets and baubles so central to the Protestant mind may tell us something about why so many American writers were attracted to the subject of the eloquent Indians.

(1986: 217)

However, Heckewelder's objections can be seen more profitably not so much as Protestant, but as a general eighteenth-century attitude towards language, for the stricture against metaphor is deeply embedded in the Catholic Condillac's thinking (see, for instance, Andresen 1982). In all cases, the Indian culture and language – to the mind of the European and of many American settlers – did not achieve that golden, *rational* mean: either they had no sexuality or too much sexuality; either they had no grammar or too many verb endings; either they had no language or too much language. The Indian could not win, and did not win.

THE AMERICAN RESPONSE

In early nineteenth-century America, the charge of barbarism, levelled against either American English or the American Indian languages, could not be taken lightly. The early nineteenth-century (Euro-)American had to decide, in effect, how closely he or she chose to associate, either physically or culturally, with the aboriginal American.

It had always been part of the settlers' lives to be in speaking contact with the Indians. Given this contact, the portrayal of the Indians in the earliest settlers' records differs from, say the Voltairian or Rousseauian portrayals, in that these representations of Indian speech suggest at least a rudimentary perception of a language barrier, however unflattering these representations actually were to the Indians. An unusual study of the stereotyped broken English of the Indians, handed down to the present through Westerns and comic strips, such as "me heap big chief" and "you like um fire water," is carried out in Leechman and Hall (1955) who reach as far back as 1675 for representations of Indian Pidgin English.

John Heckewelder (1743–1823)

One of the most important documents on Indian life to be produced in the early nineteenth century was written by a man who had chosen a very close association with the Indians. John Heckewelder, a Moravian missionary, spent the greater part of his life from 1762 onward among the Delaware. He was appointed assistant in 1771 to another well-known missionary and specialist in Delaware, David Zeisberger (1721–1808). Heckewelder was elected to the American Philosophical Society in 1797.

In 1819, Heckewelder published his important *Account of the History, Manners, and Customs of the Indian Nations, who once inhabited Pennsylvania and the Neighbouring States* (1881 [1819]). This work, incidentally, according to Simpson (1986: 203), served as one of Cooper's major sources. Also incidentally, the review of this work by Pickering is the one where Pickering first propounds his wish to study man "through the medium of his noblest and peculiar faculty of speech" and to establish a science which should be "proudly called *Universal Grammar*" (1819: 179). It is also the review which Humboldt read and which inspired Humboldt to correspond with Pickering (see Mueller-Vollmer 1974: 260). Heckewelder's title, which includes the words "the Indian Nations, who once inhabited Pennsylvania," presages the major theme of the nineteenth-century westward expansion, for by Heckewelder's time, the Delaware, the *Lenni Lenape (original people)* had already been almost entirely replaced by the *Wapsid Lenape (white people)*. The lament over the vanishing tribes was articulated as early as Benjamin Smith Barton's *New Views* and in his Dedication to Thomas Jefferson (1797: iv).

Space does not permit an examination of the richness of Heckewelder's *History, Manners, and Customs*. Rather, it is Chapter 9, "Languages" (1881 [1819]: 118–27), and the correspondence between Heckewelder and Peter Stephen Duponceau "respecting the Indian languages" appended to the work that draws our attention, for here American linguists are responding directly to the European portrayal of the American Indian languages. In the chapter on "Languages," Heckewelder dismisses the French missionary Sagard-Théodat's analysis of Huron in a brief paragraph. Heckewelder decries the fact that there is no good Dictionary of Iroquois. There is only

> a large vocabulary of the Huron, composed by Father Sagard, a good and pious French Missionary, but of very limited abilities, and who also resided too short a time among that nation to be able to give a correct account of their language. He represents it in his preface, as poor, imperfect, anomalous, and inadequate to the clear expression of ideas, in which he is contradicted by others whom we have reason to believe better informed.
>
> (1881 [1819]: 120)

That better-informed source is David Zeisberger, who considered the Iroquois (of which Huron is a dialect) as a rich and comprehensive idiom. Of Zeisberger's work, Heckewelder writes: "We do not, unfortunately, possess a single grammar of any of these dialects; we have nothing, in fact, besides the fragment of Zeisberger's Dictionary," a sad circumstance which is explained by the fact "that a grammar which [Zeisberger] composed of [Huron], and the best part of his Dictionary, are irretrievably lost" (1881 [1819]: 120). To the list of the various "lacks" in the study of the American Indian languages must be added the lack of survival of important materials.

In the chapter on "Languages," Heckewelder also states that Delaware is a kind of "universal language, so much admired and so generally spoken by the Indian nations," (1881 [1819]: 124), and he goes on to correct the various false classifications of

Delaware by such commentators as Carver, Lahontan, and even the celebrated Professor Vater, the compiler, who ventured a classification of the Delaware "in his excellent continuation of Adelung's Mithridates." It is the particular object of Hecke-welder's publications "to satisfy the world that the languages of the Indians are not so poor, so devoid of variety of expression, so inadequate to the communication even of abstract ideas, or in a word so *barbarous*, as has been generally imagined" (1881 [1819]: 125).

Appended to Heckewelder's *Account* is his correspondence with Duponceau for the year 1816. Revealing the state of American Indian studies in America, as opposed to that in Europe, the correspondence focuses on points of Indian grammar, from the most detailed (Duponceau wishes to know "the proper word for *she* in Delaware, and how is it declined," 1881 [1819]: 359) to the most general information on genetic classifications of the various Iroquois and Algonquin dialects. The correspondence reveals both men to be well-read and well-versed on European language-theory in general and European views of the American Indian languages in particular. The list of names mentioned in the correspondence tells its own story: Maupertuis, Turgot, Volney, Vater, Rudiger, Adam Smith. The correspondence also gives hints to the future direction of American Indian studies and of attempts at general linguistics. A more quintessentially American statement can hardly be imagined than the one Heckewelder writes to Duponceau on the subject of the supposed irregularities in Indian pronunciation:

> To this you will add the numerous errors committed by those who attempt to write down the words of the Indian languages, and who either in their own have not alphabetic signs adequate to the true expression of the sounds, or want an *Indian ear* to distinguish them. I could write a volume on the subject of their ridiculous mistakes. (1881 [1819]: 374)

Duponceau's colleague, John Pickering, would, in fact, make such an attempt at a new alphabet in 1820, and it is entirely pertinent here to point out that when an *Indian ear* did set out to render an Indian language (Cherokee) in script in the 1820s, that ear came up with a syllabary and not an alphabet. For studies of the (half) Cherokee Indian Sequoyah (1770?–1843), or George Gist, see Greene (1985) and Monteith (1984).

Throughout the Heckewelder–Duponceau correspondence (references below are to 1881 [1819]), Heckewelder's severest criticism of European representations of Indian life is reserved for the Baron Lahontan, while his severest criticism of European language-ideas goes to "the ponderous work of a Scotch Lord named Monboddo . . . who on the authority of a Father Sagard (a French Missionary) . . . represents the language of the Hurons as the most incoherent and unsystematical heap of vocables that can possibly be conceived" (377). Heckewelder wishes to show Duponceau "by the instances of Father Sagard, and Lord Monboddo, what false ideas the Europeans have conceived on this subject" (388).

Duponceau, for his part, gives the palm for "false ideas" to Adam Smith's "elegant treatise on the origin and formation of languages," which "is certainly very ingenious." However, Duponceau continues, "it is only unfortunate that it does not accord with the facts, as far as our observations can trace them" (406–7). Duponceau concludes: "In Philology, as well as in every other science, authorities are to be weighed, compared, and examined, and no assertion should be lightly believed that is not supported by evident proof faithfully drawn from the original sources" (417). Even "the celebrated" Professor Vater of Leipzig is taken to task by Duponceau for his statement that "The Chippewas have no forms" (*Die Chippewaer haven fast keine formen*) (367). Duponceau strikes the guiding note for the future of American linguistic relativism when he writes:

> let us suppose that a Huron or a Delaware is writing a treatise on the origin of language, and in the pride of pompous ignorance attempts to make similar observations on the English idiom. Following Lord Monboddo's course of reasoning, he will say: "The English is the most imperfect language upon earth, for its words have no analogy to each other. They say, for instance, '*a house*', and the things that belong to a house they call '*domestic*'. They say, '*a year*', and 'an *annual* payment,' for a sum of money payable every year."
>
> (378)

Taking this reasoning to its logical conclusion, Duponceau then states: "Such would be the language of our Huron philosopher, and he would be about as right as Lord Monboddo" (378). Of

Sagard-Théodat, Duponceau concurs with Heckewelder that the French missionary "was perfectly bewildered in the variety of its forms, and drew the very common conclusion that what he could not comprehend was necessarily barbarous and irregular" (378–9). On the difference between languages that form verbs with and without the use of auxiliaries, Duponceau comes to the very modern conclusion: "I do not, therefore, see as yet, that there is a necessary connexion between the greater or lesser degree of civilisation of a people, and the organisation of their language" (389). As clear as this statement is, it would take the whole of the nineteenth century to assimilate. We turn, now, to a study of the man and the intellectual background which led to such a statement.

Peter Stephen Duponceau (1760–1844)

Of all the early American linguists, Pierre Etienne Duponceau has attracted the most attention from modern scholars. Good accounts of his life and career exist in Belyj (1975), Smith (1983), and Guice (1987), but perhaps no better synopsis is available than that of his necrology written by his long-time friend and fellow linguist, John Pickering (1849b [1844]).

Duponceau was born in France and was groomed for the Church, but early on abandoned that path in favor of language studies. At the age of fifteen, he left the countryside for Paris, where he was private secretary to Court de Gébelin, who, according to Pickering, was "the well-known author of the voluminous, though now neglected work, the *Monde primitif, analysé et comparé avec le Monde Moderne,*" which, in Pickering's judgment, "amidst a mass of the antiquated philology of seventy years ago, still contains some general views and speculations, that are not wholly unworthy of attention" (1849b [1844]: 163). Duponceau came to the United States in 1777, became a citizen of Pennsylvania in 1781, was admitted an attorney of the Court of Common Pleas at Philadelphia in 1785, and became an attorney of the Supreme Court in the following year. Because of his acquaintance with the civil and continental law of Europe and with foreign languages, he was in demand for matters involving international law and practice. He produced an impressive list of writings on legal matters and Pennsylvania history (see Pickering 1849b [1844]: 166).

He was elected to the American Philosophical Society in 1791 (whence his acquaintance with Heckewelder), and was president of that society from 1827 from 1827 until his death, as well as president of the Historical Society of Pennsylvania from 1837 to 1844. Pickering notes that in the latter part of Duponceau's life, after he had acquired a competent fortune by his profession, he devoted most of his time to his favorite study of *General Philology* which Pickering identifies as the "science which has employed the first intellects of the old world, from . . . Leibnitz to . . . William Humboldt" and to which Duponceau's contributions had been "honorably recognized in Europe, by the voice of all Germany, and by the award of the [Volney] prize of the French Institute [in 1835, for his *Mémoire*, published 1838], and his election as a corresponding member of that distinguished body" (1849b [1844]: 168). In addition to Duponceau's interest in Indian languages, Pickering reports his interest in the science of music and in the study of writing systems, most notably the Chinese in his 1838 dissertation which aroused considerable controversy among international scholars and won him the distinction of a forty-three page review in the *Journal Asiatique*. Anecdotal evidence for Duponceau's interest in writing systems is provided by Pickering who recounts that Duponceau had early in life studied the *"Russian*, which at that period was a *terra incognita* to scholars in general." Upon his arrival in the United States, Duponceau "kept his journal in the French language, written in the *Russian character*" (1849b [1844]: 168).

Duponceau's first published work in linguistics was his "English Phonology" (1818, read before the American Philosophical Society, 1817), which he sent both to Jefferson and to Pickering. Pickering responded by sending Duponceau his *Vocabulary* and thus the life-long friendship between the two men was formed (M.O. Pickering 1887: 266–7). In addition to securing the friendship with Pickering, Duponceau's "Phonology" certainly provides one of the first efforts at analyzing and comparing the different sounds of the world's languages, at studying "Phonology," that is, "knowledge of the sounds produced by the human voice" (1818: 228). While he is not yet ready to devise a universal alphabet representing "all the sounds and shades of sounds actually existing in human languages," he is willing to identify "the curious and interesting science, which, until a better name can be devised, I would denominate the *Phonology of Language*" (1818: 231).

The "Phonology" is also a beautiful synthesis of the variety of forces that shaped early nineteenth-century American linguistics. First, Duponceau was a non-native speaker of English, indifferent to the hot topic of Americanisms (unlike his friend, Pickering, who was thoroughly engaged in the issue) but with an ear attuned to *variety*: the sound of English as opposed to French, the differences between American English and British English, the very different sounds of American Indian languages. Perhaps Duponceau had even picked up on the rhythms of Afro-American speech or those of American Indian Pidgin English. The American experience with language has always been one of variety, and in early nineteenth-century American "melting pot" polyglot communities, this meant experience with *phonetic* and *phonologic* variety. As evidence of the degree to which studies of American English and the American Indian languages were fused in Duponceau's work, he opens his treatise of *English* phonology with observations about the difficulties of representing the sound *W* in Lenni-Lenape, that "whistling" sound that attracted the attention of Bréboeuf. Duponceau describes the sound and a Delaware syllable-structure constraint, when he identifies *W* as

> a consonant, the sound of which is produced by a soft whistling; however barbarous this sound may appear to one who has never heard it, when pronounced, or rather whistled has a pleasing and delicate effect on the ear, although it is frequently followed by the consonant *d* or *t*, as in *Wdanis*, daughter, *Wtehim*, Strawberries, *Wtellsin*, to do so, &c.
>
> (1818: 230)

He is led to the conclusion that "The epithet *barbarous* is much too soon and too easily applied, when we speak of sounds and of languages that we do not know" (1818: 230). With this sentence, he corrects Sagard-Théodat's, Monboddo's, and Herder's phonetic misapprehensions.

Second, Duponceau's entire project in "English Phonology" issues straight out of the political conception of language and its concern for written representation (see Chapter 1, pp. 49–51). Duponceau's purpose is to develop an

> alphabet of sounds . . . which the learned at least, might understand, and which might be made use of to convey to the

mind through the eye, a tolerable idea of the pronunciation of idioms yet unknown, and to represent the sounds of languages foreign to each other in a manner more fixed and determinate than has hitherto been done.

(231)

He acknowledges that such a universal alphabet could not yet exactly represent all of the subtle varieties of sounds, but he is ready to attempt the first phonology of English. Such whimsical names as *aulif*, *arpeth*, *airish*, *azim*, *elim*, *oreb*, and *oomin* are Duponceau's designations for the seven vowels.

Third, this concern for establishing a universal alphabet ties him, once again, directly to French Ideology, in particular to Volney. This Ideologue's most important contribution to linguistics was his project for the universal phonetic alphabet on which he worked for twenty-five years and to which he was inspired by the evident inaccuracies of the transcriptions of non-Western European languages in the vocabularies such as Pallas's (see Auroux, Désirat, and Hordé 1982). Volney's work, *L'Alfabet européen appliqué aux langues asiatiques*, was communicated to the American Academy of Arts and Sciences by Duponceau, after which Pickering applied both Volney's and Duponceau's principles to his *Essay on a Uniform Orthography for the Indian Languages of North America* (1820b). Relying on such diverse sources as Sir William Jones, John Eliot, John Heckewelder, and Sebastian Rasle, Pickering carried on the tradition of Volney and Duponceau of utilizing the Roman characters and of respecting the principle of using one distinct letter for each distinct sound. In this work, Pickering establishes, for instance, the convention of using the *cedilla* placed under the vowel to mark the nasal vowels in his proposed Indian alphabet. He attributes the idea to Duponceau's suggestion, which was calqued on the *Polish* orthographic practice (1820b: 16).

Despite Volney's, Duponceau's, and Pickering's contributions, it has been Karl Lepsius (1810–84) who has received historical credit for the alphabet on the basis of *Das allgemeine linguistische Alphabet* (Berlin, 1855). Lepsius devotes a page or two to Volney, dismissing his method as neither "scientific nor . . . practical"; and of Pickering, Lepsius passes the damaging judgment that: "[Pickering] took writing systems backwards rather than forwards" (1855: 10–11).[13] Unfortunately for Pickering (his historical fate, anyway), he asserted his plan to be "founded upon the idea of taking the common European sounds of the vowels as the basis of the alphabet" (1820b: 37–8), thus somewhat justifying Lepsius's judgment. Duponceau, on the other hand, had had the far subtler idea to study the "component sounds of the English oral language, *considered in the abstract*, and *independent of the signs* which are used to represent them" (1818: 239, emphasis mine; see also Rousseau 1981: 75).

The idea for which Duponceau has received the most attention is his typological observation on the American Indian languages, publicly introduced first in his "Report to the Historical and Literary Committee to the American Philosophical Society" of 1819, but privately sketched out in his 1816 correspondence with Heckewelder. The phrases with which Duponceau is most closely associated are those where he claims "a wonderful organization which distinguishes the languages of the aborigines of this country from all other idioms of the known world" and, again, where he refers to "those comprehensive grammatical forms which appear to prevail with little variation among the aboriginal native of America, from Greenland to Cape Horn" (1819: xiv; revived first in Haas 1969b: 239–40). With these observations was launched the question of "Grammar or Lexicon" in American Indian classifications through J.W. Powell. Haas (1969b) thoroughly treats the influence of Duponceau's statements in nineteenth-century American Indian studies, and her arguments need not be repeated here.

More at issue in the context of this present work is Duponceau's deeply grounded commitment to Ideology, which approach is very different from that assumed by Grimm and elaborated by Humboldt. In his correspondence with Heckewelder, Duponceau confirms the degree to which he is indebted to French thought:

> M. Maupertuis, in his Essay, took great pains to shew the necessity of studying the languages even of the most barbarous nations, "because," said he, "we may chance to find some that are formed on a *new plan of ideas*." M. Turgot, instead of acknowledging the justness of this profound remark, affected to turn it into ridicule, and said he could not understand what was meant by *plans of ideas*." If he had been acquainted with the Delaware language, he would have been at no loss to comprehend it.
>
> (1819: 365)

Maupertuis's phrase *plan of ideas* was to figure in the theoretical underpinnings of all of Duponceau's linguistic writings. A fascinating study of an unpublished *Essai* (1825) of Duponceau is offered by Robins (1987) who reports that Duponceau divided philology into three main divisions:

1 phonology, "the study of speech sounds and their graphic representation, which should lead to a universal phonetic alphabet";

2 etymology, "the mainly historical comparison of word forms, by which the affinities of languages may be established." In this subfield of "Philology" will fall genetic classification; and,

3 ideology, "which embraces *dans sa vaste étendue* the various forms, structures, and systems of languages and the means whereby they differently group and expound the ideas of the human mind." This, according to Duponceau, "may lead to a universal grammar, showing all the different combinations of ideas that human language can achieve" (Robins 1987: 437–8). To this division of "Philology," then, typology is assigned, and this typology carries philosophical and psychological implications *à la* Volney, determined by the "general character" of the grammatical structures exhibited.

This is precisely the tripartite division accorded to philology, "the science of language," in the *Encyclopedia Americana* (vol. X, 1832). Although I have not been able to determine who contributed the entry "Philology," I am using Robins (1987) to suggest that it was Duponceau. The entry as a whole covers some thirteen pages, with equal space given to each of the three divisions, i.e. phonology, etymology, and ideology, and all three of the discussions draw on the widest possible conception of the database.

The section "Phonology" displays a broad view of "the knowledge of the sounds produced by the human voice." It opens on a discussion of what we would now call prosodic or suprasegmental features of language with strong analogies to music, then concentrates on describing segmental aspects of phonology: the vowels and the consonants. The point concerning voiced and voiceless stops (although they are not called such) in Indian languages is of interest. "There are nations," the author writes, "who confound the *b* and the *v*, the *b* and the *p*, and the *d* and the *t*, and cannot discriminate the one from the other." The case in point is

Mohawk where "it requires a very nice ear to distinguish" between the *k* and the *g*. The author continues, "The reverend Mr. Williams, a native Mohawk of mixed blood, after much hesitation, at last determined in favor of *k*" (1830, X: 86). Although reasons (such as phonetic environments) are given to support the decision of *k*, it is clear the author is supporting the analysis by virtue of the fact that Mr Williams had access to "native speaker intuitions."

The author does not set up any sound correspondences in the first division, "Phonology." In the second branch, "Etymology," there are, however, several word lists, one comparing Russian, English, and Latin, another using Russian and English and bringing in Dutch, German, and Greek. The author has a clear sense that these words are etymologically related. Using the word "affinities" to capture the relationship, the author identifies the goal of "Etymology": "Amidst all these affinities existing among so many languages, how is the mother tongue to be discovered?" The author is hopeful: "The task is undoubtedly very difficult, but, to a certain degree, perhaps, not impossible" (1832, X: 89). There is no hint that the task is to be achieved by *sound* correspondences. It is rather to be carried out through morphological comparisons.

"Philology" is defined as "a science as vast in its extent as interesting in its details." Like all other sciences, "it requires to be subjected to some methodical order, in order that a comprehensive view may be taken of its whole extent, and a regular system pursued in the study of its component parts." The author follows this with the observation that

> we do not find that any attempt has been made in Europe to give to philology its definite form, by delineating its constituent members. We are therefore obliged to adopt, as the only one that we are acquainted with, the division which Mr. Duponceau has made of it.

> (X: 84)

This entry is, furthermore, distinguished from the next entry, "Philology, *in a narrower sense*," which is

> the knowledge and criticism of the ancient languages and the works written therein, in which sense the word is commonly

used by the Germans, who give to the science in its wider sense the designation of *Linguistik* or *Sprachenkunde* (science of languages).

(X: 93-4)

Duponceau has not, however, received credit for this early attempt to give "methodical order" and "regular system" to the study of "philology." Rather he is best known for having contributed the term "polysynthetic" to language studies, polysynthetism being characteristic of the Indian languages and the process by which "words can be compounded to any extent," where "the languages [are] essentially polysyllabic, and in which monosyllables are rarely to be found" (1832, X: 92). We can now see that "polysynthetic" belongs, above all, within the third division of "Philology," namely, "Ideology." Within this third division fall the analysis of grammatical forms, "the points of view in which men have considered the ideas which they meant to express, or, rather, to awaken in the minds of others" (1832, X: 90). Although the study of differing grammatical forms tends to show that the existing languages have not had a common origin, the historical development of these forms is not the central concern of this third division of "Philology." The second division, "Etymology," deals with language history. The third division, "Ideology," belongs within a structural, *a*historical framework and not within the diachronic and evolutionist framework that was to emerge with Humboldt. In agreement, then, with Leopold (1984), we see that Duponceau's thought was consistent with the ahistoricism of French Ideology, and interestingly enough, the term "polysynthetic" itself comes first from mineralogy. According to Leopold, the term "had been applied to crystallin composites formed in series of two united crystals in order to produce a laminated structure" (1984: 68).

Duponceau can now be contrasted with Pickering, who was one of the earliest proponents of German *Sprachwissenschaft* in America. If Duponceau's approach to language was overtly political, Pickering's was not necessarily so.

John Pickering (1777-1846)

Although Duponceau has received more and consistent recent

scholarly attention, John Pickering is the more influential figure in the development of America linguistics. However, a useful full-length biography exists of Pickering, written by his daughter (M.O. Pickering 1887), whereas no such volume exists for Duponceau. As evidenced by the many references to Pickering in my story thus far, it is apparent that Pickering had a strong formative influence on general American intellectual life. He was also a highly regarded figure during his lifetime. A distinguished Classics scholar and graduate of Harvard (1796), Pickering was, in fact, so well regarded for his linguistic abilities that he was elected Hancock Professor of Hebrew at Harvard in 1806 and then offered the chair of Greek Literature at Harvard in 1812. He turned both of these positions down. He was elected to the American Academy of Arts and Sciences in 1810, was its president in 1839, and was elected to the American Philosophical Society in 1820.

Pickering and Duponceau shared much in their friendship, beginning with their professions: they were both lawyers, tying them, at least in their day-to-day existence, to the political conception of language (and to Sir William Jones). Thus, they were both "gentlemen scholars," like Jefferson and unlike Webster. Again, like Jefferson, they shared a leisurely, wide-ranging interest in language studies, from the Classics to American Indian languages, Duponceau concentrating more on Algonquin, Pickering rather more on Iroquois with his Cherokee studies. They were both involved with the study and elaboration of writing systems. They both corresponded with the leading European linguistic lights of the day, both in France and in Germany.

In another sense, however, they were complementary figures: Duponceau resided in Philadelphia, that early seat of American intellectual activity. Pickering lived in Boston, which was to eclipse Philadelphia in intellectual importance, one sign of the times, perhaps, being the organization of the Boston Society for the Diffusion of Useful Knowledge in 1829, in which Pickering was chosen vice-president. Pickering, furthermore, was the younger by seventeen years, and this generational difference emerges in their slightly different orientations. Duponceau was immersed in French thought. Pickering was partially critical of it (e.g. see his opinion of Volney's interpretation of Indian religion, 1820b: 105) and would become instead an ardent advocate of German learning.

Furthermore, Duponceau, allied to ideology, was committed to language as a form of social, animal behavior (ideology is part of zoology) that seems to underly anthropological approaches to language studies, still today. A strongly political conception of language obscures the line between animal and human behavior. Pickering, by way of contrast, wished to study man "through the medium of his noblest and peculiar faculty of speech" (1819: 179), that peculiar faculty which would ultimately *separate* him from the lower animals and lower forms of animal communication. It was Pickering's phrase about the "noblest and peculiar faculty" that Humboldt homed in on and that underlies, again still today, rationalist approaches to language, those (mechanical and autonomous) approaches which seek to successfully analyze language *apart* from its social setting and as a *special* form of human behavior. Although, throughout Pickering's writing on language, as throughout Duponceau's writing on language, there is not yet mention of language being tied evolutionarily to *race* – we are, after all, still pre-Darwin – and Pickering still sees primarily a *horizon* in the variety of the world's languages, not a *hierarchy*.

In a comprehensive account of Pickering's linguistic views, it cannot be entirely irrelevant that Pickering should have taken such a strong early purist position against "Americanisms," calling for a reliance on the written standard and the authority of the works of "Milton, Pope, Swift, Addison, and other English authors, justly styled classic" to determine the legitimacy of the words at issue in his *Vocabulary*. Then, too, Pickering showed himself to be more conservative than Duponceau in his approach to the universal alphabet and failed, as Lepsius pointed out, by tying himself in his use of the Roman alphabet to the phonetic values of the Western European languages. Following William Jones, Pickering chose the Italian phonetic values for the vowels.

Although Pickering was to soften his position on Americanisms, he did not ease up on Webster. In the Boston *Courier* of 1837, for instance, an article appeared signed only "W," but undoubtedly written by Pickering. It unequivocally declared Webster (who was, by then, an octogenarian) and his learning out of date. "W" writes:

it will no longer do to rely upon the old books that were the authorities at the period when Dr. Webster laid the foundation of his Saxon learning . . . [such as] the laborious and really valuable, though extremely defective work of Hickes . . . and Lye's splendid, but unsafe work.

"W" follows this with the pithy remark that

we have no doubt . . . that the student will acquire more just notions of the *Anglo-Saxon* language and grammar from a few weeks' study of the illustrious modern Danish scholar, Rask, than from years of hard labor in the ponderous folios of Hickes and Lye, which, after all his labor, will still lead him into error.

"W" – Pickering – is still not through. Given the relationship of Anglo-Saxon to English and the further relationship of English to the "northern dialects":

the works of the modern German scholars rise to a still higher degree of importance; and, yet, strange to tell, none of the philologists in England [one thinks here of the legacy of Horne Tooke], or in our own country, appear to have derived any benefit from them. To judge from the labor of lexicographers in our language, the reader would hardly know that such men as Adelung . . . Humboldt, Grimm, Bopp, Rask, and others, of our own times, ever existed.

(quoted in Read 1966: 179)

Pickering is undoubtedly correct for wanting to keep the American public abreast of innovations and for taking to task Webster's egregious lexicographic mistakes. Nevertheless, the negative by-product of such an article was to cast a shadow across the whole of Webster's effort and his essentially political conception of language.

Pickering's ties to Germany are of particular interest in the history of American linguistics, and the relevant materials are not readily accessible to American scholars, as are Pickering's writings in general hard to come by.[14] The record of Wilhelm von Humboldt's side of his fourteen-year correspondence with Pickering is published in Mueller-Vollmer (1974). Many of Pickering's letters to Humboldt appeared in M.O. Pickering (1887). Pickering was also in personal contact with Bopp, who sent him his *Die celtischen Sprachen*, when it first came out in 1839, and Pickering was elected as a Corresponding Member of the Philosophical and

Historical Class of the Royal Academy of Sciences of Prussia in 1840 (M.O. Pickering 1887: 469–70). Despite the harsh criticism Pickering received from Lepsius after his death, during his lifetime at least, the two men were in epistolary contact (M.O. Pickering 1887: 504).

Through Francis Lieber (see below), Pickering's well-known contribution to the first edition of *Encyclopedia Americana* (1830), in the Appendix of volume VI entitled "Indian Languages of America" (1830–1), was translated into German in 1834 with the title *Ueber die indianischen Sprachen Amerikas* and was bought by such important university libraries as Goettingen's. It is also apparently through his contact with Pickering that Humboldt picked up (among other things) on the terms *einschliessender* "inclusive" and *ausschliessender* "exclusive" plural that figure in Humboldt's *Ueber die Kawi Sprache* (1838). These terms would eventually be handed down to Gallatin and Trumbull and finally used by Boas as "inclusive" and "exclusive" in his 1911 *Introduction* (see Haas 1969a, b). Furthermore, from materials at the Boston Mission Society, Pickering supplied Humboldt in the 1820s with data from the Pacific languages, specifically a Feejee (Fiji) vocabulary. Polynesian data had been absent in, for instance, *Mithdridates*.[15]

However, as with Duponceau, Pickering's contribution to the codification of the study of linguistics in America has been largely overlooked. In addition to his 1819 and 1820 reviews, he welcomed in his 1822 review of Adelung's *Uebersicht aller bekannten Sprachen und ihrer Dialekte* (1820) "the epoch of a *new science,*" namely, "the *comparative science of languages.*" This science, which studies "the *phenomena* of language (if we may so speak)" (1822: 29–30) is, of course, in this context of the review of Adelung, most associated with Germany and the German language. However, through Pickering's correspondence with Duponceau, it can be shown how very original was this idea of the science of language with the American Pickering. An 1821 letter on the subject of Pickering's notes on Eliot's *Grammar* (precisely the one where Pickering introduces the terms "inclusive" and "exclusive"), Duponceau is prompted to write to Pickering about Pickering's new idea:

The idea of the phenomena of language is new and beautiful. . . . It will give rise to more new ideas and things than you are aware of. A noble book is wanted in philology, – the Phenomena of Human Language. You are worthy of writing the book, since the idea is yours; if you do not, it will be written, for this is a mother-idea that will create a new title in philological literature. Could jealousy enter into my composition, I should be jealous of that idea, which I would give much to have conceived and developed as you have. Humboldt has understood it, and paid its author due homage for it.

(M.O. Pickering 1887: 313)

Pickering has not, however, been given due homage for the idea in the general history of linguistics, as is characteristic of most of American linguistics before the twentieth century.

Pickering's work is delicately balanced between the new German methods and his experience as an early nineteenth-century American, that is a person highly aware of the political dimensions of language and participating in the liberal, expansionist spirit of the early decades. In his "Indian Languages of America" of 1830–1, Pickering is overtly critical of Humboldt's "ingenious and profound Dissertation on the Forms of Languages (*Ueber das Entstehen der grammatischen Formen und ihren Einfluss auf die Ideen-Entwicklung*, 1822)" and chastises the Baron for not allowing the processes of the American Indian languages to be "genuine grammatical forms (*aechte formen*)" (VI: 582). Even though, Pickering writes, "these facts [of the American languages] have attracted the attention of the learned in Europe as well as in this country", he is aware that "they have not been able entirely to remove the prejudices that have been so long entertained against the languages of savage nations" (VI: 581). Pickering relies heavily on Duponceau and spends several pages arguing against just those European prejudices. Despite his conservatism, Pickering was a continual defender of the worth and integrity of the Indian languages, beginning in the 1820s, when he vigorously defended the work of Heckewelder and Duponceau against Lewis Cass's very negative review (1826) of Heckewelder, which confirmed the negative stereotype of the Indian that already existed in the popular American imagination.

Pickering's "Indian Languages" is a "state of the art" overview of all the Indian studies to have come before him. It is clear from this article that phonology is not the main concern of his approach to the Indian languages. Pickering takes us through the various Indian parts of speech from a section on the "Article" on through "Adverbs, Prepositions, Conjunctions, Interjections" and ends with a reproduction of Guest's (*sic*) Cherokee syllabary. In this article, Pickering draws most of his examples from Cherokee and spends approximately half of the entire appendix on the Indian verbs. In this way, Pickering's "Indian Languages" is a kind of *grammaire générale* for the American languages, a last expression in the American nineteenth century of the French eighteenth century.

Pickering's work thus directly complements the work of Albert Gallatin and his genetic classifications.

Albert Gallatin (1761–1849)

In the general scheme of American linguistics of the time, Gallatin was interested in the "etymologic" (i.e. genetic) – not the "ideologic" (or structural) – classification of the American languages. Gallatin addressed the question of numbers, first entertained by Jefferson: how many different languages (stocks, or families) were there? Barton, Duponceau, and even Pickering had given their various opinions on the question, but their interest was not primarily in determining a firm answer to that particular question. It was Gallatin's purpose to try for a definitive answer. Gallatin produced two important classifications of the North American Indians, the first his "Synopsis" of 1836, the second in 1848 under the title of *Hale's Indians of North-west America, and Vocabularies of North America*. In the first, Gallatin opens on the comment that the classification was made at the request of a "distinguished friend, Baron Alexander Humboldt" in 1823 (1836: 1), thus acknowledging the German influence from the very beginning. It figures, as well, in his concluding remarks, when in Section VI, Gallatin introduces the first signs of an evolutionary optic into American Indian studies when he identifies the grammatical processes as deriving from "natural causes" and "resorted to in the most ancient times by other nations" (1836: 208).

As Haas (1969b) has shown, Gallatin might have begun in 1836 in the manner of Duponceau and based his classification on structural factors, but he ended, in 1848, in determining *by their vocabularies alone* the different languages of the Indians within the United States. His substantive contribution to the genetic classification of the Indian languages was his ascertainment of thirty-two distinct families, in and north of the United States. This 1848 work and its change in methodology from the grammatical to the lexical as the basis of genetic classification was, according to Haas (1969b), to be a landmark in the history of the genealogical classification of the North American languages, not to be superseded until J.W. Powell (Chapter 4).

The philosophy behind Gallatin's change in methodology is present in 1836 and is directly related to already established ideas about the nature of progress in language. Gallatin suggests, in effect, in the last section of his *Synopsis* that grammatical forms remain constant while "progress of knowledge" is indexed through the addition of new words. Taking the language situation in Europe as an example, Gallatin determines that "the most uneducated men, those who in Europe speak only *patois* of the written language, deviate from the established rules of grammar, but use grammatical forms to the same extent as the best masters of the language" (1836: 207). The statement sounds like a less poetic version of Sapir's famous phrase: "When it comes to linguistic form, Plato walks with the Macedonian swineherd, Confucius with the head-hunting savage of Assam" (1921: 219). Now, since for Gallatin, the difference of language use between "the uneducated" and "the best masters" does not lie in their ability to use grammatical forms, it must, then, lie in their vocabularies, the *size* of their vocabularies. Gallatin leaves this part of his thinking unarticulated, but it is certainly implied:

> Notwithstanding the great progress of knowledge during the last four centuries, though new words have been introduced and others became obsolete, though languages have been polished and adorned, the grammatical forms remain the same as they were four hundred years ago, and have been found sufficient for the communication of new ideas and of all that may have been added to our knowledge.
>
> (1836: 207)

From this observation, Gallatin concludes that "experience shows that the changes have everywhere applied much more to words than to grammar." Words, then, will show the differences over time, if one is assured (as was Gallatin) that the grammatical forms and structure have remained the same. When Gallatin writes that "grammatical forms were as necessary, for the most common purposes, and when the knowledge of man and his sphere of ideas were most limited, as in the most advanced state of civilization" (1836: 206), the implication is that grammatical forms are (relatively speaking) everywhere the same, while the distinction between a "limited" and "an advanced state of civilization" with regard to the "knowledge of man and his sphere of ideas" must then be the number of words created in a speaking community to express that knowledge. My interpretation of the importance in Gallatin's thinking of the relative size of the vocabulary is motivated by my reading the history of American linguistics for all three arcs at once. That is, there is a strong tradition in the dictionary-orientation of English studies to extol the number of words in English. There is the equally strong tradition in Indian studies to disparage the numbers of ideas expressed by Indian words (Huron has "few ideas"). Although Gallatin does not come right out and say it, the tradition behind the phrase "limited sphere of ideas" echoes in the closing pages of Gallatin's "Synopsis."

Consistent with his time, Gallatin subscribes to the Mosaic chronology. Also consistent with his time is his methodology. He emphasizes cultural "revolutionary time" in identifying words, especially the great quantity of words introduced into the European languages in the previous four centuries, as the indicators of change. Gallatin does not, of course, yet have the idea of evolutionary time, the slow workings of random mutation and natural selection during which the species must have evolved to their present-day diversity. As for linguistic diversity, a rereading of Gallatin's "Prefatory Letter" and his conclusion shows how very much Gallatin's effort was part of a larger picture, since he places his study within the general question of accounting for the *global* diversity of languages (1836: 5). He examines the question of the increase in uniformity or decrease in uniformity of the number of language families in the entire world and buttresses his discussion, and indeed his entire exposition, with frequent references to Asian, African, and European languages. Needless to say, he supports his American classification with a wide range of data. Gallatin's direct quote from LeJeune of the forms: "'I see a man,' *Niouapaman iriniou*" versus "'I see a stone' . . . *Niouabaten*" (1836: 25) is a nice improvement over Herder's discussion of the same, for

Herder does not trouble himself to actually cite the Indian forms.

In addition to his "landmark" genetic classifications, Gallatin helps shape the history of American linguistics through the variety of professional societies in which he took a leading role. Gallatin was, for instance, instrumental in establishing the American Ethnological Society in 1842 and was named first president. The society's original roster included, among others, Henry Schoolcraft. The American Ethnological Society was to gain a certain prestige in ethnological circles which it would enjoy over the next twenty years until its dissolution in 1870 and reformation as the Anthropological Society of New York. Before 1842, Gallatin had been active in the American Antiquarian Society of Massachusetts. The next year, in 1843, he was the founding president of the New-York Historical Society, a society which, again, included Henry Schoolcraft. Gallatin's (surprisingly negative) opinion of the American Indians might best be summed up in his inaugural address to the New-York Historical Society where he describes the glorious discovery of America which was "a land inhabited only by Savage Tribes" (1843: 11). Duponceau and Pickering were not given to making such statements and were rather defenders of Indian territorial rights, but, after all, Gallatin had been Secretary of the Treasury under Jefferson and was more concerned with acquiring land than assuring the Indians their rights.

From the occasional *Transactions* and *Bulletins* of the American Ethnological Society, it is apparent that the Society construed the term *ethnology* to include a mixture of geography, philology, history, archaeology, travelogue, and even literary criticism and Biblical history. The titular change from *ethnology* to *anthropology* in the late 1860s indicates the degree to which American ethnologists had become increasingly sensitive to European orientations, for nearly all European societies of that time preferred the term *anthropology* to *ethnology* (see Bieder and Tax 1976). The point to be made here is that up until the 1840s, American researchers – linguists and ethnologists – were self-defining, relying on their own resources and determining their own theoretical directions. They were not, however, isolated from European language-discussions, but fully participated in discussing the general issues of the day. The period after the 1840s shows a return to a dependence on Europe. It shows as well – again with reference to Europe – the decline of the amateur and the rise of the professional.

Francis Lieber (1800–72) and the Encyclopedia Americana

Francis Lieber is one of the more surprising figures to emerge in this history of American linguistics.

Lieber was born in Berlin and took his university degrees from Jena in 1820, before coming to the United States in 1827. Shortly after his arrival and on the model of the German encyclopedia *Conversations-Lexikon*, he embarked on the editing of that first great codification of general American scholarship, the *Encyclopedia Americana*, marshalling the talents of such men as Edward Everett, George Bancroft, George Ticknor, John Pickering, and Peter Stephen Duponceau. The first edition appeared in thirteen volumes between 1829 and 1833. In 1835 he was appointed to the professorship of history and political economy in South Carolina College (whose chancellor bore the interesting name DeSaussure) in which position he remained more than twenty years. In 1857, when the Civil War approached and Lieber's stands against slavery made him unpopular in the South, he accepted an equivalent professorship in Columbia College in New York where he was subsequently elected to the chair of political science in the Law School of the same institution. He remained in that position until his death.

Like Duponceau, Lieber was a non-native speaker of English with his ear finely tuned to the *varieties* of American speech. Like Duponceau and Pickering, he was a professional lawyer and wrote widely on law, in particular political ethics, and on language. Unlike Duponceau and Pickering, he was fully a part of the American university academic system; and although he collaborated with both Duponceau and Pickering, he was never elected into the American Philosophical Society. He was, however, active in the Boston Society for the Diffusion of Useful Knowledge. Among his many German contacts were his correspondences with both Humboldts. He corresponded as well with Henry Schoolcraft and Albert Gallatin.

A full account of Lieber's linguistic interests remains to be undertaken. Surely, one of his most important contributions remains unpublished in a ten-volume set of Notes on Language which are at the Huntington Library (San Marino, California). These manuscripts include observations on Negro speech, pidginization, language in contact, the general processes of language change, and what we would now call code-switching. For now, we must rely on Heath (1982) and her study of these manuscripts. Heath has determined that Lieber was a "man ahead of his time" in his concern with "processes of language change and language in social contexts. He collected and commented on the development of pidgins and creoles, language varieties within English, and the language of the powerful and the powerless" (Heath 1982: 247). In addition, Lieber attempted to describe and name processes of change which occurred as a result of dialect convergence as well as

> the interrelationships of specific registers of individuals in social or professional contexts. He noted that when two speech communities which shared a minimum of linguistic competence and common cultural understanding come together, each must adopt special strategies for communication. These strategies in turn lead to processes of language change.
>
> (Heath 1982: 247)

Language change for Lieber could occur as either simplification (acquisition, adaptation, pidginization, or analytization) or amplification, which leads to shifts in syntax and lexicon. In close consistency with all the American language studies before him, Lieber's views on language are socially grounded and in tune with variety which was a fundamental part of the American experience with language in the nineteenth century. Heath also notes that the type of linguistic relativism that Lieber recommended and practiced was to decrease markedly after the mid-nineteenth century in American language studies with a return to prescriptivism (1982: 248), an observation which accords well with the general spirit of liberalism and relativism encountered earlier in, say, Duponceau.

Another of Lieber's important contributions to language studies is his 1850 study of "The Vocal Sounds of Laura Bridgman." The relationship of this study to the nineteenth-century American tradition of sign language and the deaf will not be taken up here (see Introduction, p. 20, note 2). However, Lieber's opening statements on language in that study will be quoted (albeit briefly), for they capture attention. "Language," Lieber writes:

> consists of signs, representing ideas. These signs are selected by the person who speaks, in accordance with the ideas prevailing

in his own mind, in order to produce the reversed process in the individual spoken to; they are used for that process – the most wonderful and important on this earth – of conveying ideas from one distinct individual to another; for the communion of mind with mind, through sensuous impressions, made in skilful succession, and in accordance with general laws. Why, then, do all languages consist of phonetic signs? There is no tribe known making exclusive use of ocular communion, conveying ideas chiefly by visible signs.

(1880 [1850]: 443)

First, these statements tie Lieber firmly into (franco-american, social-context-oriented) sign theory and provide an important relay from the *grammairiens philosophes* and the Ideologues to Whitney's sign theory.

Secondly, these statements are closely related to the statements made in the entry "Language" for the *Encyclopedia Americana* of 1830. Although it is not clear to me who wrote that entry, Lieber informs us in an editorial note that it is at least the same person who contributed the entry "Philology" (vol. VII, 1831), thus, possibly it was Duponceau. Like the entry "Philology," the entry "Language" bears Duponceau's perceptions of linguistic relativism, particularly in the closing remarks on grammatical forms, that "we must not confound *perfection* with *cultivation*," as well as the fact that "Languages were made for the purpose of communication between men, and all are adequate to that end" (VII: 416). The entry "Language" opens, however, on a definition of language as "God-given" where ideas are communicated "by signs" (VII: 408) and proceeds to a long passage on the "visible signs" of the "deaf and dumb." The substantialist conception of language is in full evidence in the entry "Language" with the following statement that "speech alone is properly entitled to the name of language, because it alone can class and methodize ideas, and *clothe them in forms* which help to discriminate their various shades, and which memory easily retains" (VII: 410). The article continues that those who are deprived, by nature, of the sense of hearing will make the best use they can of the senses which they possess. "We have known a young woman [Laura Bridgman?], born deaf and blind," the author reports, "who, to a certain degree, could understand, and make herself understood, by means of touch.'' However, for the most part, ''speech is the basis of all other modes of communication between men, and all of them, whatever be their forms, reach the mind only through the recollection of ideas, as clothed in the words of a spoken language'' (VII: 410).

Linguistic relativism is in full force throughout Lieber's writings on language. In an essay entitled ''On the Study of Foreign Languages, especially of the Classic Tongues,'' which was written as a letter to Gallatin in 1837, it seems that Lieber is going to extol the superiority of Greek and Latin. Contrary to that expectation, however, Lieber's arguments take him to a position that sounds remarkably like twentieth-century structuralism. Very little of the first two-thirds of the letter is devoted to the wonders of Greek and Latin. Most of it centers on a discussion of French, German, and English vocabularies, with some Greek and American Indian. Lieber notes, for instance, how the French have no one specific word for *to ride*, but rather two ideas, either *se promener* or *aller* plus *cheval* (1880 [1837]: 505). He follows this through to a discussion of the lack of correspondence among the various languages even in the word *horse* (as the one-word German *Rappe* = two English words, *black horse*), which leads him to state that

> This dissection of one image we best call the *division of ideas* – the most important subject, perhaps, in the whole province of the philosophy of languages . . . . We have seen that different languages may proceed on a different division of ideas. They actually do so in most cases, and on this very point rests mainly the great advantage of studying foreign languages.
>
> (1880 [1837]: 506)

From there, Lieber proceeds to dissect the nuances found in French *langue* and *langage* but not in English, then moves on to a discussion of the nuances of German *Glaube* as opposed to English *faith* and *belief* and balances all these against *Treue*. He concludes that

> These interesting inquiries into the division of ideas, and the difference of this division in different languages, by which we discover a different affinity and affiliation of thoughts and notions, a different perception of things, and a consequently

different ramification of ideas; in short, a different logic of nations, may be continued without end.

(1880 [1837]: 507; emphasis mine)

Then suggesting the well-known Saussurean bubble, Lieber says that "words describe a circle within which lies their meaning, and there can hardly be found in the different languages any two such circles which cover precisely the same space." He continues:

The circle of one word may cover half the circle of the corresponding word in another language, or the greater part, while part of its own circle is covered by another word in the first language, yet again by this same word may be covered part of the circle of quite another word, with an infinite variety of *affiliation of ideas*.

(1880 [1837]: 510; emphasis mine)

Lieber proceeds to make use of the language of the North American Indians, citing Mohegan *netáchgan* "brother," as opposed to *gegapan* "unmarried brother," which contrasts with the French *garçon* for "unmarried male adult" as well as English *bachelor* and *spinster* for unmarried male and female adults respectively (1880 [1837]: 515). If it were not for Lieber's next remarks on the grammatical structure of the Indian languages, I would be tempted to twist a phrase from Dell Hymes, who once stated (personal communication), in reference to Boas, that it took a German Jew to truly appreciate the Indian languages and to make a case for linguistic relativism. On the basis of what Lieber has said so far, I would agree with Hymes that it *did* take a German Jew, except that it was not Boas, it was Lieber.

Lieber's next statements, however, plant him firmly in the nineteenth-century vein of typologizing. Citing the process of *polysynthetism* in connection with the Indian languages, Lieber wishes to improve on Duponceau's terminology by introducing the term "holophrasis," that is, "words which express a complex of ideas" or "words which express the whole thing or idea, undivided, unanalyzed" (1880 [1837]: 518). The Mohegan word for *giving something to eat* would be holophrastic. By contrast, words such as the Latin *res*, English *to beat*, and the Greek *lógos* would be polyphrastic (1880 [1837]: 518–19). All languages exhibit both processes, but languages differ in their character according to the degree to which they exhibit one process or the other. Furthermore, holophrastic words are necessary for "energy of style" (520), so that "the poet wants frequently holophrastic words" (521), while "elegance of language requires analytic words" (522). Lieber finishes his essay in the manner one would have expected him to begin, that is by observing that since Greek abounds in both processes, it is by far the richest and most perfect language ever created; and he closes it on the importance of Greek in the American educational system.

Several decades later, Lieber continues with this notion of *holophrasis* with particular regard to the American Indian languages in his "Plan of Thought of the American Languages" included in Henry Schoolcraft's *Archives of Aboriginal Knowledge* of 1860 (vol. II). Lieber is very aware that "holophrastic is a relative term" (1860: 349). He invents the charming image that American Indian languages – like Sanskrit – have a tendency "to form or to use single words which to us appear like clusters of grapes." These he calls *bunch words*. However, Lieber then opens the door to the evolutionary framework that was to bedevil linguistics for the rest of the century when he observes that "as man begins with *perceiving* totalities, and then generalizes in his *mind*, so do children and early nations show the strongest tendency to form and use . . . *bunch words*" (1860: 347).

To these languages, Lieber opposes French, with its strongly *analytical* tendencies, all the while recognizing, again, that *analytical* is a relative term. With this terminology, however, the subjacent attitude carried over from eighteenth-century language philolosophy can surface: we have here the Indian–infant image, where the Indian is a child and his/her language childlike, with grammatical processes belonging to the language-acquisition stage (holophrasis).[16] By implication, then, the process of analysis belongs to the world of the rational European–adult. Through his choice of terminology, Lieber opens the door to the non-relativist, evolutionarily oriented period of language studies which was to prevail in the second half of the nineteenth century.

3

THE INSTITUTIONALIZATION OF AMERICAN LINGUISTICS: 1842–94

THE AMERICAN ORIENTAL SOCIETY

In 1828, soon after his arrival in America, Francis Lieber wrote his parents an enthusiastic letter about his plans for the *Encyclopedia Americana*. In this letter, Lieber judges Mr Duponceau to be "one of the most learned men in America" and acknowledges that he himself is "deeply engaged in the study of the language of the North American Indians." He is evidently pleased that "many men in Germany are engaged in this study, especially William von Humboldt." In fact, so enthusiastic is Lieber in this letter that he wishes "to propose to Mr. Duponceau a plan greatly approved of by Mr. Pickering," which was the founding of "a society for the promotion of the study of the Indian language" (Perry 1882: 81). Whether or not Lieber ever did propose this plan to Duponceau is not, unfortunately, revealed in any of Lieber's subsequent letters. What is known, however, is that no such society was ever established. Instead, the first American society devoted exclusively to language proved to be one which featured study not of the languages of the North American Indians but of the *other* Indians, i.e. Sanskrit, in the context of the American Oriental Society.

In the same year that Gallatin helped organize the American Ethnological Society, that is, in August of 1842, John Pickering called an informal meeting at his law offices of a few gentlemen interested in oriental literature. They drew up a constitution for the American Oriental Society and, at the first official meeting in October, elected Pickering president. Although Pickering was to die only four years later, that is, before the *Journal* began in 1849, it is evident from the list of officers for 1846–7 that he had succeeded in a few short years in getting the fledgling society off the ground.

The membership list included the names of Duponceau, Pickering, and Webster (all deceased by that time), as well as Edward Everett (then president of Harvard), Horatio Hale, and Francis Lieber. Among the distinguished honorary members were Bopp, Grimm, and Alexander von Humboldt, along with the archaeologist Jean-Jacques Champollion-Figeac and the orientalist Amédée Jaubert, both listed as members of the Institute, Paris.

In 1846, the corresponding secretary was Edward Eldridge Salisbury (1814–1901) of New Haven, who was to be one of the society's main pillars in the early years. Salisbury's name and endowment form the chair of Sanskrit and Comparative Philology at Yale to this day. In 1850, Salisbury brought a student of his into the organization, William Dwight Whitney, a young and promising Sanskritist at Yale. Whitney went on to become the society's librarian from 1855 to 1873, corresponding secretary from 1857, upon succeeding Salisbury, until 1884, when he was elected president, in which office he served six years. In 1884, Maurice Bloomfield also became especially active in the society, serving as director until 1924, vice-president in 1906 and again later, and president in 1910–11. In group-oriented, organizational terms, then, Pickering's influence over the coming generation of American linguists is marked.

Pickering's intellectual orientation was to have equally far-reaching effects over the next several generations of American linguists. First, of course, is the fact that the very organization of the American Oriental Society – as opposed to one for the North American Indians – reflects Pickering's fundamental conservatism, or, rather, his desire to imitate the Europeans, for the American Oriental Society was inspired by the establishment of the Asiatic Society in Calcutta (1783). Pickering's Eurocentrism had surfaced throughout his life in other ways: initially, as a student at Harvard, his deep grounding in the Classics and "Philology in the narrower sense"; his subsequent campaign against "Americanisms"; later, the very plan of his Indian alphabet, which was "founded upon the idea of taking the common European sounds of the vowels" as his basis.

In his presidential address to the American Oriental Society in 1842, Pickering also cast the form for American linguistics for the next half century. A conservative, Pickering always strove for a great, comprehensive grasp of whatever subject he approached. He had already displayed his ability to oversee and to synthesize in his *Encyclopedia Americana* article on the Indian languages. There, he summed up, and in relatively few pages, the issues and answers to a wide range of questions that had formed the tradition of American Indian languages studies for the past two hundred years. So it was in his presidential address that Pickering offers, once again, an *état présent* of philologic–ethnographic (read: "linguistic") research, in Europe as well as America. He displays not only his impressive Classical formation but also offers a vision for future research. He says that the object of the society is not only to inquire into the history, language, and literature of the *Orientals*, but also:

> It is . . . our intention to extend our inquiries beyond the Eastern *Continent* to the uncivilized nations, who inhabit the different groups of islands in the Indian and Pacific Oceans, from the eastern coast of Asia to the western coast of America; comprising that region of the globe which has been called Polynesia.
>
> (1849a [1842]: 5)

By acquiring this knowledge from these researches, Pickering hopes: "to furnish some useful additions to the materials already existing, for the completion of the general ethnography of the globe" (1849a [1842]: 5). Facing east, beginning first with Greece, then on to Egypt and Africa, Pickering proceeds to roam the globe over the next forty pages, heading ever eastward, wrapping the world until he arrives at the American Indians he knew so well. His vision for the future of language study is still one of expanding spatial horizons, not one of evolutionary hierarchy. Exhorting his fellow members to elevate themselves "to such a height as is indispensable for the survey of so vast a subject," he offers a bird's-eye view of the subject, which at present, he is only able "to distinguish and trace out the general outlines." Because of this, Pickering "must be reconciled to the omission of numberless details, which in the general view successively fade away and vanish in the distance" (1849a [1842]: 6). He leaves those "numberless details" to future generations, and it will be precisely William Dwight Whitney who answers Pickering's call in his *Language and the Study of Language* of 1867 where, in Lecture IX, he provides a similar survey of the world's languages, given in an order similar to Pickering's, with as much linguistic data as

Whitney could provide at that time. Although Whitney makes absolutely no mention of Pickering, it is difficult to believe, since Whitney joined the organization the year after the address was published, that Whitney did not read it and did not use it as his model. Whitney has since been credited with having been the first to succeed in writing a book on general linguistics which based itself on "real linguistic data rather than abstract speculations" (quoted in Koerner 1973: 74).

Still in this address, Pickering makes his last bid for the science of *philology*, or general philology. He says that it is: "a science, comparatively, of recent date, and the ultimate results of which, in ascertaining the relationship and history of nations – even of those which are not known to have ever had *written* languages – can hardly yet be justly appreciated" (1849a [1842]: 51). Pickering is not staking any theoretical claims for the boundaries of the science. Consistent with his vision of horizon, Pickering understands general philology "spatially" as opposed to "historically," and his survey presupposes Duponceau's ethnographic, *ideologic* approach. Pickering's "methodology" is one of globe-trotting, areal classification taking precedence over the genetic. As Duponceau had laid it out, the subdivision of philology known as *etymology* would investigate genetic relationships, but both Duponceau and Pickering were more interested in the subdivision *ideology*. These American divisions for this new science of language were soon to be eclipsed by the mid-century codification of *Sprachwissenschaft* in Germany and August Schleicher's separation of *Geisteswissenschaft* from *Naturwissenschaft*.

In this context of Schleicher and Germany, Pickering's address reveals much about the state of American language studies in 1842 *vis-à-vis* those in Europe. Pickering makes a point of registering American "firsts": he praises Duponceau who "first gave to the European world just and philosophical views of the families of aboriginal languages of this continent," and he signals Duponceau's glorious reception in France "where philological knowledge has been so highly prized" and "where the great value of his learning was justly estimated" (1849 [1842]: 51). Pickering mentions, modestly, his own "first" in having devised for the unwritten dialects of the Sandwich Islands of Polynesia "a systematic orthography" which is "now generally adopted in other dialects of the Pacific" (1849a [1842]: 52). Although he considers that Europe and the United States "constitute but one literary community," he must relish the "low state" of ethnographical and philological science in Britain, for he quotes at length British commentators who rail about the very same thing. British backwardness may be summed up in the name of one man: Horne Tooke. Pickering quotes a "learned Englishman" to the effect that:

> Horne Tooke dug more deeply than his competitors, and by no means without success; but, for want of practical knowledge, he often labored in the wrong vein, and as often failed to turn the right one to the utmost advantage.
>
> (1849a [1842]: 56)

All this, of course, stood in stark contrast to Germany, "that genial soil of profound learning." It is Pickering's opinion that it should be a

> high gratification to every American who values the reputation of his native land, to know that some of our young countrymen are now residing in Germany . . . with a view to the acquisition of the Sanscrit language; and that we shall one day have the fruits of their learning among us.
>
> (1849a [1842]: 42)

Pickering ends his address with high hopes for the future contributions to general philology to be made by Americans.

However, something more is at stake in this address, for Pickering begins it with a comparison of the situation of the American gentleman scholar to that of Sir William Jones and other British residents in Calcutta. Pickering laments that "under a free form of government, like ours . . . almost every man is called upon to have some agency in the management of public affairs" (1849a [1842]: 5, see also Chapter 1, note 4, p. 259). Thus, in the young America, there is no proper leisure, as there is in "older and larger states" for "an extraordinary subdivision of labor" (1849a [1842]: 3–4), that is, for full-time scholarship as there was (in unstated but heavily implied terms) in the German states. Now, let us remember that Pickering had turned down not one, but two chaired professorships at Harvard (1806, 1812). With all the benefit of hindsight, Pickering's comments seem tinged with "bad faith," for it seems that what Pickering is responding to here is the extraordinary successes of the German university system and the intellectual prestige associated with it. When Pickering turned down those chairs, he could not have predicted the stunning advances of German institutional research by the mid-1840s.

To set the stage in America, the year 1842 stood on the threshold of the last great surge of American expansion with the Mexican War (1846–8). It was just before that war, in the summer of 1845, in fact, that the first journalistic use of the phrase "Manifest Destiny" appeared in an anonymous article in the *United States Magazine and Democratic Review* (July–August). The phrase caught the spirit of the divine sanction for the territorial expansion felt in the young nation, the right to overspread the continent for the free development of its multiplying millions – an event well presaged by Adams, Rush, and Webster. A civil war was also in the offing, and the mood of the "boundlessness" of American possibilities was to retreat into the effort at "consolidation," in geographical expansion as well as in language studies. Pickering not only felt the push for consolidation, he was a force behind it.

The establishment of the American Oriental Society was closely contemporaneous with the revival of prescriptivism, which had abated in the 1830s and 1840s. In the periodization of Drake (1977), the years 1851–75 mark a return to prescriptive standards in the center of which was the "Great Dictionary War," a kind of civil war in language studies. According to Drake, the appearance of the quarto edition of *Worcester's Dictionary* in 1860 "set off a rivalry between it and the Goodrich revison of the *New Webster*, a rivalry in which apparently nearly every literate person took sides" (1977: 19). George Marsh, for one, took aim at Webster in his *Lectures on the English Languages*, delivered at Columbia College in 1858–9 and published in 1860. He cites "a celebrated lexicographer" and ridicules him for suggesting that the etymology of *issue* coincides with Ethiopic *watsa* (1860: 63). He gives other evidence that many of Webster's etymologies are unfounded and claims the best etymologies yet written in the United States were done by Webster's rival, Joseph Emerson Worcester (1784–1865). It follows from this attack on Webster (however well-founded) that Marsh would also deny Webster's desire for a national language and literature. In this volume, Marsh states plainly: "The three great literary monuments, the English Bible, Shakspeare [*sic*], and Milton, fixed the syntax of the sacred and the secular dialects'' (1860: 265) and are unlikely to be improved upon.[1]

The Webster–Worcester rivalry took the form of lawsuits and litigation that were to last for decades and hinged on that issue so central to the political conception of language: authority. By 1860, the dictionary had become the final authority in language matters and, in so doing, had also become big business. The popular debate over a dictionary indicates the degree to which the political conception of language still prevailed in America, a conception which was actually to be reinforced by particular developments in American history: three great waves of European immigration began after the Civil War, and these new citizens sought entry into ''polite'' society through the passport of linguistic ''correctness,'' while the many native-born Americans were equally committed to the idea of linguistic conformity as a means to upward mobility.

The North American Review, characteristically, provided a forum for the public debate. In 1860 (vol. 91), there appeared an article, in fact, reviewing Marsh's *Lectures on the English Language*. The subject of the review might be said to be that of Americanisms, a subject on which the last word had evidently *not* been said by Pickering in his *Encyclopedia Americana* entry of 1830. The *North American Review* article begins by criticizing those English critics who are

> unwilling to acknowledge that *we* have any . . . inheritance in and power over the common language . . . [and] have been too ready to stigmatize all the contributions which the vigor of American life, or the new exigencies of American literature, have made to the language, as innovations, corruptions, barbarisms.
> (507)

In the next breath, the author refers to ''much foolish talk about a national American literature'' and to a disposition

> to claim that there is, and of right ought to be, full license allowed to this great, free American people to modify the language . . . quite independently of foreign models, so as to adapt it to the peculiar wants and characteristics of the American mind.
> (508; quoted also in Drake 1977: 20)

Of this last claim the author does not approve, and though the author is relieved that "we do not find many writers going so far as to insist upon an American language," he is firmly against those writers who do insist "upon being absolved from all allegiance, and even from any special deference, to English use and authority" (508). The author ends the article with an observation on the differences between the "best" speakers of British English and the "best" speakers of American English. In Britain, he maintains that "the liberally educated . . . aim always to speak their best, and so have a style of colloquial English peculiar to themselves, as pure and simple as it is elegant," while "here the same class of men allow themselves to use the language of their inferiors in culture." This practice, the author concludes, "if not abandoned, will oblige us always, as now, to look to the mother country for the highest examples of spoken English" (528). John Pickering may well have approved of these arguments.

Now, what of the study of American Indian languages? In the 1860s, the public debate over the status of the Indian languages was apparently over. In the 1820s, the works of Eliot, Edwards, and Cotton were being reprinted, and the pages of *The North American Review* had been full with Pickering's reviews of these re-editions, as well as the reviews of Heckewelder, both for and against. The attack against Heckewelder came in a lengthy review by Lewis Cass in 1826 whose tone is set by Cass's statement to the effect that "The range of thought of our Indian neighbors is extremely limited" (22: 79). Pickering (under the pen-name of Kass-ti-ga-tor-skee, or "The Feathered Arrow") vigorously counterattacked Cass and the latter's egregious misinterpretations, and in such prominent places as *The New York Review* and *The United States Review* for 1826.

By the 1860s, however, *The North American Review* had lost interest in the Indian languages as a subject. There is an article in volume 90 (1860) on the Indians (as well as an unfavorable review of Darwin's *Origin of the Species*), but this article deals only with the territorial rights the Indians did and did not have in the eyes of the American government and is not interested in Indian language, manners, or customs. Now, Pickering had headed his first Kass-ti-ga-tor-skee rebuttal with a quote in Massachusetts from Eliot's *Bible* which reads "A nation whose language thou knowest not, neither understandest what they say." However, by

1860, Duponceau and Pickering were long dead. Pickering's intellectual legacy was the American Oriental Society, and Pickering's successors in that society did not inherit his interest in the Indian languages.

A small, but insightful light is shed on the development of American linguistics through a letter dated 1852 written by one William W. Turner to Professor Edward Salisbury. This letter indicates how difficult it was in 1852 to get American Indian language material published. Turner had submitted "A Grammar of the Choctaw Language" both to C.C. Felton, Professor of Greek Literature at Harvard and to Salisbury, Professor of Arabic and Sanskrit Languages and Literature at Yale. The grammar was never published, and the reasons for its failure can only be surmised. However, Turner's letter was published in the second volume of the *International Journal of American Linguistics* with the comment that:

> Neither are the services of professors of Greek Literature or of the Oriental languages required to pass upon present-day products of American linguistic researches. In this field, the specialist has at last come unto his own; and opportunities for publication are afforded not only through the Smithsonian Institution's Bureau of American Ethnology but also through various other channels, and lastly through the newly founded International Journal of American Linguistics.
>
> (MacCurdy 1921-2: 75)

Whatever this letter may indicate for the bad times Indian language studies suffered in the 1850s and the better times to come after Powell and on to Boas toward the turn of the twentieth century, the letter also indicates, in the context of my story, that the 1850s were a significantly *worse* time for Indian language studies than they had been in the opening four decades of the century.

To return to Pickering's comments on German learning in his presidential address of 1842: Pickering is indicating that a change has already arrived on the intellectual landscape, a change that was ultimately to affect negatively the study of the Indian languages. That is, the "gentleman scholar" was losing the prestige he had enjoyed in those early decades. It may not seem the case at first that Pickering should have suffered from any loss of prestige. In *The Launching of Modern American Science 1846–1876*, Robert Bruce paints a lively and exciting picture of Boston as the city of science in the 1840s. In 1846, Josiah Whitney, for instance, called Boston "the only city in America where anything of any account is done for science" (Bruce 1987: 82), and Bruce cites as evidence of scientific fertility in Massachusetts the startling figures that with less than 5 per cent of the nation's population, that state produced more than 20 per cent of the leading scientists (1987: 83). Boston boasted many advantages: it was considered a desirable place to live, had good fishing and shipping, thus good finance and industry, and a spirit of enterprise bolstered by strong New England Puritanism which viewed science as "witness to God's handiwork," It had the Lowell Institute, wealthy patrons, culture, ideals, and a *richesse oblige* attitude of science as a worthy cause (1987: 33–4). John Pickering and his American Oriental Society certainly are part of the scientific story in Boston of the 1840s.

Most of all, however, by 1842, an event across the Atlantic was affecting the Boston intellectual climate, that "event" being the extraordinary rise in prestige of the German university system, the "event" which Pickering had not foreseen in 1806 and 1812, when he turned down his academic appointments. With the rise of the German university came the concomitant loss of prestige for the talented amateur, the "gentleman scholar." Again, Bruce (1987) argues convincingly that the German university – and "there were a score of them by 1846" – had achieved unparalleled heights of scholarship, while nothing even resembling a modern university or even a serious graduate program yet existed in the United States. The German university was a model for all other intellectual communities to follow. It was, above all, dedicated to research. It lengthened education by four or five years, gave freedom to its faculty and to its students in a seminar method, all of which encouraged specialization. Free and easy communication among the various universities assured not only transfer of information, it also promoted co-ordination of scientific development, so that the university could guide its students to areas which needed investigation. In addition, the system of university rank helped promote a desire for position and helped keep up professional standards and responsibility (Bruce 1987: 8).

It is no wonder, then, that between the years 1820 and 1920

nearly nine thousand American students crossed the Atlantic to enter the prestigious lecture halls, seminars, and laboratories of German universities (Herbst 1965: 1). In the lists can be found the names of Edward Salisbury, who from 1836 to 1840 studied Arabic first with Sylvestre De Sacy and Garcin de Tassy in Paris before going on to Berlin to study Sanskrit with Bopp; William Dwight Whitney, who in 1850 went to Germany to study three semesters with Bopp, Albrecht Weber, and Karl Lepsius in Berlin and two under Rudolph von Roth in Tuebingen, earning his doctorate from the University of Breslau in 1861; Basil Gildersleeve, first editor of the *American Journal of Philology*, who studied for three years at Berlin, Bonn, and Goettingen, receiving his PhD at Goettingen in 1853; Francis Child, first professor of English at Harvard (1876), who studied in 1852–3 at Goettingen and Berlin; Maurice Bloomfield, a student of Whitney's, who spent the years 1879–81 studying in Berlin and Leipzig; Louise Pound (1872–1958), who took her PhD at the University of Heidelberg in 1900; Truman Michelson, who, after earning his PhD at Harvard in 1904, studied in Berlin and Leipzig in 1904–5; and Leonard Bloomfield (Maurice's nephew), who studied at Leipzig and Goettingen in 1913–14 with August Leskien (the translator of Whitney's *The Life and Growth of Language*), Karl Brugmann, and Herman Oldenberg.

The impact of German *Wissenschaft* on American language studies cannot be overestimated. It is, in fact, an integral part of the story of American linguistics in the nineteenth century.

THE CHALLENGE FROM GERMANY

Benjamin Franklin had been the first to lead the way to Goettingen toward the end of the eighteenth century, and he was followed, at the beginning of the nineteenth, by Ticknor, Cogswell, Everett, and Bancroft. These four New England men brought the new critical methods in the natural and the social sciences stateside. By 1820 German thought was already beginning to capture the imagination of the Boston intelligentsia. Philadelphia, the bastion of French Enlightenment thought, was falling into an intellectual slumber. The fresh New England mood is best summed up in a glowing tribute to Edward Everett, the educator, by one of his pupils at Harvard, Ralph Waldo Emerson. Emerson gives the sense of new day dawning in these words:

Germany had created criticism in vain for us until 1820, when Edward Everett returned from his five years in Europe, and brought to Cambridge his rich results, which no one was so fitted by natural grace and the splendor of his rhetoric to introduce and recommend. He made us for the first time acquainted with Wolff's theory of the Homeric writings, with the criticism of Heyne. The novelty of the learning lost nothing in the skill and genius of his relations, and the rudest undergraduate found a new morning opened to him in the lecture-room of Harvard Hall.

(1911 [1883]: 330)

However, Emerson, the sage of transcendentalism, did not at first witness the triumph of his brand of German philosophy. Emerson's brand came from Friedrich Schelling (1775–1854), the foremost German natural philosopher at the beginning of the nineteenth century who had defined Nature as unconscious reason in the process of becoming, struggling to gain consciousness of itself. As Emerson would phrase it in Chapter IV, "Language," of his 1836 essay *Nature*:

There seems to be a necessity in spirit to manifest itself in material forms; and day and night, river and storm, beast and bird, acid and alkali, preexist in necessary Ideas in the mind of God, and are what they are by virtue of preceding affections, in the world of spirit. A Fact is the end or last issue of spirit.

(1985 [1836]: 43–4)

Similarly, in that same essay, Emerson suffuses language with a spiritual nature. He acknowledges that words used to convey a spiritual import arise, originally, from sensible things. However, for Emerson, "the process by which this transformation [from material to spiritual] is made, is hidden from us in the remote time when language was framed" (1985 [1836]: 33). Although the original processes are lost to us, Emerson states that "the same tendency may be daily observed in children." Then, using an Indian–infant comparison that has become familiar, he adds that: "Children and savages use only nouns or names of things, which they continually convert into verbs, and apply to analogous mental acts" (33). Emerson declares a "radical correspondence between visible things and human thoughts" which leads him to the

131

Rousseauian observation that "savages, who have only what is necessary, converse in figures. As we go back in history, language becomes more picturesque, until its infancy, when it is all poetry" (36–7). The goal of his meditations, that is, "for the universe [to become] transparent", sounds at first like Condillac, but when he adds that "the light of *higher laws* than its own, shines through it" (43), he allies himself to Germany.

In Germany, Humboldt had identified language as the organic embodiment of collective consciousness, a quasi-independent entity controlling an individual's thought and expression. Interest in the sign, *Zeichen*, that had preoccupied most of the French eighteenth century, was too small an entity to serve as the most interesting object of meditation. For Humboldt, the word was to be situated as an intermediate entity between the sign as a product of collective (i.e. social) analysis and the image which was, at the same time, a product of arbitrariness or of voluntary choice (*Willkuer*) as well as a product of the impression of objects. At this crucial point, then, Humboldt's thought can be seen to oppose Kantian synthesis to Condillac's analysis. Humboldt's synthesis is a transcendental synthesis, based on the model of sexual union, where two impulses, that of the union of spontaneity–understanding on one side and of receptivity–imagination on the other, "marry" to create new beings. The synthesis of Humboldt's "senses" are not the classic senses with which Condillac endows his statue, but the senses are sexual organs, directed to the *other*. Emerson's imagery is parallel, again in the chapter "Language" from *Nature*: "All the facts in natural history taken by themselves," Emerson writes, "have no value, but are barren like a single sex. But marry it to human history, and it is full of life" (1985 [1836]: 35).

For Humboldt, this concept of synthesis is as the basis of his celebrated formula of language as *energeia*. Language is no longer a cold, passive instrument (organon) of thought as it had been for Condillac, but the active, passionate, formative organ of thought. From this it follows that Humboldt has a very different disposition towards the arbitrariness of the sign than Condillac. The arbitrariness of the sign, for Condillac, is bad. It was Condillac's goal to eliminate the space of the arbitrariness, to make language conform to the *ordre de la nature*. By contrast, Humboldt views the arbitrariness of the sign as positive, as the space of liberty from the "order of nature." This liberty is, however, subject to other "orders," namely social and geographic contingencies, as well as one's individual disposition. Thus, when Condillac complains that the indetermination of significations makes us reason amiss and must be eliminated from language, Humboldt gives a positive interpretation to that indetermination, for without it, spontaneity (*Selbsttaetigkeit*) of thought would be impossible. Through this "spontaneity" or *individuelle Taetigkeit*, Humboldt stresses language as the "noblest faculty," that ability which qualitatively separates man from the "lower animals." For Humboldt as for Emerson, the causes or reasons for the acquisition of that ability in the early development of language are lost to us in the misty recesses of time.

However, the late-eighteenth-century speculative philosophy of a Hegel or a Schelling, which would give rise to Humboldt and Emerson, was by no means an instant success in the United States. By 1815 – again that date – the continental European revolt against the speculative philosophy of a Hegel or a Schelling had begun. German speculative philosophy jarred, furthermore, with American common-sense philosophers, whose affinities lay with Scottish moralism. In the 1820s and 1830s, that is, following the successes of Bopp and Grimm in philology, and Rudolph von Virchow (1821–1902) in anthropology, the methods of "hard" empirical research, verification, and induction were winning the scientific day in American classrooms and lecture halls. American students were seeing the arrival of the "scientific age" of German scholarship, while the "philosophic age" was receding into the past. By mid-century, German science stood high with an army of giants: "Helmholtz, Ohm, and Mayer in physics; Gauss in mathematics; Liebig, Woehler, Bunsen, and Mitscherlich in chemistry; Bessel and Encke in astronomy; Von Baer, Mueller, Schleiden, and Schwann in biology, [Alexander von] Humboldt in geography" (Bruce 1987: 9).

However, American history had its own momentum in the nineteenth century, and as Jurgen Herbst tells the story, although transcendentalism and Hegelian social thought might not have immediately made it into American academe, they did appear with the resurgence of nationalist sentiments during and after the Civil War. This resurgence coincided "with the disappearance of moral philosophy into the emerging disciplines of history, political science, political economy, and sociology" (1965: 66). After mid-century, major shifts in discipline boundaries were underway, and the Germans were drawing all the lines.

In language studies, the divisions of the German *Wissenschaften* – with a clean cleavage between the realm of *Geisteswissenschaft* proper and that of the *Naturwissenschaften* – were to take their theoretical shape from August Schleicher (1821–68). By mid-century, Schleicher had staked out the landscape in his *Die Sprachen Europas in systematischer Uebersicht* (1983 [1850]). The status of language studies, the "real" or "scientific" part of language studies, i.e. linguistics, hinged on the question of whether it was a physical science: *Naturwissenschaft*; or a moral science: *Geisteswissenschaft*. Schleicher identified that part of language study belonging to *Geisteswissenschaft* as *Philologie* and distinguished it from "die Wissenschaft der Sprache," i.e. "linguistics," which belonged to the division *Naturwissenschaft*. The former was a "historical discipline" and viewed language as a means to study the literature and culture of a people and thus dealt with all that is subject to human will. The latter was concerned with language *per se*, that is language which, like an organism, is dominated by "unalterable natural laws" – at least in phonology and morphology. Linguistics is therefore a natural science, and since it is founded on phenomena outside the realm of free will, is it open to direct investigation and strict observation.[2]

Thus, *Geisteswissenschaft* studies mankind's cultural history, while *Naturwissenschaft* studies the natural history of man. With this separation, the morphological hierarchizing, which has come to be so well identified with nineteenth-century language studies, became a part of "the natural history of man." Schleicher takes up the morphological typologies worked out by Humboldt and gives them their evolutionary twist by identifying a rising development from isolating to agglutinative, then on to the highest stage, inflectional. Since known language history does not support this theory, Schleicher identifies the prehistoric growth of language according to this "natural" pattern and distinguishes it from the historical period of language. The separation between the two periods and the two theoretical realms is clear: the laws of physical science, *Naturwissenschaft*, express generalizations about timeless causal relations between forces of relatively constant intensity; the so-called "laws" of the moral sciences (subject as they are to human will) are less exact generalizations (Christy 1983: 45) and therefore less "scientific."

One of the more prominent linguists in the mid-nineteenth century to take up Schleicher's distinction was Friedrich Max Mueller (1823–1900). Mueller wrote in 1865 that he had always taken it

> for granted that the science of language . . . is one of the physical sciences, and that therefore its method ought to be the same as that which has been followed with so much success in botany, geology, anatomy, and other branches of the study of nature.
>
> (quoted in Christy 1983: 45)

Through Mueller, the distinction of the branches had crystallized: *Sprachwissenschaft* deals with *Natur*, that is, ultimately, with acts of God and unknown causes; *Philologie* deals with the *Geist*, acts of man and known causes.

Into the issues we can now map the position of Mueller's most vigorous nineteenth-century critic, William Dwight Whitney.

WILLIAM DWIGHT WHITNEY (1827–94)

In addition to his chronologically central place in this narrative of linguistics in America from 1769 to 1924, William Dwight Whitney is also the central intellectual figure in my story from three points of view: 1) Whitney's thought about language derives from American sources which have been described thus far and will fundamentally influence that which is to come; 2) almost single-handedly, Whitney institutionalized American language studies and gave language studies an organization that is still in place today; 3) Whitney presents a fully integrated thought, such that in order to discuss language studies in the second half of the nineteenth century, I can focus on one individual, instead of having to create a mosaic out of an overview of the work of several. I do not intend to cover the full range of Whitney's work, only that part which fits into my American framework, and that part actually covers quite a wide range of his professional activity.

Of Whitney's life and career, it is usually mentioned first that his older brother Josiah Dwight Whitney was an eminent geologist and introduced brother William to Lyell's *Principles*, thus helping to usher uniformitarian methodology into language studies. Next, it is usually mentioned that when Josiah returned from Europe in

1845, he brought with him 341 volumes for his library, including Bopp's Sanskrit grammar which he passed along to the 18-year-old William. Later, when William was to join Josiah's geological survey of the Lake Superior region in the summer of 1849, he took Bopp's grammar with him. Thus, William was prepared in the fall of 1849 when he went to Yale for a year of Sanskrit under Salisbury. Following this, Whitney went to Germany in 1850, and upon his return in 1853, he embarked on a career at Yale whose glories would only increase, never to diminish until (abruptly) after his death. Whitney's career marks the full academic institutionalization of linguistics in the United States.

The most provocative detail in Whitney's life, from my perspective, is the fact that his father owned the Northampton Bank and that the young William worked for three years as a clerk there between 1846 and 1849. It so happened that the day after he began his study of medicine in a physician's office (October 1, 1845), he contracted measles. Now, during his convalescence, he first read Bopp's grammar. Immediately thereafter, however, William went to work at the bank. The intersection of language and money occurs in Whitney's writings, as one of the coordinates of the political conception of language which identifies language and nation. It is also the case that in the non-centralized American banking system of the mid-nineteenth century, thousands of unit banks independently supported the post-1840s territorial expansion. Whether or not the Northampton Bank had a direct stake in the westward expansion, I have not been able to discover, but the financial mood of the time was "invest in the West," and Whitney's stint in the bank coincided with the Mexican War and the Gold Rush. His expansionist ideas for the English language are unambiguously expressed in his work.

As wonderfully influential as Josiah Dwight seems, an illuminating anecdote concerning the brothers Whitney is recounted by Bruce (1987). Both Josiah and William were members of the prestigious Academy of Sciences (established by an act of Congress and signed by President Lincoln in 1863), and Josiah brought before the Academy a personal vendetta against a fellow geologist named Benjamin Silliman. It seems that Josiah, in his 1860 geological survey of California, ignored the promise of certain oil and gold deposits which Silliman later discovered and touted. Enraged, Josiah wished to expel Silliman from the National

Academy on the grounds that Silliman wanted only to make money from his discoveries, and Josiah blamed Silliman for the failure to obtain legislative funds for a further survey. Bruce writes, however, that "it was obvious then and is now that Whitney's own arrogance, sharp tongue, indifference to economic payoffs, and repeated failure to meet deadlines were to blame" (1987: 316). In any case, Josiah savagely hounded Silliman out of academe and tried to get him expelled from the National Academy, charging him with falsifying geological reports for profit. Josiah was 'strangely dilatory" in backing up his charges, however. When the Academy dismissed Josiah's case against Silliman, "Whitney and his brother William quit the Academy in a huff, but Silliman remained a member and lived to see his gold and oil reports spectacularly borne out by events" (Bruce 1987: 316). The point of this gossipy anecdote – as is the point of any anecdote – is to represent the complexities of a personality, and to suggest the multiplicities of influence that Josiah might have exerted over William.

It is, however, not my intention to tarnish Whitney's family, or to diminish the distinction of either brother's career. William Dwight's was unusually distinguished. He was celebrated at home and abroad from Kazan to Paris. Whatever the distinction of his career during his life, it did not survive his death. In the past one hundred years, Whitney's thought and writings have been fragmented by later linguists, The collective fragmentation of Whitney's work is symptomatic of the zero value of historical perspectives that has existed, up to the present, in American linguistics.

Whitney in Historical Perspective

With regard to Whitney's fate, it is entirely relevant that the main Neogrammarian tract, i.e. the "Vorwort" to *Morphologische Untersuchungen* by Osthoff and Brugmann (1878), does not mention Whitney's name. Osthoff and Brugmann do give a rather balanced account of the background and goals of their school, duly acknowledging the work of such men as Steinthal and Scherer. However, they do not mention the linguist who "surely played the greatest role in incorporating Lyell's uniformitarianism into linguistics – William Dwight Whitney" (Christy 1983: 78). According to

Christy, it was Whitney, and not Scherer, who first advocated and practiced Lyell's uniformitarian principle in linguistics. Once again, the American contribution to linguistics was written out of the historical record as determined by nineteenth-century Germany.

Whitney had another chance in the nineteenth century to achieve some significant place in general linguistic history and the history of general linguistics. At his death, the First American Congress of Philologists dedicated their meeting held at Philadelphia, December 27–8, 1894, to his memory. Those readers interested in numerology may note that this was thirty years to the day before the founding of the Linguistic Society of America. In any case, Whitney's memorial meeting was an event to remember. An astonishingly august list of foreign scholars sent letters for the occasion: Graziadio Ascoli (Rome), Auguste Barth (Paris), Otto von Boehtingk (Leipzig), Peter von Bradke (Giessen), Michel Bréal (Paris), Karl Brugmann (Leipzig), Georg Buehler (Vienna), Edward Cowell (Cambridge, England), Berthold Delbrueck (Jena), Richard Garbe (Koenigsberg), Victor Henry (Paris), Alfred Hillebrandt (Breslau), Julius Jolly (Wuerzburg), Hendrik Kern (Leiden), August Leskien (Leipzig), Alfred Ludwig (Prague), Friedrich Mueller (Vienna), Hermann Oldenberg (Kiel), Richard Pischel (Halle), Reinhold Rost (London), Rudolf von Roth (Tuebingen), Emile Senart (Paris), and Ernst Windisch (Leipzig).

Ferdinand de Saussure was also invited to write, but with his usual "epistolophobia," as Jakobson (1971) puts it, the forty-page draft was never finished and never sent. The gist of Saussure's reply can be summed up in the words:

> Of the different attempts . . . to extract from the mass of results accumulated by comparative grammar some generalizations about language, all were frustrated or without general value, except that of Whitney, which from the very first was on the right track, and which today need only be patiently carried on.
>
> (quoted in Jakobson 1971: xxix)

Jakobson reports, again, from an incomplete and unpublished manuscript, that Saussure wrote: 'The American Whitney, whom I revere, never said a single word on the subjects [of the theory and method of linguistic science] that was not correct.'' Saussure adds, "However, as all the others [linguists past and present], he

did not imagine that language [*langue*] needed a systematics"
(Jakobson 1971: xxxvii).[3] An entire chapter devoted to Whitney's
influence on Saussure is found in Koerner (1973; see also Koerner
1979).

In the twentieth century, Whitney's influence extended into
other countries. Jakobson traces Whitney's influence first to Jan
Baudouin de Courtenay (1845–1929) at Kazan, and then on to
Moscow University in 1901–2 through the head of the Moscow
linguistic school, F.F. Fortunatov (1848–1914), who named as one
of the few recommended manuals for his *General Course* Whitney's
The Life and Growth of Language. In agreement with Whitney,
Fortunatov pointed out the close relationship between language
and society. Fortunatov, like Whitney and Saussure, was critical
of Schleicher's oversimplified and mechanistic view of the Indo-
European ancestor language (see Jakobson 1971: xxv–xxvi). After
all this initial praise, however, Whitney fell into oblivion, to be
recently revived by European historiographers.

In the United States, a slightly different story unfolds. Hardly
a decade after Whitney's memorial meeting is found the following
reference to Whitney in the closing arguments of Sapir's Master's
Essay on "Herder's 'Ursprung der Sprache'" (1907). In the
context of valorizing the Herder–Humboldt approach to language,
Sapir first praises Max Mueller with these words:

> As the last general linguist to discuss language problems from
> the standpoint that maintained the existence of a wide,
> impassable gulf between man and the lower animals, and stoutly
> denied any genetic relationship between animal cries and the
> rude beginnings of human speech, should perhaps be mentioned
> Max Mueller. Like Herder and Humboldt, he saw in language
> the distinguishing mark that separated man from the brute
> world, and was never tired, to the end of his days, of arguing
> that this possession of language was the death-blow to
> Darwinism.
>
> (1984 [1907]: 388)

Sapir continues that Mueller adhered to the idea of the inter-
relation of language and reason, and of their simultaneous growth,
which, again, was common to Herder and Humboldt. So
impressed was Mueller by this theory of the essential identity of
language and reason that his slogan in later days was, Sapir

writes: "Without reason no language; without language no reason." However, Sapir continues that it is well known that "his assertion of this principle brought on a fruitless logomachy with William Dwight Whitney" (388). Sapir was twenty-three years old at the time he wrote these words, and I do not believe he ever again referred to Whitney in his work. In any case, we have here a clear indication that, after Whitney's death, for the early twentieth century, German thought had come to the United States and was prevailing.

A further indication of German pre-eminence comes in Bloomfield's first book *Introduction to the Study of Language* (1914) which states quite plainly its debt to Whitney and the path he opened up. However, Bloomfield also wishes to "update" Whitney by incorporating the recent advances in linguistic science, and this, for Bloomfield of 1914, means incorporating Wundt's *Voelkerpsychologie* – yet another indication of the extent of influence of German thought after the turn of the twentieth century.

Whitney's thought has subsequently not survived intact into the late twentieth century. A fragmentation has occurred, and Whitney has been interpreted slightly differently in each of the three arcs of development I have identified in the development of American linguistics. Taking each of the three arcs in turn, one finds that:

1   Whitney did not write on American Indian topics. He studied the "other" Indians. He was a Sanskritist, not an Americanist. Dell Hymes, in "The Americanist Tradition," notes that: "It is worth remembering that the sanest, most constructive nineteenth-century scholar to interest himself in Indian languages, Whitney, had no field work with them" (1983: 118). This lack of field work experience predicts that Whitney's contribution to Amerindian studies (such as it was) would not be kept alive. We will return to Whitney's "sanity" with respect to the Indian languages.

Josiah Dwight, on the other hand, is given credit by J.W. Powell in his *Introduction to the Study of the Indian Languages* (1880: vi) for having helped him with devising an alphabet.[4]

2   As for the study of American English, arguably the most influential scholar of the twentieth century, H.L. Mencken, dismisses Whitney in the same breath as he does Witherspoon, Worcester, Fowler, Cobb, and their like, those "American

philologists, so-called," Mencken writes, "of the early days [who] were uncompromising advocates of conformity to English precept and example, and combated every indication of a national independence in speech with the utmost vigilance" (1936 edn: 60). Mencken had no use for Whitney's *Essentials of English Grammar* (1877), and the work has thus fallen into oblivion. Whitney merits a three-page mention in Finegan's *Attitudes toward English Usage. The History of a War of Words* (1980), confirming Whitney's conservative and authoritarian approach to English grammar, although Finegan does note that Whitney's criterion for "bad" usage is sociological and not inherently linguistic. "For the first time," Finegan writes, "an American broke loose from the circularity of preferring the usage of the best speakers and writers while identifying such models by the character of their English" (1980: 65). Whitney receives a similar two pages in Drake's *The Role of Prescriptivism in American Linguistics, 1820–1970* (1977).

3   In the third arc of development, that of European influence on American scholarship and of the rise of general linguistics, we have already seen that Whitney's memory fared initially better than in the first two arcs.

As a result of Whitney's strong association with Sanskrit, it so happens that the more recent historical retrospectives written by American linguists typically place Whitney in the sphere of influence of Germanic Indo-European studies. These recent historical retrospectives, by Stephen Anderson (1985), Michael Silverstein (1971), William Labov (1972), and Charles Hockett (1980), form an interesting composite of the present evaluation of Whitney's thought.

Anderson has judged the overall effect of Whitney's work to be preparatory rather than substantive, commonsensical rather than strictly original:

> [Whitney] was known less for revolutionary or even novel ideas than for the balance and common sense with which he confronted the often rather mystical excesses of much other nineteenth-century thought about language . . . . His own work was completely within the framework of his time, presaging in no important way the sort of structuralism that would soon dominate the field.
>
> (1985: 195–6)

So, while Whitney might not have fallen into the errors of the nineteenth century, neither did he rise out of his century to have any particular impact on the present century. Anderson conveys something humdrum hovering over Whitney's "common-sense" approach to language. One has the impression that any other linguist of the nineteenth century with this common sense could have done as well.

Silverstein, by way of contrast, awards Whitney a "first." "It is hackneyed to insist," Silverstein writes, "that Whitney was almost the first to stress the 'cultural' nature of language, in modern terms" (1971: viii). Here, one has the idea that Whitney did make a personal, perhaps even original, contribution to linguistics by recognizing and stressing language as "social fact." Silverstein excellently exposes Whitney's view of language change through a discussion of Whitney's views on the opposition of *material* and *form* and "phonetic economy" (1971: xvi–xxi). Silverstein's discussion leads one to see the implications of Whitney's thought: 1) that a unilinear evolutionary schema is fitting and proper and that Indo-European languages are the "highest" and most developed; 2) that written records are indispensable to insure historical reconstructions, since the directionality of change can only be determined *a posteriori*; 3) that the "exceptionlessness" of sound changes is tautological, because every change has a context of productivity and application and that phonological structure must, of necessity, mirror historical processes. Whitney was codifying a view of historical regularism that was already in Bopp and others, but in giving it a general theoretical explanation, he gave a basis for Neogrammarianism, which he himself never espoused and devoted much time to arguing against. Silverstein concludes that

in Whitney's case, as in the cases of later writers, like Franz Boas and Sapir in certain phases . . . the dynamic alternations of shape in elements of a language in different constructions, is primarily a reflection of historical processes, the geological evidence, so to speak, of what must have gone on through time. We miss a clear idea of independent systemic status of such alternations.

(1971: xxi)

So, Whitney falls short, but he is still very good. If it is the case that, as Silverstein writes, "we must reverse our priorities from Whitney" and look first to the system, then to the items in it, Silverstein acknowledges that it is also the case that "we are only now coming to empirical grips with Whitney's truth [i.e. his view of the processes of the life of language in society] *and* Saussure's truth" (1971: xx).

Silverstein's generally more positive impression of Whitney is mitigated by Labov. Now, Labov does place Whitney at the head of the "social" group of linguists represented by Whitney, Schuchardt, Meillet, Vendryes, Jespersen, and Sturtevant. While this privileged place ought to have earned Whitney Labov's praise, Labov criticizes Whitney's intuitive and anecdotal social approach and cites it as one of the four reasons why the "asocial" linguists, i.e. Paul, Sweet, Troubetzkoy, Bloomfield, Hockett, Martinet, Kurylowicz, Chomsky, and Halle, have eclipsed the "social" linguists in the twentieth century. Labov, like Anderson, sees the "common sense" in Whitney's approach, but this is precisely Labov's point of criticism. Labov writes:

> When we read the comments of Whitney, Meillet, Jespersen, or Sturtevant we cannot argue that any of these authors *knew* more about society's impact on language than anyone else; they were simply willing to talk about it more . . . . We find to our dismay that Whitney lives in a world of "facts" which are obvious to him but not to us, the kind of commonsense "experience" which has never been questioned.
>
> (1972: 269)

Labov argues that thought-experiments with castaways take the place of actual data for the "social" linguists, and this limitation in their own work, according to Labov, has contributed to their position having been of secondary importance in twentieth-century *socio*linguistics.

I will go farther and place Whitney's thought-experiments in their larger historical context, that of the armchair *grammarien philosophe* who would mentally abandon two children in a desert in order to rationalize the origin and progress of language. The most influential implementer of this technique was, of course, Condillac in his 1746 *Essai*. In this larger context, then too, Whitney's work may be considered non-innovative and traditional. However, now we have the hint that Whitney's thought belongs to a different tradition from the mechanical one that everyone thinks he should belong to; we also have a hint as to why he fails to measure up to preconceived notions of what Whitney should have been doing or how he should have been doing it.

Finally, Hockett presents a fresh perspective on Whitney. In the informal context of the oral archives of *First Person Singular*, Hockett mentions the satisfaction he felt as a student assimilating Bloomfield's 1933 *Language*. Then:

> just a few months ago, I finally had reason to undertake a serious study of William Dwight Whitney's general writings. I knew that Bloomfield had overtly acknowledged his debt to Whitney; nevertheless, I was overwhelmed to discover the extent of that debt (and thus our own), and amazed at the variety of topics on which Whitney's remarks, allowing for a difference of terminology and style, are as valid and profound now as a century ago.
>
> (1980: 160)

The satisfaction Hockett the student felt in Bloomfield's synthesis turned to amazement, years later, when he discovered the full extent of Bloomfield's debt to Whitney. Hockett was caught off-guard, surprised by Whitney's originality and modernity.

Here, let us distinguish the difference between being original and claiming originality. In light of American linguistics of the past thirty years, and especially since Kuhn's *The Structure of Scientific Revolutions* (1962), it has been most important to foment revolution – or, at least, claim to be doing so. Before Kuhn, and well back into the nineteenth century, scientists, including Whitney, held the additive or meliorist model of scientific progress. Whitney belonged to this tradition of "place a stone in the bright temple of knowledge." In the eighteenth and nineteenth centuries, scientists were concerned with modestly laying the foundations of knowledge, laying the bricks, or even, with pride, placing the keystone into the great arch of knowledge.[5] Whitney did not claim originality, and no one since him has claimed it for him in the history of American linguistics. Of course, Whitney's work was within the framework of his own time. So is Anderson's, so is mine. How – or why – should it be otherwise?

However, let us put claims for or against one's own, or another's, originality to the side. Let us look, instead, for the reason behind Whitney's relative oblivion *vis-à-vis* Bloomfield and Saussure, his two greatest twentieth-century admirers. I argue that the cause of this oblivion is the same as the one that lies behind the fragmentation of Whitney's thought in the history of linguistics, American and otherwise. It is the same one which assures that Whitney will *not* posit an independent system within language. It is the same one that gives rise to Labov's impatience at Whitney's mere "willing[ness] to talk about" society's impact on language, which implies that Whitney did not really "do anything about it" (i.e. get out in the field to gather Labov-style sociolinguistic data). It is the same one which sends the odor of fuddy-duddy prescriptivism and authoritarianism wafting around Whitney's writings. The unifying reason behind all these objections to Whitney's thought and writings on language derives from his basic conception of language. It is not mechanical, it is *political*.

Whitney and the Political Conception of Language

Whitney fully belonged both to his century and to the century-old conception of language that had been elaborated in America since Webster and modified by Pickering. By this point in my narrative, it should be a well-established feature of American linguistics that Whitney mentions neither Webster nor Pickering.

Nevertheless, clear echoes of Webster can be heard in Whitney's version of the linguistic Manifest Destiny for (American) English. Like Webster before him, Whitney is still interested in predicting the future of English, which he, again like Webster, understands as unfolding in an overt and specifically social and political context. In his first, most complete and possibly best-known work in general linguistics, namely *Language and the Study of Language: Twelve Lectures on the Principles of Linguistic Science*, Whitney writes:

> The English is already, perhaps, spoken and written as mother-tongue by a greater number of persons than any other existing dialect of high cultivation; and its sphere seems to be widening, at home and abroad, more rapidly than any other. If it ever becomes a world-language, it will do so, of course, not on account of its superiority as a form of human speech – since no one ever yet abandoned his own vernacular and adopted another because the latter was a better language – but by the effect of

social and political conditions, which shall widen the boundaries of the English-speaking community.

(1887 [1867]: 470)

Unmistakably claiming social and political conditions for the spread of a language, Whitney discounts any kind of inherent "superiority" of English as a reason for its world-wide spread. Whitney continues, in the next breath, with pride: "Yet we cannot but be desirous to convince ourselves that it is worthy of so high a destiny."

As a further part of his American heritage, Whitney is imbued with the idea of language as *res-publica*, an *institution*, a democratic institution. "The speakers of a language thus constitute a republic," Whitney writes, "or rather, a democracy, in which authority is conferred only by *general suffrage* and for due cause, and is exercised under constant supervision and control" (1887 [1867]: 38; emphasis mine). In a variety of passages, Whitney – like Thomas Sheridan before him (see above p. 33) – compares the linguistic act to voting (*suffrage*) or ratification: "The community ratified his act [of naming]" (1887 [1867]: 38); or, again, speaking of the differences between British and American English, he mentions those words that "we [Americans] have originated yet others which they [British] have not accepted and ratified" (1887 [1867]: 173). More forcefully, Whitney writes:

The whole process of language-making and language-changing, in all its different departments, is composed of single acts, performed by individuals; yet each act is determined, not alone by the needs of the particular case, but also by the general usages of the community as acting in and represented by the individual; so that, in its initiation as well as its acceptance and ratification, it is virtually the act of the community, as truly conventional as if men held a meeting for its discussion and decision.

(1887 [1867]: 148)

Whitney's reference to *men* holding the meetings for "discussion and decision" is entirely accurate. Women did not get the political vote in the United States until 1920. Whether or not they have always had the linguistic vote is a question that is open for "discussion and decision."[6]

Again echoing Webster and Jefferson and Franklin and any other American who ever wrote on the inconsistencies of English spelling, Whitney makes a plea for orthographic reform, and in the broadest expansionist terms imaginable:

> If we expect and wish that our tongue become one day a world-language, understood and employed on every continent and in every clime, then it is our bounden duty to help prepare the way for taking off its neck this heavy millstone [of English orthography]. How heavy, we are hardly able to realize, having ourselves quite forgotten the toil it once cost us to learn to read and speak correctly; yet we cannot help seeing how serious an obstacle to the wide extension of a language is a mode of writing which converts it, from one of the easiest in the world, to one of the hardest, for a foreigner to acquire and use.
>
> (1887 [1867]: 469–70)

Whitney reiterates that "a reformation is greatly to be desired, and perhaps, at some time in the future, a way will be found to bring it about" (469). He was to employ some of his energies to just that goal with the establishment of the Spelling Reform Association in 1876, although I have been unable to discover just what this society did nor how long is existed.

On the subject of linguistic authority, then, it follows that Whitney adheres strongly to the written tradition, and on this score, he sounds less like Webster and more like Pickering and Marsh. As is characteristic of the those who hold the political conception of language and who consciously acknowledge the sources of *power* for the speakers of a particular language, Whitney unambiguously identifies the source and center of linguistic authority to be the *written* language. On speaking of the language situation in America, Whitney writes that it is inevitable that:

> the languages of the various nationalities which have contributed to our later population should disappear, swallowed up in the predominant English . . . . Nor could it be doubtful which was the predominant element, to which the others would have to conform themselves. In any cultivated and lettered community, the cultivated speech, the language of letters, is the central point toward which all the rest gravitate, as they are

broken up and lose their local hold.

(1887 [1867]: 171)

Whitney recognizes the power of the written word and argues for the centrality of literature in these terms:

> Literature is the most dignified, the most legitimate, and the most powerful of the forces which effect the conservation of language, and the one which acts most purely according to its true merit, free from the adventitious aids and drawbacks of place and time.

(1887 [1867]: 173)

Like Pickering, Whitney steers a middle course between Websterian yeoman rule and British elitism for speaking norms. Whitney is willing to concede that: "We have been content hitherto to accept the inferior position [*vis-à-vis* British usage]" (173) because of "our acknowledgement of her superior authority in matters of learning and literature" (172–3). Given this, Americans "have been able thus far to restrain our respective lines of linguistic growth from notable divergence. Though we are sundered by an ocean, there have been invisible ties enough between us to bind us together into one community" (173). However, like Webster (and the later Pickering), Whitney also points out that

> Our [American] increasing numbers and our growing independence of character and culture will give us in our own estimation an equal right [to determine our own speaking norms] . . . and we shall feel more and more unwilling to yield implicitly to British precedent.

(173)

In any case, the American Whitney (unlike Marsh and his reviewer) is more than well aware that: "Aristocracy and exclusiveness tend to final overthrow, in language as in politics" (150).

For Whitney, then, it was consistent with his whole conception of language to work on the ten-volume *Century Dictionary* (1889–91), a Websterian effort if there ever was one, with, of course, impeccable etymologies. The entry "language" sounds remarkably like Beauzée's *Encyclopédie* definition: "the whole body of uttered signs employed and understood by a given community as expression of its thoughts.'' Under ''linguist'' we find as the first definition something like ''polyglot,'' i.e. ''a person skilled in the use of languages; one who can speak several languages,'' while only as the second definition do we find ''student of language; a philologist.''

It was also entirely consistent that he write *Essentials of English Grammar* in 1877. Whitney was aware of the social nature of language in a political sense, not a sociolinguistic, Labovian sense. Whitney was not ''out in the field'' gathering data. He was in the classroom setting speaking norms. The subtitle of his English grammar reads *For the Use of Schools*. In this effort, he aligns himself with Webster, although with the built-in ideas of 'good'' and ''bad'' English. It is this facet of Whitney's work which no doubt drew Mencken's censure, although, as Finegan points out (see above p. 141), Whitney's identification of ''good'' and ''bad'' is sociological:

> By good English we mean those words, and those meanings of them, and those ways of putting them together, which are used by the best speakers, the people of best education; everything which such people do not use, or use in another way, is bad English.
>
> (1892 [1877]: 3)

As a result, Whitney maintains (probably based on his own usage) the very stuffy distinction between *shall* and *will* (119–20). I found no pronouncements on the double negative, which Webster supported, but prescriptive grammars wished to eliminate.

On the double negative, Webster had supported it on the ground that it was ''nearly impossible . . . ever to change a usage which enters into the language of every cottage, every hour and almost every moment'' (quoted above pp. 38–9). Webster did not advocate going into every cottage to record every usage at every moment. He, like Whitney after him, was interested in having everyone speak the same norm, such that common (linguistic) consent equals the band of national union. On the score of this desirable band of national union, Whitney, like Edward Everett before him, vaunts the fact that ''the general language of America, through all sections of the country and all orders of the population, became far more nearly homogeneous, and accordant with the correct standard of English speech, than is the average language of England" (172). Homogeneity of national speech is the goal of those committed to a political conception of language.

Now, Webster had predicted a separation between the two national Englishes, British and American, that would inevitably occur with time. One hundred years later, however, Whitney, closer to the real possibility of English as a world language, perceives (like Franklin) that English has a better chance of attaining that highly to be desired goal if the language of England and America stay relatively the same. Whitney, like every other American who ever wrote on the subject, saw that American English was going to develop on its own, away from British English. The recognition of this inevitable separation in the speaking communities was, in part, behind Whitney's designation of literature as the highest authority: "What we have to rely upon to counteract this separating tendency and annul its effect is the predominating influence of the class of highest cultivation, as exerted especially through the medium of literature" (1887 [1867]: 173). Since Whitney wrote before the widespread use of telephones, it is not difficult to see why he chose the written word as the most unifying form of communication among geographically far-flung speakers of English, all the while believing in the idea of "best" models, both speaking and literary.

Whatever was going to be the fate of English in the world, the national fate of American English was unfolding before Whitney's eyes in its rapid spread across the North American continent. The English language was on its way to becoming a representative of "Modern civilization, with the great states it creates, and the wide and active intercourse among men which it prompts and for which it affords the needed facilities." With all of these advantages, this modern civilization "is able to establish upon unoccupied soil, and then to maintain there, a community upon a scale of grandeur to which ancient times could afford no parallel" (1887 [1867]: 172). The key phrases here are *unoccupied soil* and *scale of grandeur*. The multiplying millions of (American) English speakers were to achieve "a scale of grandeur" for their civilization by establishing it upon "unoccupied soil." However, Whitney is well aware that the soil is not quite totally "unoccupied," and we already know the answer to the question of what languages American English was displacing in its spread: the American Indian languages. When discussing the subjects of the increase and decrease of diversity of language, Whitney opines:

As, here in America, a single cultivated nation, of homogeneous speech, is taking the place of a congeries of wild tribes, with their host of discordant tongues, so, on a smaller scale, is it everywhere else: civilization and the conditions it makes are gaining upon barbarism and its isolating influences.

(1887 [1867]: 181)

Notice here the key phrase, "*congeries* of wild tribes, with their host of discordant tongues," which implies "barbarism" and "isolation," and which is opposed to the "single cultivated nation of homogeneous speech," the political equivalent of "civilization." Just so does Whitney characterize the ancient Indo-Europeans of whose – significantly – "extended and elaborate political organization no traces are discoverable," thus making these people "doubtless a *congeries* of petty tribes, under chiefs and leaders, rather than kings, and with institutions of patriarchal cast" (207; emphasis mine). The American Indians, like the ancient Indo-Europeans, endured in a sociopolitical state of barbarism and isolation, a direct result of the smallness of their speaking community. For Whitney, here as elsewhere, might makes right; the bigger the state, the better; or even, then "survival of the fittest," to evoke here the well-known Spencerian phrase.

For the first time in the historical record, there appears the suggestion of a *quantitative* sense of "primitive," which arises out of Whitney's political conception of language. A primitive language might be defined, quite simply, by its relatively *fewer* speakers. A language of high cultivation has relatively *more* speakers. The "primitiveness" is not necessarily to be found *in* the language, that is, in its structure, in the perdurable, evolutionarily transcendent (Humboldtian) core. It is rather to be found in the extent of the power of a language. That power is numerical: it lies in the numbers of speakers, which is directly bound to the power of the literary language by which means a language is able to extend its influence over large territories and to get more speakers, in ever-widening circles, until, of course, the language becomes a world language – what Whitney identified as the "bounden goal" for the speakers of English. In another famous book entitled *Language*, this one by Sapir, does such a quantitative sense of "primitive" emerge:

Under primitive conditions the political groups are small, the tendency to localism exceedingly strong. It is natural, therefore, that the languages of primitive folk or of non-urban populations in general are differentiated into a great number of dialects. There are parts of the globe where almost every village has its own dialect.

(1921: 151)

Here, "small" equals "primitive conditions." Although Sapir plainly refers to "political groups" as a basis for identifying the range of a language or dialect, what is missing in Sapir's passage, of course, is a sense of the desirability or undesirability of the relative size of that political group.

However, Whitney (unlike Sapir) is not ready to abandon the *qualitative* judgments regarding languages. As Silverstein shows, for Whitney, the material, i.e. the grammatically independent lexical items, and the formal, i.e. the subordinate, grammatical affixes (especially inflections), form two poles of a continuously variable process. Certain parts of language are highly structured into formal classes, other parts are not, and "this can be explained by how long they have been undergoing the constant process of combination and adaptation," what, for Whitney, "seems to be a unilinear evolutionary tendency" (Silverstein 1971: xvii). Such a view would not be incompatible with the evolutionary psychology of the Englishman Herbert Spencer (1820–1903).

With regard to his view of the American Indian languages, then, Whitney first stresses the old, essentially eighteenth-century argument about the "number, variety and changeableness of the different [Indian] tongues" and notes that before the arrival of the Europeans, the continent seemed to have been peopled by these "congeries of petty tribes, incessantly at warfare, or standing off from one another in jealous and suspicious seclusion" (1887 [1867]: 346). Whitney did not uphold the prejudice according to which unwritten languages could not be subjected to the comparative method, as Haas and Hymes have pointed out, and he did call for the *reconstruction* of their older forms. It is presumably in this sense that Hymes accords Whitney his "sanity." However, Whitney also made clear his opinion, echoing here Duponceau (but without reference to Duponceau), about the "single type or plan" of the Indian languages which existed from "the Arctic Ocean to Cape Horn." Whitney calls this the incorporative or polysynthetic type. Of this type, Whitney adds an opinion *not* expressed in Duponceau, but found in Humboldt that

> It tends to the excessive and abnormal agglomeration of distinct significant elements in its words; whereby, on the one hand, cumbrous compounds are formed as the names of objects, and a character of tedious and time-wasting polysyllabism is given to the language.

Whitney exemplifies this "excessive," "abnormal," "cumbrous," "tedious," and "time-wasting polysyllabism" with "the three to ten-syllabled numeral and pronominal words of our western Indian tongues; or the Mexican name for 'goat,' *kaw-kwauh tentsone*, literally 'head-tree (horn) -lip-hair (beard),' or 'the horned and bearded one''' (1887 [1867]: 348).

Whitney has become known for his use of "real live data" in his general writings on language. He was certainly familiar with the American traditions in the study of the native Indian languages and cites, for example, Gallatin as his source for the Cherokee data he uses, as well as Schoolcraft (by way of Steinthal). He does not, however, cite any particular source for the Mexican data, above, nor again for a further example of "unwieldly aggregation," i.e. incorporation or polysynthetism:

> the Mexican says "I-flesh-eat," as a single word, compounded of three elements; or if, for emphasis, the object is left to stand separate, it is at least first represented by a pronoun in the verbal compound: as "I-it-eat, the flesh;" or "I-it-him-give, the bread, my son" for "I give my son the bread."
>
> (1887 [1867]: 349)

In this case, Whitney does not give the "real live" Mexican data. Curiously enough, this example will acquire particular echoes in American general linguistics through Bloomfield (see Chapter 5). I have found no record of this example in Gallatin or Duponceau or Pickering. I believe Whitney culled it from Humboldt.[7]

It is not surprising that Whitney accorded no particular importance to the study of the American Indian languages with which speakers of American English were in an intense rivalry for territory. He was, above all, an orthodox Sanskritist. When the privileged place of Sanskrit among the Indo-European languages was contested, he continued to underline the importance of

Sanskrit in the Indo-European family and the special place of Indo-European studies within general linguistics (Rocher 1979: 11). Whitney took a theoretical and methodological position that assured the central position of Sanskrit, and he had a personal investment in the importance of the study of that language. He does lament, in passing, that the study of American Indian languages is not well represented in American education and tips his hat to the Smithsonian (at which location he gave his "twelve lectures" in 1864, as well as at the Lowell Institute in 1864–5) for its work (1887 [1867]: 352–3). However with all of his "pull," he personally did not promote American Indian studies, nor would he have found any reason to do so.

Throughout his writings, Whitney hammers home his points about the fundamentally social and institutional character of language, and his statements on the subject can be multiplied indefinitely. They all fall consistently in a line with Marsh who, in 1860, advocated the theory "which regards language as wholly arbitrary, artificial, and conventional, as a thing of human invention," distinguishing it from "things organic, products of the laws of nature" (1860: 260). Following Marsh, Whitney insists that "speech is not a personal possession, but a social," and that "it belongs, not to the individual, but to the member of society" (1887 [1867]: 404). He claims repeatedly that "No item of existing language is the work of an individual, for what we may severally choose to say is not language until it be accepted and employed by our fellows. The whole development of speech, though imitated by the acts of individuals, is wrought out by the community" (1887 [1867]: 404). Whitney's conception of language is fundamentally *political*, in that, for Whitney, language equals the sum total of the beliefs of a community. In fact, he says exactly that:

> A language is living, when it is the instrument of thought of a whole people, the wonted means of expression of all their feelings, experiences, opinions, reasonings; when the connection between it and their mental activity is so close that the one reflects the other, and that the two grow together, the instrument ever adapting itself to the uses which it is to subserve.
>
> (1887 [1867]: 32)

No clearer statement of the language–nation intersection which supports the political conception of language can be found.

Whitney also held that individuals in the given community are infinitely diverse and variable. It follows, then, that to assure the ultimate homogeneity of that community which gives the language its power, Whitney underscores pedagogy, the central goal of education being, according to Whitney, "to learn to speak and write" – albeit – "correctly" (1887 [1867]: 17). Whitney was committed to the teaching of "correct" English and, in a tradition dating back to Jefferson, also actively committed to the teaching of foreign languages. Whitney not only taught Sanskrit from 1854 on, but also, for additional income, taught French and German at Yale College and at the Sheffield Scientific School of Yale, out of which activity came several grammars and dictionaries of French and German. He continued this extracurricural teaching for some sixteen years until Salisbury funded a chair for him in 1869 (see Silverstein 1971: xiii).

Whitney's conception of language, with its overt identifications of the sources of power, is political: the power of the written word and the power that comes from sheer numerical superiority. Whitney was content to see American English overspread the continent and prevail over the native American languages, but only on sociopolitical grounds, not on racial ones. Several decades before Boas's pronouncement to the same effect, Whitney declared a disjunction between race and language. In observing that we do not produce our speech from within, but acquire it from without, Whitney derives the following lesson that

> no individual's speech directly and necessarily marks his descent; it only shows in what community he grew up. Language is no infallible sign of race, but only its probable indication, and an indication of which the probability is exposed to very serious drawbacks.
>
> (1887 [1867]: 372)

Whitney's conception of language was, finally, political in the sense that he espoused a "common-sense" linguistic science, a democratic and "popular" view of language and held a belief that the science of language and its principles could and should be accessible to all. Much has been made of the fact that Whitney wrote in "popular" as well as "learned" journals. The "common sense" that Anderson, for instance, feels in Whitney's approach to language is exactly what Whitney was striving for. In an 1875 article, "Are Languages Institutions?," published in the *Contemporary Review*, Whitney divides opinions respecting language into two principal opposing classes: the "positive" or the "common-sense" class versus the "sentimental" or the "metaphysical" class. The first represents the "unlearned popular view of speech, that of the general body of cultivated people, that which has the most votaries among the students of physical science." The latter tends toward an "admiring contemplation of language, in its comprehensive relation to the human mind and human progress, and toward its study in and through the processes of mental action that underlie its production and use." Whitney holds the first, more popular doctrine to be also the "truer, and, in the proper sense, more philosophical" (1875: 716). The other, he maintains, is "founded on the insecure basis of combined misapprehension and exaggeration" (1875: 716). The latter group is represented by Steinthal, Renan, and Mueller "who are teaching . . . error, and sustaining it by untenable arguments" (1875: 725). Whitney might also have been reacting against Emerson, although the seemingly self-imposed American ban on mentioning other Americans prevents Whitney from invoking Emerson's name.

The "secure basis" of Whitney's "common-sense" approach is to be found in his sign theory. Language, he writes in this same article, "is a body, not of thoughts, nor of physical acts, but of physically apprehensible signs for thought" (1875: 724). Signs, for Whitney, "are arbitrary and conventional; arbitrary, not because no reason can be given for the assignment of each word to its use, but because the reason is only a historical, not a necessary one" (1875: 717). Whitney also writes here that "Everything in the study of language, as in most other studies, depends upon the way in which one approaches the fundamental questions" (1875: 716). Thus, it is only appropriate that we turn now to the fundamental question of Whitney's approach to signs.

On Signs

As a product of the American nineteenth century, Whitney's insistence on the deeply institutional character of language goes hand-in-hand with his interest in signs as "arbitrary and conventional" expressions of the shared beliefs of the members of the society. I identified this tradition in Chapter 1 as a part of a confluent franco-american tradition. Thus, I would interpret Whitney in regard to his influence on Saussure not so much a *source* for Saussure, but rather a relay between Saussure and the French eighteenth century.[8]

From the very first chapter of *Language and the Study of Language*, Whitney gives a prominent place to a discussion of signs. Like Gallatin and Marsh, Whitney is interested in the quantity of signs available to the speakers of a given language, here English. He is interested in the "mass." In English, there is "an immense mass" of signs roughly equivalent to words. The "encyclopedic English language," as Whitney terms it, the English of the great dictionaries – that is, the *word power* of English as I shall interpret it in "commonsensical" or "folk-linguistic" terms – contains, by Whitney's estimation, more than a hundred thousand words. Whitney continues:

> If all the signs for thought employed for the purposes of communication by those who have spoken and who speak no other tongue than ours were brought together, if all obsolete, technical, and dialectic words were gathered in . . . [then] the number mentioned would be vastly augmented.
>
> (1887 [1867]: 18)

This mass of signs does not exist for Whitney as a *system* of signs. Let us examine this statement. In explaining in a passage why language does not equal thought, Whitney does indeed refer to the possibility of a language as "the most perfect *system of signs*," that is, he suggests that "even the most perfect systems of signs, the most richly developed language will not allow one person to reveal all that the mind contains to another person" (1887 [1867]: 111; emphasis mine). Again, arguing against "the absurdity in the doctrine that words and thoughts are identical," Whitney does indeed state that "nothing brings more distinctly to light the true nature of language, as a *system of arbitrary signs for thought*, learned and made auxiliary to the processes of thought" than a comparison of speech with sign language employed by the "deaf and dumb" (1887 [1867]: 410; emphasis mine). Whitney contends that the signs of the deaf–mute answer the same purpose that our spoken signs answer for us.

However, for Whitney, these references to any *system* of signs are not at all the *système*, in Meillet's formula, *où tout se tient*. Whitney's sense of disorganized mass prevails over the sense of system. Although he refers, as shown above, to language as a "system of signs," he is just as apt to write that: "Every spoken language is a *congeries* of individual signs, called words; and each word . . . was learned by every person who employs it from some other person who had employed it before him" (1887 [1867]: 32; emphasis mine). Here, the use of "congeries," an aggregation or mass of entities, recalls Whitney's description of the American Indian and even the ancient Indo-European political groupings which were small and non-homogeneous and non-regulated either by the written language or by an institutionalized educational system.

Whitney's emphasis on congeries also points to his focus on the individual as the unit of historical change. For Whitney, the *whole* and unique individual, completely integrated into the society in which he lives, is the agent of change:

> Every existing form of human speech is a body of arbitrary and conventional signs for thought, handed down by tradition from one generation to another, no individual in any generation receiving or transmitting the whole body, but the sum of the separate givings and takings being effective to keep it in existence without essential loss. Yet the process of traditional transmission always has been, is now, and will ever continue to be, in all parts of the world, an imperfect one.
>
> (1887 [1867]: 32)

To rephrase Sapir who was to write that "All grammars leak" (1921: 38), Whitney sees the "leakage," i.e. the inherent imperfections in language-use that permit language-change, occurring not in the abstracted entity of "language itself," not in some autonomously defined "grammar," but in the collection of individuals who compose the speech community. For Whitney, it is not the "grammars" but the speech communities which leak (see Silverstein 1971: xiv). Again, the regulation of this leakage was ultimately to be effected in the classroom where all the individual variations in the speech community would be levelled – or rather, would be reformed to the "best" models.

Around the contrast between Whitney's description of signs and Saussure's revolves the entire transition from the eighteenth- and nineteenth-century political conception of language to the twentieth-century mechanical conception of language. Whitney writes that: "Language is made up of signs for thought, which, though in one sense parts of a whole, are in another and more essential sense isolated and independent entities" (1887 [1867]: 54). These isolated and independent entities – words – are, above all, *material*: 1) they are material in the sense that they are historically derived; 2) they are material in the sense that they are not *formal*. For instance, Whitney calls the word *house* material, while the final *s* of *houses* stands in formal relation to it and "in like manner *men* from *man*" (1872: 77; 3) finally, they are material in the sense that each word "covers" some external "reality." They are isolated and independent *one from the other* "within language," but they are "pinned into" some external "reality," or rather to that portion of external reality which the generations of the speakers of a community have "wrought out" previously and which the living speakers continue to "work out." Even when that reality corresponds to something only external to language but still abstract, e.g. thought, language is material and substantial, in such a way that "material and form are not separable from one another" (1872: 90). Continuing the tradition begun in the eighteenth-century, Whitney writes that language affords thought its "dress," its "apparatus" (1887 [1867]: 406).

Thus, for Saussure language is form and not substance, while for Whitney, language is primarily substance and only secondarily form. For Whitney, language is not a system of signs *où tout se tient* which is internally regulated and formally abstracted away from context or, even, from use. In fact, as Koerner has pointed out, Whitney uses "speech" and "language" as synonymous terms (1973: 83). Language is only language when it is used, each use representing an act of "voting for" or "ratification": of a *particular* word in a *particular* grammatical construction which expresses a *particular* idea. There is no pure, or purely formal act of voting, empty and devoid of content. Each vote is a vote for something.

Language, seen as a product of history, necessarily entails a recognition of the variety of languages, those products of different histories. Whitney classifies this diversity in an article "Logical Consistency in Views of Language" (1880) – what Rocher has called Whitney's "intellectual testament" (1979: 13) – into three types: phonetic, structural, and significant. Whitney acknowledges both phonetic and structural (what "we are accustomed to call grammatical'' 1880: 328) diversity, but downplays the variety in these two categories, for: "Of the vowel-system the extreme members *a* and *i* and *u* are never wanting, hardly ever also the intermediate *e* and *o*, in all their minor varieties of coloring" (1880: 328); similarly, although structural differences classed as isolating, agglutinative, polysynthetic, inflective, and so on seem to exist, Whitney is dissatisfied with these terms, finding "the whole subject . . . the least valuable part of theoretical linguistics: 'agglutinative' and 'inflective,' especially, are mainly terms for sciolists to conjure with" (1880: 329).

The very interesting diversity among languages, for Whitney, lies in "the significant differences of language, differences in the assignment of certain combinations of sounds to certain senses," which "are even more striking than the phonetic and the structural." Differences in the third category of signification, for Whitney, are *radically* different, for "there is no underlying similarity [in significant differences], as in the other two cases [phonetic and structural differences]" (1880: 329). These "significant differences" are, like everything else in language, products of history. In *Language and the Study of Language*, Whitney notes that the resources of a language are increased by attributions to the same word of different meanings. He takes the examples of *board* and *post* and *head* and runs through the various etymological extensions of these words, noting that "a *cluster* of derived uses is gathered" about these words (1887 [1867]: 107), emphasis mine). These clusters are necessarily particular to the individual group of speakers who have "worked out" these extensions through time. The word "cluster" also suggests the helter-skelter nature of these extensions. In words reminiscent of Francis Lieber (see above pp. 117–18), Whitney writes that "there is no limit to the extent of which the roots of being of almost every word *ramify* . . . through the whole structure of the tongue to which it belongs" (1887 [1867]: 248; emphasis mine). These myriad ramifications found in every language assure that "the variety of human expression is well-nigh infinite." Whitney does not claim that the ramifications themselves are structured or predictable in any way. They are not motivated by forces internal to "language itself" and outside the realm of human will, nor, then, could the "whole circle of human speech" (1887 [1867]: 248) which Whitney is interested in comprehending exist apart from the society of speakers which speak it.

The identification of the human will "as determined by circumstance, by habit, by individual character" (1896 [1875]: 266) as the significant factor in language production, use, and change is, as I have been arguing throughout these first three chapters, diagnostic of the political conception of language. Whitney's descriptive terminology, *ratification*, *general suffrage*, supports the same conception. So does his discussion of *value*, which is further embedded in the intersection of language and money, both being institutionalized systems of exchange. However, whereas the concept of "voting" is topicalized in Whitney's writings by its frequency and its overt acknowledgement of the sources of power, Whitney's ideas about *value* and money are not topicalized, but deeply embedded in his discussion. This non-topicalization of *value* is consistent with Whitney's content-oriented approach to language where *value* is non-theoretical, that is, "material" and "real," and attached, like everything that has to do with language, to individual use and attitudes.

An interesting case in point of Whitney's content-orientation with regard to language and money is the example he chooses to illustrate his ideas about "etymologic study." At the end of Lecture VI of *Language and the Study of Language*, Whitney comes closest to making what one might call a "structuralist" statement in embryo, that is, *if* one wished to make of Whitney a precursor to Saussurean structuralism. I do not, however, and wish rather to show where Whitney's thought is discontinuous from Saussure's. On the subject of "etymologic study," Whitney states first that it is *not* limited (as, Whitney notes, is a common misapprehension) to simply tracing out the correspondence of words. This tracing-out, of course, is the fundamental stage, but it is only that. After cautioning the student of language against losing himself in the "infinity of detail" that he inevitably encounters when dealing with etymologies, Whitney points out that "the history of words is inextricably bound up with that of human thought and life and action, and cannot be read without it" (1887 [1867]: 247). The mere history of a word does not give us the "meaning" of the word. We fully understand no word, Whitney writes, until we understand the motives and conditions that called it forth and determined its form.

In this context, then, it can be neither arbitrary nor insignificant that Whitney takes, for his illustration, the example of *money*.

"The word *money*, for example," Whitney writes, "is not explained when we have marshalled the whole array of its correspondents in all European tongues, and traced them up to their source in the Latin *moneta*." What is needed to "truly" understand *money*, to achieve "perfect mastery of this single term," is the following additional knowledge:

> all the historical circumstances which have caused a term once limited to an obscure city to be current now in the mouths of such immense communities; the wants and devices of civilization and commerce which have created the thing designated by the word and made it what it is; the outward circumstances and mental associations which, by successive changes, have worked out the name from a root signifying "to think"; the structure of organ, and the habits of utterance – in themselves and in their origin – which have metamorphosed *monéta* into *móney*.
>
> (1887 [1867]: 247–8)

What is striking in this passage is not only the fact that Whitney points out the etymologic origins of *money* in the root signifying *to think*, as well as the collocation of "civilization" and "commerce;" it also suggests that it is the intersection of "historical circumstances" and "mental associations" that made the term what it came to mean. If one abstracts away the historical circumstances (as Saussure was to do), one is left with the mental associations. These mental associations, when structured, then, form the paradigmatic axis, an axis that might be understood as the residues of earlier "workings out" of associations. However, when Saussure abstracted these associations away from history, he also necessarily abstracted them away from "circumstance." Whitney is not, however, a pre-structuralist, for there is no sense in which language-use (language = speech) could ever be abstracted away from circumstance and, thus, from history. Language is no more a theoretical, abstract construct than is money, as Whitney's above example involving money demonstrates.[9] Whitney could not and would not have wanted to theoretically abstract the concept *valeur* away from language use, any more than he would have abstracted *langue* away from the society and beliefs of its speakers.

At the center of the political conception of language are the problems of consciousness and change. As a matter of fact, Whitney's refusal to abstract concepts like *value* and *language* hinges on his approach to these problems. Whitney suggests, at one point, that

> language-making is always done unconsciously and by the way, as it were: it is one of the incidents of social life, an accompaniment and result of intellectual activity, not an end toward which effort is directed, nor a task in whose performance is expended force which might have been otherwise employed.
>
> (1887 [1867]: 286)

However, it does not follow that this *unconscious* behavior is *not* a product of the will. Whitney acknowledges that, since all human communities have language, "it was just as much a part of the Creator's plan that we should talk as that we should breathe, should walk, should eat and drink." The only question for Whitney is, "whether we began to talk in the same manner as we began to breathe, as our blood began to circulate, by a process in which our own will had not part" (1887 [1867]: 399). His unequivocal answer to that is "No."

Whitney is constantly putting language-use within the realm of human will and is always pointing, as had Condillac before him, in the direction of "consciousness" and "mastery" of the language. Again like Condillac, Whitney identifies the "element of reflection" as the mental activity most closely associated with "consciousness." Whitney is not, however, seeking to fix the language with *no* change, only *slow* change, and the introduction of "the element of reflection" is merely "conservative" in its effect, rather than arresting change completely. "A people that think of their speech, talk about it, observe and deduce its rules and usages," Whitney writes, "will alter it but slowly. A tendency to do this sometimes forms a part of a nation's peculiar character" (1887 [1867]: 148). The tendency to do this certainly forms a part of the European and American traditions.

Whitney's version of language change is directly involved with the nature of the force by which language changes are effected. The nature of the force is language use, and language use "lies wholly within the domain of voluntary human action, its modification can lie in no other domain. That is to say, language is changed by the action of men's wills, and by nothing else" (1880: 335). Whitney refines his point: "This does not by any means imply that the will is exerted directly toward the change of language, any more than the will of a fugitive is directed toward his own discovery when by voluntary action he leaves the tracks by which he is followed" (1880: 335). Here, then, is drawn an ingenious middle ground between Condillac's enlightened consciousness and the post-Freudian discovery and exploration of the linguistic unconscious, as found in, say, Saussure or Boas.

Whitney goes so far as to speak of phonetic articulations in terms of consciousness and will. In writing against Lepsius's views on consonants, Whitney writes: "Is not each one as distinct a product of the voluntary action of the articulating organs, consciously directed to its production, as in any vowel?" (1861: 206).

Now we have entered the territory of German scholarship, Neo-grammarianism, and that tradition of language studies I earlier identified as a mechanical conception of language. How does Whitney, with his political conception of language, respond to the challenges of German scholarship?

Whitney and Linguistic Science

It follows from everything above that Whitney views linguistic science to be a branch of the moral sciences and not the physical sciences. However, can there be a "true" science of language without identifying some part of language which the linguist can observe "objectively?" As a kind of answer (to this not explicitly asked question), Whitney writes:

A considerable class of linguistic scholars, fearful lest they should not otherwise make out language to be a sufficiently exalted and sacred thing, confound it with thought, and arrogate to the instrumentality a part of the attributes which belong only to the agent.

(1887 [1867]: 434)

One might read into this statement the idea that these same linguistic scholars might be fearful lest they should not otherwise have a true science of language without making language a suffi-ciently exalted and sacred thing, i.e. a sufficiently objectified thing, worthy of independent study. The objectification of language – the separation of speech from the speaking agent, implied in the above quote, that is, the *mechanization* of language

– is what Whitney was ultimately against. In his insistence that language could be studied as a product of the human will and subject to conscious actions and still be a science, he was fighting a rising tide. The wave was forming in Germany.

As quoted above, "everything in the science of language depends upon the way in which one approaches the fundamental questions." What is clear from Whitney's approach to the fundamental question about the postulation of a "science of language" is that it is not logically contingent upon first formulating an autonomous level in language that will be the linguist's privileged territory. Whitney's non-autonomous view of language is compatible with his elaboration of a "science of language." Whitney's approach is not less scientific than Saussure's or Bloomfield's; it is not some almost-but-not-quite-pre-structuralist attempt to conceive of a science of language. It is a full-blown effort which happens to be discontinuous from Saussure's and Bloomfield's efforts, and it emphasizes different aspects of language that Saussure's and Bloomfield's conceptions leave out. In the *Century Dictionary*, (1889–91) under the entry "linguistics," we find the following definition: "the science of languages or of the origin and history of words; the general and comparative study of human languages and of their elements. Also called *comparative philology*." Whitney then cites Marsh: "In *linguistics* . . . language itself, as one of the great characteristics of humanity, is the end, and the means are the study of general and comparative grammar" (Marsh 1860: 52). It is the phrase "language itself" that draws our attention, for this is the focus of "linguistics," that is, "language itself" as it is found in its "natural" setting, i.e. society. Whitney is very clear about distinguishing between linguistics and comparative philology. In what sounds reminiscent of the *Encyclopedia Americana* entry for "Philology" (read: linguistics) as "the science of language" which the Europeans had not given a definite form to, Whitney writes at the end of *The Life and Growth of Language* that:

> while Germany is the home of comparative philology, the scholars of that country have . . . distinguished themselves much less in that which we have called the science of language. There is among them (not less than elsewhere) such discordance on points of fundamental importance, such uncertainty of view,

such carelessness of consistency, that a German science cannot be said yet to have an existence.

(1896 [1875]: 318–19)

Whitney first wrote those words in 1875, just before the first expressions of Neogrammarianism, and he repeats a version of them in his "Logical Consistency in Views of Language" where he once again deplores "the present semi-chaotic condition of linguistic science" (1880: 327).

If developing a scientific approach means, as it clearly did for Whitney, the postulation of an interrelated set of principles to guide research, then Whitney surely had a scientific approach to language. Whitney was the first to introduce the principle of uniformitarianism to language study. The appropriate passages of Whitney's work where he sets out this uniformitarian method of geology and its application to linguistics is well developed in Christy (1983: 78–89) and need not be repeated here, as well as Whitney's clear-headed refusal to be misled by the parallel between linguistics and the physical science of geology into thinking that language study is any other than a moral science.

In identifying the study of language as a branch of the moral sciences, that is, in defining the fundamental nature of language as an institution, Whitney could logically carry through on the idea of the arbitrary nature of the linguistic sign. The non-necessary nature of the link between sound and meaning, furthermore, allowed him to explain the force of phonetic change in terms of the principle of economy (see 1877). Perhaps the two most serviceable forces he identifies in the process of language-making and language-use emerge as a result of the coupling of his political conception of language with his emphasis on speech as a product of the voluntary action of the individual. On the one hand, Whitney writes, "each independent mind working unrestrainedly according to its own impulses" would impress upon the development of speech its own history. Whitney identifies this force as "centrifugal force," such that "linguistic development is . . . made up, as we may fairly express it, of an infinity of divergent or centrifugal forces" (1887 [1867]: 155). At the same time, "there is not wanting an effective centripetal force also, which holds all the [centrifugal forces] in check." This "centripetal force" is otherwise known as the "necessity of communication" and it acts to resolve the infinity of divergences, "giving value to that part of each which makes in a certain direction, and annulling the rest" (1887 [1867]: 155). Whitney held to the end of his life that phonetic change, for instance, is individual and sporadic. He does not pursue the idea that centripetal force gives value to any *particular* change in any *particular* direction, an idea that will show up several decades later, albeit with a transcendent core, as Sapir's "Drift" (1921: 147–70).

Whitney's approach to language is rich both in theory and in practice and is strongly grounded in the American political conception of language. As such, it is discontinuous both in content and in practice from Neogrammarianism. Although Whitney alone could not change the course of thinking about language in Germany, he held a firm grip on linguistic thinking in America in the second half of the nineteenth century. In fact, he was, quite possibly, the most influential American educator of his time. As Silverstein reports from his reading of the correspondence to Whitney preserved in the Yale archives, Whitney virtually controlled the academic appointments in various departments around the country, since these appointments "were subject to his recommendation, if not advice and consent" (1971: xiii).

Under the direction of Charles Lanman, the man who had helped Whitney revise his *Sanskrit Grammar*, a number of professional societies assembled in joint and special session at the University of Pennsylvania for the Whitney Memorial Meeting. The list of the societies alone demonstrates how pragmatically involved Whitney was with the professionalization and institutionalization of the science of language in America:

The American Oriental Society, organized 1842;
The American Philological Association, organized 1869;
The Spelling Reform Association, organized 1876;
The Archaeological Institute of America, organized 1879;
The Society of Biblical Literature and Exegesis, organized 1880;
The Modern Language Association of America, organized 1883;
The American Dialect Society, organized 1889.

After Whitney's death in 1894, a new perspective in American linguistics was to develop. As Silverstein notes, Whitney's death coincided with "the rise of Franz Boas's career in Washington and New York. Boas would be the next great influence in American linguistics, on the foundation of empirical anthropology and the study of "exotic," unwritten languages (Silverstein 1971: xiii). In the succession from Whitney's framework to Boas's, it is completely within the American tradition that Boas will never once refer to Whitney.

4

THE ARCS OF DEVELOPMENT
SEPARATE: 1875–1900

In the last quarter of the nineteenth century, the three arcs of development in American linguistics begin to separate in a way that has come to look to us today as somehow "natural," that is, as somehow reflecting naturally occurring fault lines within the subject matter itself, within language. However, if we retrace the paths of separation of the three arcs, we discover that there is nothing "natural" about existing intradisciplinary boundary lines. Rather we discover that the boundary lines are, in large measure, the products of the late-nineteenth-century institutionalization of language studies that came in Whitney's wake.

In order to retrace this institutionalization, I have chosen the date 1875 only to mark a clean quarter-century, although it also coincides with the publication of Whitney's second book on general linguistics, *The Life and Growth of Language*. The year 1876 would serve my purposes just as well. Johns Hopkins University, the first PhD-granting institution in the United States, opened its doors in 1876. From the very beginning, the influence of Johns Hopkins in American language studies (and across the humanities) was great. For instance, it was in 1876, after a successful series of guest lectures at Johns Hopkins, that Francis Child, a professor of rhetoric and oratory at Harvard and one of America's leading scholars, received the offer of a position at Johns Hopkins; and as a result, he was released from the rhetoric course he had taught at Harvard for twenty-five years and made Harvard's first professor of English language and literature. However, Johns Hopkins's influence was not merely that of a threatening university "raider," but, more importantly, that of a great institutional purveyor of German thought.

As for Germany and the date 1876, Karl Verner published "Eine Ausnahme der ersten Lautverschiebung" in 1876, wherein he formulated Verner's Law; and August Leskien, in that same year, expounded his hypothesis that sound laws admit of no exceptions in *Die Declination im Slavisch-Litauischen und Germanischen*, thus ushering in what would come to be known as the *junggrammatische Richtung*, or Neogrammarianism. In fact, as Koerner (1977) sees it, the year 1876 marks a distinct turning point in linguistics on both sides of the Atlantic. For the history of linguistics in America, I would interpret the turning point in terms of the decline of the political conception of language and the rise of the mechanical. The date also happily coincides with Robert Bruce's periodization for *The Launching of Modern American Science 1846 to 1876* (1987), for Bruce chooses 1876 as the year by which American science and technology had been fully formed and were on the rise.

The year 1879 might serve just as well to periodize the separation of the arcs of development. In that year, John Wesley Powell founded the Bureau of American Ethnology, thus marking a significant step in the professionalization of American anthropology. At the other end of my periodization, I chose the year 1900, again for convenience as the century mark. It also dovetails with Brinton's death and Boas's appointment to a full professorship at Columbia University, both in 1899; with Powell's death in 1902, as well as with the founding of the American Anthropological Association in 1902. The development and codification of American anthropology clearly plays a role in the history of American linguistics in that, with the separation of the arcs of development, a field known as "linguistic anthropology" must be carved out as something distinct from "linguistics" with no qualifying adjective. With the progressive dismantling of the political conception of language, which had built in the language–nation intersection, and with the concomitant rise of the mechanical conception of language, which became coextensive with the field of "linguistics," the concept of "nation" shifted disciplinary ground from language studies to anthropology, where it surfaces in Daniel Brinton's work at the end of the nineteenth century.

We will trace the separation of each arc of development in turn.

THE ARC OF DEVELOPMENT OF ENGLISH STUDIES

First, the "theoretical exigencies" of Whitney's political

conception of language insured that the study of (American) English would occupy a central place both in his writings and in his teaching program. In America after Whitney, English studies continued to act, for some decades, as a "natural" gateway into comparative Indo-European philology as well as into "linguistic science." However, it was a "historically contingent" occurrence that just at the time American higher education was institutionalizing itself in the last quarter of the nineteenth century, the German model of education was most influential.[1] With the massive influence of German-styled education came also the content of German scholarship. In language studies, this meant, in a word, Neogrammarianism, and the English-language-oriented bridge into general linguistics did not survive beyond Leonard Bloomfield's first text, *Introduction to the Study of Language*, published in 1914 (see Chapter 5).

As a result, certain approaches to language study theoretically coherent in Whitney's approach to language in the nineteenth century, e.g. the research program of dialect studies, were marginalized in American linguistics in the twentieth century. The results of dialect studies came to be regarded as anecdotal in twentieth-century language theory and took on the role of entertaining curios in the classroom.

A case in point of the anecdotal role assumed by dialect studies can be illustrated by one pair of words: *grease* and *greasy*. This particular pair of words has become so much a part of "classroom linguistics," that is to say that it has become so much a part of the oral tradition of American linguistics itself ("folk-linguistic linguistics"?), that I hardly need here state the phonetic features involved in the *grease/greasy* alternation or to present the geographical distribution of the features involved in the alternation. Although this example is a perennial favorite in introductory courses to linguistics,[2] it has not played the same theoretically pivotal role in any claims about the nature of language or about the way one should go about doing linguistics that Grimm's Law and the Great Vowel Shift have played both in classrooms and in schools of thought about language. In fact, I did not know, until I ran across what I think might be the original article on the subject, that a man named George Hempl from the University of Michigan, Ann Arbor, wrote it and published it in the first issue of *Dialect Notes* in 1896.

Hempl's study of *grease* and *greasy* certainly seems anecdotal, since he opens his article by indicating that it is based on "insufficient data," thus making the results "tentative" (1896: 438). Hempl's findings also acquire an added anecdotal dimension in that some of his observations can be confirmed in the classroom, i.e. "non-scientifically," especially where there is a geographic mix of students. In 1990, one might still elicit from an informant an observation that Hempl made almost one hundred years ago, namely: "An interesting psychological problem is presented by the fact that some people who normally say 'greasy' with *s*, pronounce the word with *z* when speaking of a disagreeable greasiness" (1896: 443–4).

However, Hempl's approach is not as anecdotal as it first appears, and his study exhibits, as well as any, what was at stake for American linguists of the period. First, after presenting his data and his discussion, Hempl comments on the various geographic distributions of *s* and *z* in the noun and adjective. He then notes that in the West, the earlier usages were largely those of the South and the Midland but later yielded to, or compromised with, those of the North, to which Hempl adds, in italics *"but to a different extent in different parts of the language complex"* (1896: 442). I note here the use of the phrase "language complex" which suggests the following.

1 Hempl allowed for a more varied language community than the basically unified one which was a political goal for Whitney. Whitney had no difficulty acknowledging variation not only within the community but also within the individual. In *Language and the Study of Language*, Whitney stated very clearly that: "Nor must the word community, as used with reference to language, be taken in a too restricted or definite sense. It has various degrees of extension, and bounds within bounds: the same person may belong to more than one community, using in each a different idiom" (1887 [1867]: 156). It was the very recognition of this lack of uniformity in the multiply-overlapping speaking communities that justified Whitney's pedagogic program for linguistic unity in the service of achieving a unified, democratic "nation." Hempl, on the other hand, has no interest in levelling the differences.

2 Hempl's word "complex" suggests that he conceives of a more ordered, or structured, language community than Whitney, who

chose the word "congeries" to designate not only the external organization of (primitive) language communities but also the internal organization of (any given) "system of signs." Behind Whitney's use of "congeries" lies his belief in the individual, the entire, conscious, and idiosyncratic individual, as the basic linguistic unit.

Second, Hempl is grappling with the question of "correct" usage and, once again, comes to a different conclusion than the one Whitney would have reached. Hempl spends several pages discussing the probable historical source of the *s*/*z* alternation. He notes that "dictionaries until recently recognized the voiceless *s* in the noun only, and prescribed the sound of *z* in the verb and the adjective" (1896: 439). He notes further that *s*/*z* alternation is no doubt similar to: "'the house', but 'houzez,' and 'to houze'; 'louse,' but 'louzy,' etc." (1896: 439). He suggests that "it is possible that at one time all English-speaking persons gave the noun *s* and the verb and adjective *z*" (1896: 441). However, Hempl is interested in explaining the present frequent use of *s* in the verb and adjective and thinks it "much more likely . . . that in the larger part of the English-speaking territory the group never thoroughly conformed to the category: '*s* in noun; *z* in verb and adjective'" (1896: 441). That is, he suggests that the use of *s* in the verb and adjective is original and posits its origin from the older *ss*, which has been retained "just as it has in other such words: 'release', 'increase', 'cease', etc." (1896: 441). The point here is that Hempl finds the "school-teacher and the dictionary" which teach that "'*s* in the verb and adjective is 'wrong'" are themselves wrong in that this prescriptive rule of pronunciation "introduces a disturbing element in the natural development of usage" (1896: 441). Here, Hempl is distinguishing between "natural development" and "prescriptive rules" and prefers "natural development," i.e. "historically correct." This argument is akin to Webster's preference for the historically prior double negative over the prescriptive "innovation" of the single negative (see above pp. 38–9).

Hempl clearly recognizes "frequency of use" as a factor that determines language change, particularly with regard to prescriptive usage. He notes, for instance, that "where natural usage is influenced by the school and the dictionary (until recently advocating *z* in the verb and adjective), this influence is the more apt to prevail the more often the word occurs in general conversation, where it may be "corrected" (1896: 443). He points out that the word

> "greasy" may be heard often enough at school and in general intercourse, but "to grease" is rarely heard except in the barnyard – of greasing wagon wheels – and in the kitchen – of greasing pans. These factors naturally reduce the percent of *s* in "greasy."
>
> (1896: 443)

Now, one hundred years and several generations later, Hempl's data provide excellent material for a longitudinal study, but I wonder whether the results could be other than very narrowly conceived, for dialect geography in the last hundred years has been a decidedly unglamorous branch of linguistics.

In fact, dialect studies in the twentieth century seem to have had their own history, apart from "general linguistics." This *separate* history accounts for Dell Hymes's correct and intuitive sense "that the field of English studies as a whole has kept certain kinds of studies of the English language going, and been a source for them, when they were not the center of linguistic attention" (1980: 211–12).

Symptomatic of the changes in orientation in American linguistics occurring in the last quarter of the nineteenth century is the re-evaluation of the place of Anglo-Saxon in English studies. In 1825, with the opening of the University of Virginia, Thomas Jefferson, fully committed to the intersection of language and nation, had considered the study of Anglo-Saxon of prime importance for determining the 'true" laws of the English-speaking peoples. Sixty years later, at the Second Annual Convention of the Modern Language Association, a Professor Hart of the University of Cincinnati expressed his doubts "as to the value of Anglo-Saxon in a course of English Literature . . . . There is no continuity of *thought* between England before and after the Norman Conquest. The interest in Anglo-Saxon is chiefly linguistic and historic" (1884: xi). Professor Hart is explicitly denying the "Saxon myth," which had, no doubt, run its course by that time; and one hundred years after the American Revolution, it is easy to understand how the appeal Jefferson made to the political dimensions of learning Anglo-Saxon were no longer felt to be pressing, or, indeed, of any real interest to Professor Hart or to anyone but a linguist.

At the same time, in identifying the study of Anglo-Saxon as being "chiefly linguistic and historic," Hart is implicitly supporting the separation of the study of language (linguistics) from the study of the expression of the thoughts of the speakers of that language (literature). In the German science of the day, which was gaining popularity in the United States, Hart's distinction coincides with the division of *Naturwissenschaft* and *Geiteswissenschaft*, with *Sprachwissenschaft* falling firmly with the circle of the former and *Literaturwissenschaft* the latter.

After 1883 and the founding of the Modern Language Association, whose interests must have been perceived to be different from those of the American Philological Association established fifteen years earlier, the arc of development of English studies distinctly separates and defines itself. The rise of the institutional identity of the field of "English" is evidenced by the figures from the first Modern Language Association convention, which tallied merely thirty-nine teachers of English representing twenty leading colleges as against the figures from 1900 which showed major universities in all sections of the country offering graduate degrees in English literature (Applebee 1974: 27–8; see also Franklin 1978, 1984). Now, the very first professorship of English in the United States allied language and literature, when at Lafayette College Francis March received the title of Professor of the English Language and Comparative Philology in 1857 and held it until 1906 (Parker 1967: 345). However, elsewhere by the turn of the twentieth century, that position had, in practice, split into two: English literature and (English) linguistics. English studies had come a long way from Benjamin Franklin's proposal of 1750 (see above p. 49).

THE ARC OF DEVELOPMENT OF AMERICAN INDIAN STUDIES

Although most histories of American Indian linguistics written in the twentieth century assume that Indian studies had a separate history all along, I maintain that this separate history becomes completely justified only in the last quarter of the nineteenth century. In this period of academic institutionalization, it is easy to see – in retrospect – that American Indian language studies were *not* institutionalized along with English and the Classics and Indo-European studies, for we have only to look around today to witness the results of the *lack* of that academic institutionalization. Again, Dell Hymes has long been aware of the situation. At one of the three symposia held in honor of the golden anniversary of the Linguistic Society of America in 1976, Hymes chided the linguistic community when he stated that:

> It ought to be embarrassing, shocking, that there is not a minimum of one chair in Native American languages at each of the state universities. (I am not sure that there is one such chair in the entire country.) There ought to be Institutes of Native American Languages, venerable Institutes that would now be celebrating or approaching their centennials.

> (1983: 121)

It is also easy to determine – again in retrospect – why American Indian language studies should have been marginalized in academe. I have traced the marginalization of American Indian language data back to the seventeenth and eighteenth centuries, and, despite forceful arguments to the contrary, the Indians and their languages continued to be negatively perceived, such that the lack of academic institutionalization of Indian linguistics seems an inevitable consequence of all the history that had gone before.

That is retrospect. In the early 1870s, the marginalization of the Indian languages does not appear to be necessarily predetermined. For Whitney, as for Pickering before him, American Indian data is certainly not marginalized in his conception of "linguistic science." Although Whitney does not give the study of Indian languages the same methodological status as Sanskrit in historical linguistics, he does not privilege Sanskrit data in his studies of "linguistic science," and he does not hesitate to use data from the Indian languages in his two major texts on general linguistics. Although Whitney does not pursue or promote American Indian studies himself, he is aware of their importance as a valuable part of the global database on which one must necessarily ground any statements about general linguistics. Nor even is data from the American Indian languages immediately marginalized in the early philological journals that were coming into existence in the 1870s and 1880s. The first volume of the *Transactions of the American*

Philological Association (1869–70) has not one but two articles in it by James Hammond Trumbull (1821–97), an independent scholar from Hartford, Connecticut. In the first seven volumes of the *Transactions*, Trumbull contributed five articles.

In the first issue of the *Transactions*, Trumbull's first contribution, "On the best Method of Studying the North American Languages," begins with what amounts to the ritual disparagement of all previous studies of the Indian languages. It also serves as an excellent history of American Indian language studies. That is, Trumbull shows he is fully aware both of a long tradition, by quoting everyone back to Eliot, and of its relationship to general philological interests, by quoting Whitney's hard-headed logic on the subject of the methods of comparative philology applied to "exotic" language families (1869–70a: 58–9; 67). The tone and content of Trumbull's article make it apparent that the subject of Indian languages was not a narrowly conceived domain of language study but had a greater bearing on all philological research. Articles on Indian languages were, therefore, appropriate to the *Transactions* and pertinent to its readers.

In both articles, Trumbull takes careful aim at prevailing misconceptions about Indian languages, particularly mistaken *European* conceptions. Trumbull no longer has to confront directly Herder or Burnet or Adam Smith, as did Heckewelder and Duponceau. Trumbull is, rather, having to argue now against Humboldt, Steinthal, Max Mueller, and, sure enough, Sagard-Théodat, that bad penny who keeps turning up (1869–70a: 65, note). Although Trumbull still upholds the idea that the Indian languages are of the "polysynthetic type" and claims that "the American languages differ from the Indo-European both in grammatical structure and in their plan of thought" (1869–70a: 59), he does devote quite a lot of space to unravelling the idea that one Indian word of eleven syllables can be adequately translated by only four or five English words. He cites Massachusetts: *wut-ap-pe'-sit-tuk-qus'-sun-noo-weht-unk'-quoh* as requiring for its accurate translation eight or ten English words with at least eleven syllables: "he, falling down upon his knees, worshipped [or, made supplication to] him" (1869–70a: 60).

Without direct reference to Whitney, Trumbull seems to be taking issue with Whitney's opinion of the "tedious and time-wasting polysyllabism" of the American languages expressed in

Language and the Study of Language (1887 [1867]: 348; quoted above p. 153). Significantly, in his next study of general linguistics, *The Life and Growth of Language*, Whitney softens his opinion on the Indian languages by stating merely that "the tendency is toward the formation of words of immense length, and of an intricate structure that gives expression to a host of things left by us to be understood." Whitney then cites "the longest word in Eliot's Massachusetts Bible" having eleven syllables, which is precisely "*wut-appesituqussun-nooweht-unk-quoh*, which renders 'kneeling down to him' in our own version; but it really means 'he came to a state of rest upon the bended knees, doing reverence unto him'" (1896 [1875]: 261–1). Whitney shows himself open to revision.

In his second contribution to the first volume of the *Transactions*, "On some Mistaken Notions of Algonkin Grammar," Trumbull praises "scholars like Pickering and Gallatin," who have worked on the Indian languages "with moderate success," but he tempers that (faint) praise with the observation that for every Pickering and Gallatin "there have been fifty who were content to glean a few surface-specimens and spare themselves all trouble of assay or analysis" (1869–70b: 105). He then sets out to correct some of those mistakes. What is needed, of course, is for linguists to release their analyses from the Latin and Greek models and to refrain from seeking a relationship between the languages of America to those of Asia and Europe before discovering the relationship of American languages to one another. Here again, Whitney follows through on Trumbull's advice. In the same passage of Whitney's quoted above, Whitney writes now of the American languages: "our grammatical terminology does not at all suit these languages; we are involved in contradictions and absurdities as soon as we attempt to apply it to them" (1896 [1875]: 260). In the following pages, which lead into Whitney's exposition of "Language and Ethnology," Whitney advocates the cautious plan of limiting reconstructions to geographically contiguous territories before comparing any language to "every unrelated dialect in existence" (1896 [1875]: 267) – a practice exercised on the American Indian languages from the eighteenth century through the early twentieth.

Given Whitney's subsequent support of Trumbull's contributions, Trumbull would have had every reason to be confirmed in the positive attitude he displayed in all of his articles in the

Transactions for the contributions to be made to "general philology" of the study of the American languages. That there has been "little progress in dealing with the problems which the almost innumerable languages of America present," Trumbull writes, "need not surprise or discourage us." The reason for Trumbull's unconcern? Because "the science of language is yet in its infancy" (1869–70a: 57).

Trumbull, and then by extension, Whitney, were not alone in thinking the study of the American languages formed a part of the future of "the science of language." So did the American Philological Association. At the preliminary meeting of the association in 1869, attended, of course, by Trumbull and Whitney, the organizing members identified its scope as "the whole field of philological investigation." They established a schedule of seven subsections, of which "American aboriginal languages" was one, along with Oriental languages, Latin and Greek, Modern European languages, and English, added to which was "the science of language, and history of philology" and "linguistic pedagogy." This schedule was published in the *Transactions of the American Philological Association* (*Proceedings* 1869: 6).

The American Philological Association consciously conceived of itself as the American society for "the science of language" – what we would now call "linguistics." In his contribution to the first issue of the *Transactions*, Whitney (the first president of the organization) identified "the recently established French association," i.e. the Société de Linguistique, as having a "kindred object with our own" (1869–70: 84). Incidentally, the Société Linguistique de Paris, established in 1865, was the first society to bear the name "linguistics," and it, too, conceived the American languages as being a necessary part of its program (see Swiggers 1984b; also Auroux 1983). Again, in the report of the preliminary meeting of the American Philological Association, the organizers make specific reference to the one European society which, more nearly than any other, offered a model for them to follow, namely, the Sammlung der deutschen Philologen und Schulmaenner (*Proceedings* 1869: 6). The Americans, however, conceived of their "domain of philology" as very broad and foresaw a continuing need for "local and specific societies," e.g. the American Oriental Society, while the American Philological Association would act more as the umbrella organization.

However, a glance through the first twenty years of the association's *Transactions* confirms that, however broadly the organizers conceived the domain of philology ("the science of language," in the American usage back to Pickering), the reality of the association's activity was very narrow indeed. For all practical purposes, it could be said to have been a vehicle for Latin and Greek scholarship with attention to issues relevant to the German-speaking world. After Trumbull stopped publishing, the American Indian languages were practically absent. Although, in principle, American Indian languages had gotten "in on the ground floor" of American linguistics, we can see that during the 1870s and 1880s, Americans were recasting and narrowing their definition of "science of language" and closely patterning it on the German model.

THE ARC OF DEVELOPMENT OF "LINGUISTIC SCIENCE"

In order to understand the development of "linguistic science" in the last quarter of the nineteenth century, we need to return, as always, to Whitney. The importance Whitney placed on Sanskrit as the centerpiece of Indo-European studies insured that his work would be strongly bound to German trends and ideas. Although to the end of his days Whitney was strongly opposed to the theoretical model of language and the "linguistic science" of the *Junggrammatiker*, his students were not necessarily equally opposed. New schools attract young students, and Whitney was already approaching fifty when the Young Turks of Leipzig burst in on the linguistic scene. Within a generation or two after Whitney, the German approach to linguistics was fully integrated into American linguistic theory, mostly by way of Johns Hopkins University, with a strong push from Maurice Bloomfield.

The opening of Johns Hopkins in 1876 did not mean the immediate end of Whitney's influence at Yale; far from it. In fact, Whitney was singularly instrumental in helping to establish language studies at Johns Hopkins. The *Johns Hopkins Alumni Magazine* for 1925–6 (vol. 14), claims that the Department of Sanskrit and Comparative Philology at the university was founded with the guidance of Whitney. Whitney never held a chair at Johns Hopkins, but he gave "about twenty lectures a year during the first two years" of Johns Hopkins's existence, which was "accompanied by frequent consultations with students who were interested in his subjects" (14: 34). The themes of Whitney's lectures were general linguistics, comparative grammar, and indology, and these three areas were "the themes of instruction and investigation in the Department" at least through 1925–6 (14: 34).

The first incumbent upon a chair of Sanskrit at Johns Hopkins was Charles Rockwell Lanman (1850–1941), a student of Whitney's at Yale, who helped with the second edition of Whitney's *Sanskrit Grammar* (1889, first edition 1879) and who organized Whitney's memorial meeting in 1894. Lanman was at Johns Hopkins from 1877–80, at the end of which time he was called to the Professorship of Sanskrit at Harvard. Lanman was succeeded at Johns Hopkins in 1881 by Maurice Bloomfield, also a student under Whitney, who had been a Fellow in Sanskrit at Johns Hopkins, then the first graduate from the department, and afterwards a student in Austria and Germany. Since his call to the chair at Johns Hopkins, Bloomfield was uninterruptedly head of the department until 1925 and had almost sole conduct of the department.

In 1876, Basil Gildersleeve (1831–1924), who had until then been a Professor of Greek at the University of Virginia since 1856, was called to Johns Hopkins to create the Greek department. He stayed in Baltimore until retirement in 1915. His most significant contribution to American language studies during this period was his founding of *The American Journal of Philology* in 1880, which he edited until 1920. In his "Editorial Note" of 1880, Gildersleeve admits that "to some the Greek element [in the journal] may seem suspiciously preponderant," but he assures his readership that he has secured the editorial co-operation of scholars eminent in "Comparative Grammar, in the Oriental, the Romance and the Teutonic languages," as well as in Latin and Greek (1880: 2). No mention of the American Indian languages is made.

It is an interesting sidelight that the first volume of *The American Journal of Philology* included a book review of Colonel Mallery's *Introduction to the Study of Sign-Language among the North American Indians as illustrating the Gesture-speech of Mankind* (1880). Mallery's volume happened to appear in the same series and the same year that Powell's *Introduction to the Study of Indian Languages* appeared. However, Powell's work receives no review and no mention in the journal. Furthermore, Mallery's study is reviewed by Crawford Toy (1836–1919), Hancock Professor of Hebrew and Other Oriental Languages at Harvard. Toy is generally critical of Mallery's work, advising Mallery "to urge on his collaborators the earnest study of the Indian tongues with which they have to deal" (1880: 207). Since useful studies of Indian languages were definitely not lacking in 1880, Toy's suggestion as well as the editorial decision to review a book on Indian *sign language* nevertheless points to the idea that Indian studies were suffering from a general *lack*. It also suggests that the only possible angle of interest to the readers of *The American Journal of Philology* with regard to Indian communication was the Indian's *silence* – a strategy we have encountered before, going back to Rousseau and Cooper. In any case, by the time the journal *Modern Philology* was created at the University of Chicago in 1903–4, there was no question of a place for American Indian language data, not even the "lip service" given to the review of Mallery's volume.

Although Johns Hopkins had equally strong English, Classics, and Romance Languages departments, it was the Germanic department that would eventually succeed English as the "natural" gateway into "linguistic science." The Germanic department came into prominence in 1885 but truly found its place in the American linguistic scene in 1907, when Professor Hermann Collitz was called from Bryn Mawr College to take charge of the newly established chair in Germanic philology.

Hermann Collitz (1855–1935) was German-born and German-trained, studying Classical, Germanic, and Comparative Indo-European philology at the University of Goettingen (where he received his PhD in 1878), and afterwards continuing his studies in Berlin until 1882. Collitz began his academic career as an instructor in comparative philology and Sanskrit in the University of Halle, Germany, where he became known for his work on Greek dialects and topics in Indo-European grammar. He was called to Bryn Mawr College to take charge of the department of Germanic philology, then went to Johns Hopkins, where he took charge of the courses in Gothic, Old Norse, Old High German, and Old Saxon, as well as in comparative and historical German grammar. In 1912, he started the series *Hesperia*, a collection of monographs in Germanic philology, to which, in co-operation with the English department, a supplementary branch for English philology was added.

The influence of Johns Hopkins in language studies during the last quarter of the nineteenth century and first quarter of the twentieth century is pronounced. Hermann Collitz was elected the first year's president of the Linguistic Society of America (for 1925). He was also elected, for the same year, president of the Modern Language Association. Maurice Bloomfield was elected the Linguistic Society of America's second president (for 1926), but was prevented from taking the chair because of ill health.

The German and Germanic orientation of American linguistics can be almost immediately felt from the late 1870s onwards. It is felt not only in the character and direction of undergraduate and graduate studies disseminated at Johns Hopkins, but is also reflected in the pages of the two major journals devoted to "linguistic science," namely in Gildersleeve's *Modern Philology*, where one would expect the German and Germanic influence, but also in the *Transactions of the American Philological Association* which Whitney had originally run out of his hip-pocket.

After the late 1870s, the pages of these two journals became increasingly devoted to discussing the most important phrase to come out of late nineteenth-century German *Sprachwissenschaft*: namely, "phonetic laws admit of no exceptions," otherwise known as the principle of *Ausnahmslosigkeit*. American linguists of the last two decades of the nineteenth century eagerly debated the issue, and it must be said that American linguists did not immediately accept the idea. Whitney was firmly opposed to the "dogma of the invariability of phonetic change in language," as he phrased it in his article entitled "Examples of Sporadic and Partial Phonetic Change in English" (1894). Interestingly enough, this article appeared in a volume of *Indogermanische Forschungen* dedicated to August Leskien, the man who first enunciated the principle of *Ausnahmslosigkeit* and flung it into the arena of discussion. Whitney, whose ear was ever-alive to language in its social setting and true to the belief that "linguistic science" was a *Geisteswissenschaft*, recounts from his own experience the "purely sporadic character" of the shortening of long *o* to a real short *o*, such that a shortening might be found in the word *stone* but not in the word *bone* in the same individual (1894: 33). From Whitney's point of view, acceptance of the idea of "phonetic law" (non-sporadic, non-individual, wholly unconscious, unalterable sound change) would shift the "science of language" into the realm of *Naturwissenschaft*.

Whitney had received plenty of support for his position against "exceptionless sound laws," particularly in the pages of the *Transactions of the American Philological Association*. In 1886, Frank Tarbell of Yale wrote an insightful and persuasive critique of the Neogrammarian doctrine. Neither was Collitz a firm believer in the tenet (Fay 1895), and even the French scholar Michel Bréal (1832–1915) got in on the discussion in the pages of the American *Transactions*. In a contribution entitled "On the Canons of Etymological Investigation," Bréal wrote:

> The too oft-repeated saying, that the phonetic laws act blindly, is one of those catchwords that is well not to accept uncontrolled. The phonetic laws act blindly if we admit a set of conditions that are never realized anywhere; viz. a perfectly homogeneous population coming into no contact with the outside world, learning everything by living and oral tradition, without any books, without any monuments of religion, – a population in which every one should be of the same social condition, in which there should be no difference of rank, of learning, nor even of age or sex. No sooner do you leave aside pure theory, to place yourself in presence of the reality, than you see the reasons appear which make the phonetic laws open to exceptions.

(1893: 21)

The precise wording of this passage has such distinct echoes for the modern reader that I cannot resist comparing it to Chomsky's description of the concerns of "linguistic theory" in *Aspects of the Theory of Syntax*. Chomsky argues in exactly the same terms but with exactly the opposite conclusion that:

> Linguistic theory is concerned primarily with an ideal speaker–listener, in a completely homogeneous speech-community, who knows its language perfectly and is unaffected by such grammatically irrelevant conditions as memory limitations, distractions, shifts of attention and interest, and errors (random or characteristic) in applying his knowledge of the language in actual performance.

(1965: 3)

Chomsky then adds: "This seems to me to have been the position of the *founders of modern general linguistics*, and no cogent reason for modifying it has been offered'' (1965: 3–4; emphasis mine). That is, we can see by the result in Chomsky what was at stake one hundred years before in debate over the Neogrammarian *Lautgesetz*, or sound-law, controversy, namely the status of linguistics as a science. As Chomsky implies, all those who do or did not hold a similar position to his would not count as ''linguists,'' as true ''scientists.'' He would thus identify the ''founders of modern general linguistics'' as those believing in a basically mechanical approach to language, i.e. the Neogrammarians and their followers; and that mechanical approach (as opposed to the political) began to prevail on both sides of the Atlantic at the end of the nineteenth century, at the very moment that institutional frameworks were solidifying themselves.

No one involved on either side of the *Lautgesetz* controversy seriously questioned the idea that there was something regular about phonetic change, nor, by the same token, did anyone in either camp believe in ''absolute'' laws. Even Berthold Delbrueck, a leading Neogrammarian, has been quoted over and over as saying that sound laws without exception are only to be found in heaven. The question surrounding the ''exceptionlessness'' of sound laws was not *whether* there were regularities in language and language change, but rather what was the empirical status of those regularities. Thus, the question was essentially *epistemological*, and what resulted from the debate was a new sense of the scientific position of linguistics, as Auroux (1979b) has pointed out. In other words, the question of phonetic ''law'' was a question about the representation of the proper *object* of the *science of language*. The object that emerged from the controversy was an object that existed apart from any individual, that had a particular structure, whose reality was most notably system-internal. From the point of view of historical linguistics, the beauty of positing a system-internal structure was that it would permit accurate predictions. The case in point here, of course, is Saussure's 1879 *Mémoire* in which, on the basis of the idea of system, is posited a laryngeal in the sound system of Proto-Indo-European whose existence was confirmed by the discovery of Hittite in 1906 and its subsequent decipherment in 1916. Here, then, was a true science, one whose object was the regularities to be found in language, and those regularities necessarily existed independent of the individual, not only of the individual's idiosyncrasies but also of the individual's will.

More than any other American, Maurice Bloomfield was alive to the epistemological dimensions of the controversy. In his cautiously entitled "On the Probability of the Existence of Phonetic Law," which appeared in the Johns Hopkins-controlled *American Journal of Philology*, Bloomfield begins by admitting that "the *conscious will* of any language-user undeniably stands above phonetic facts" (1884: 178). He then continues by declaring himself to be dissatisfied with the comparison recently suggested by Mueller between phonetic law and fashion, which suggests that, for Bloomfield, whatever of interest is going on in language, it is not so superficial as fashion or mere outer clothing, i.e. it won't be found on the surface of language. Further, after some more discussion, Bloomfield stakes a middle ground for "consciousness" when he notes that it would be impossible to produce any language "where the phonetic changes, either within its own special history or when compared with its kin, are exclusively sporadic or arbitrary," all the while maintaining the motivating cause as being "the *semi-conscious* whim of the individual aided by his linguistic pet-vice of laziness" (1884: 181–2; emphasis mine).

Bloomfield had opened his article by concurring with Whitney that by the very nature of the case the "inviolability of phonetic law . . . will never be proved" (1884: 178). However, mid-way through, Bloomfield takes another tack and finds reason for supporting the inviolability of phonetic law "in the fact that it has gained the adherence of a large and growing proportion of the best linguists" (1884: 182). And just how is the linguist to decide those tricky cases that seem to "fall through the cracks" between determining phonetic changes as a result of regular law or of analogy? Here is Bloomfield's answer:

> The generation of linguists who watch closely the workings of the principle [unspecified in context: presumably phonetic law], who will handle diligently and familiarly the numerous clear cases which arise from it, will not fail to acquire that quality of judgment, or better taste or tact, which will teach them to feel more and more correctly when they are face to face with these processes, how they came about, and where the words and conceptions that furnished the impetus for the inorganic changes lie.
>
> (1884: 184)

For "inorganic changes" read "mechanical," not caused by conscious will. Bloomfield's rhetorical exposition is perfect: the linguist will know when analogy and/or "phonetic law" is at work by "feel," by good judgment, "taste," and even "tact," that is, because of his experience and because the "best" linguists say so. Bloomfield is led to the conclusion that "it is not too much to say that if the doctrine of the inviolability of phonetic laws should ultimately turn out to be false, this fact would hardly detract from its value as a method" (1884: 185).

Whitney himself had opened the door to criticism when he stated on at least three occasions that phonetics and phonology had but limited explanatory power. In his 1884 article, Maurice Bloomfield is quick to point out these lapses in explanatory power, namely two passages from *Language and the Study of Language* (1896 [1867]: 95; 152), which Bloomfield quotes at length, and one passage from *Life and Growth of Language*, which Bloomfield does not quote but merely refers to (1884: 179–80). In this third passage, Whitney writes:

> It must be carefully noted, indeed, that the reach of phonetics, its power to penetrate to the heart of its facts and account for them, is only limited. There is always one element in linguistic change which refuses scientific treatment: namely, the action of the human will.
>
> (1875: 73)

As for linguistic change, then, one can either abandon the search "for the heart of the facts" of phonetic change, or one can remove phonetic change from the realm of human will. Bloomfield, following the *Junggrammatiker*, chose the latter course, and the "heart of the facts" of phonetic change came to be understood in terms of unconscious processes. Freud is hovering on the horizon.

In terms of the development of American linguistics, the real losers in the entire *Lautgesetz* controversy were not so much Whitney and his direct followers but rather, and as usual, the American Indian languages. The American Indian languages, quite simply, did not surface in the controversy. They certainly could have played a role. As Haas (1967) has shown (and above p. 88), a correspondence of *n–l–r* in Algonquian was known as early as 1643 and Roger Williams' *Key into the Language of America*. However, curiously, no one had bothered with a systematic comparison of all the sounds in a particular set of Algonquian languages until Leonard Bloomfield (1925b). Truman Michelson had worked on the Algonquian materials in 1912, well after the *Lautgesetz* controversy was over. His failure to pursue the sound shift prompted Haas to write: "Since Michelson had been trained in comparative philology in Germany [1904–95], it is not quite clear why he did not recognize this as a straightforward sound shift" (1967: 821). Soon thereafter, Sapir also published on Algonquian (1913a) but did not go much farther than Michelson in terms of intra-Algonquian shifts. Furthermore, in Chapter 8 of his 1921 *Language*, entitled "Language as a Historical Product: Phonetic Law," Sapir cites examples *exclusively* from Germanic, focusing in particular on the *foot/feet* alternation.

It would take a few more years before Leonard Bloomfield (1925b), in very much the spirit of Maurice Bloomfield (1884), would clarify "at one stroke the phonological system of the Algonkian languages" (Haas 1967: 823). Then, of course, came Leonard Bloomfield's 1928 article, which confirmed not only the regularity of sound correspondences in a non-Indo-European language, but also reaffirmed the possibility of prediction (*à la* Saussure) based on the construction of a system.[3] Almost three hundred years had elapsed between Roger Williams and Leonard Bloomfield, with materials enough to have played a part in any linguistic discussion of the 1870s and 1880s. Because of this failed opportunity for the Indian languages to have been involved in the *Lautgesetz* controversy, I cannot help but agree with Hymes that, with regard to the development of American Indian studies, "*To a great extent, the materials have not determined the scholarship; rather, the scholarship has determined the materials*" (1983: 119).

Still, the question remains: why were American Indian languages excluded from the database of the American version of the "science of language" as it was establishing itself in the last decades of the nineteenth century? Like Haas, I find it puzzling. No answer seems to be forthcoming from the writings of American scholars of the period.

Turning to the French, however, who have almost as long a history of engagement with American Indian studies as American Americanists, we find a clue. In 1924, Antoine Meillet and Marcel Cohen edited an impressive collaborative volume entitled *Les Langues du monde*. As fine an Indo-European comparativist as was

Meillet, he nevertheless expressed the doubt that for the American languages – still poorly known ("encore mal connues pour la plupart") in 1924 – one could ever expect true and complete comparative grammars ("grammaires comparées précises et complètes") (1924: 9).[4] It was against this precise passage that Bloomfield addressed his article "On the Sound-System of Central Algonquian" (1925b).

The doubts expressed by Meillet and Cohen were not aberrant for the time. Another well-known French Americanist, Paul Rivet (1876–1958), published what now looks to be a methodologically backward article in the same year, namely 1925, as Bloomfield's methodologically sound article on Algonquian. Rivet confessed doubts similar to Meillet's and Cohen's about submitting "exotic" languages to a rigorous application of the comparative method. He suggested that the lack of regular phonetic correspondences in the materials he was working with might have been the fault of the notation of the transcribers. At the same time, he was willing to consider the possibility that these "exotic" languages might not conform to "rules as strict as those found in the Indo-European languages . . . a hypothesis which does not seem to be able to be put aside on a priori grounds" (1925: 26).[5] Bloomfield's opinion on this score is unequivocal:

> A principle such as the regularity of phonetic change is not part of the specific tradition handed on to each new speaker of a given language, but is either a universal trait of human speech or nothing at all, an error.
>
> (1925: 130, note 1; quoted also in Haas 1978: 200)

Bloomfield's insight notwithstanding, old prejudices die hard. Despite Whitney's belief that the native American languages could be reconstructed along with the rest, the specter of "instability" hovering over "exotic" languages, in particular the native American, that had begun in the seventeenth century, lingered through the first quarter of the twentieth century. It is tempting to explain the lapses of Meillet and Cohen and Rivet because they were French, far from the "field," or at least "out in left field," and without ready access to good data. However, that does not explain why Michelson and Sapir missed the good data themselves, nor why the American Americanists lagged far behind their French counterparts in organizing themselves professionally. The

French were, after all, the first to establish the Congrès des Américanistes, in 1875, and later the Société des Américanistes de Paris, in 1883, both of which organizations have celebrated their centennials – events of which Dell Hymes has spoken wistfully for the American Americanist scene (see Andresen 1984b; Toumi 1984). It should also be remembered that Boas and Sapir were members of the Société des Américanistes de Paris and that Sapir published his early comparative studies of Paiute and Nahuatl in the French society's journal (Sapir 1913b, 1914). Meillet and Cohen and Rivet seem to be expressing opinions rather more characteristic of the time than exceptional, and if the American Indian languages seemed exempt from the processes of interest for the "science of language," this exemption both prompted and aggravated the division in subject matter that had occurred around the turn of the twentieth century between "linguistics" as such and "linguistic anthropology."

LINGUISTIC ANTHROPOLOGY

The last quarter of the nineteenth century marks the very distinct separation of American Indian studies from other academic and scientific language studies. The study of American Indian languages was not seen to have scientific potential within linguistics as it was defining itself at the turn of the twentieth century. Although Leonard Bloomfield established the possibility of their "scientificity" within the given terms of linguistics in 1925, the course of their institutionalization during the preceding half-century had developed along distinctly different lines from those of the Indo-European languages. The different institutional framework for their study coincided with a different framework of interests and concerns, those of "linguistic anthropology."

An institutional place for the study of American languages was established in the last quarter of the nineteenth century within the Smithsonian, that "fulcrum of scientific power in antebellum America," as Bruce phrases it (1987: 187). The Smithsonian was established in 1846, but it was not until after the Civil War that a center for the serious study of American Indian languages came into existence, namely The Bureau of American Ethnology, created by John Wesley Powell in 1879.

John Wesley Powell (1834–1902)

John Wesley Powell was first an Illinois schoolteacher with a passion for natural history, then a major in the Civil War, and finally the head of a famous expedition down the Colorado River in 1869. This last enterprise was officially dubbed the "United States Geological and Geographical Survey of the Rocky Mountain Region" in 1876. Geology, like other sciences, was becoming a profession during the late nineteenth century. So was anthropology, and Powell was the first person to be able to provide institutional support for government-sponsored research into the American Indians and their languages. Before Powell, researchers, as we have seen, had been either missionaries or "gentlemen scholars" of the type Jefferson, Duponceau, Pickering, or Trumbull. By the late nineteenth century, both the perceived need for government studies of the American Indians and the evolutionary interpretation of the history of the American Indian were firmly in place, such that with Powell: "Social organization and intellectual content . . . came together for the first time in the Bureau" (Darnell 1970a: xxxi).

The practical need perceived by the government for research into the American Indians derived from the now-familiar encounter with the Indians during the course of the westward expansion. The results of Powell's ethnographic investigations were supposed to facilitate the organization of Indian groups on reservations. With the basic information gathered about the American Indians, the government was to have a rational means of dealing with them (Darnell 1970a: 45). With the implementation of the reservation system, the government officially closed the possibility of reds and whites living side by side. The Indian languages had been theoretically marginalized from the eighteenth century onward; now the Indians themselves were being physically marginalized in "mainstream" American life. Although Powell believed in the ability of the Indians to be incorporated into "civilized" society and was the one to coin the term "acculturation," the Bureau was not interested in studying the Indians' adaptation to Western society (Darnell 1970a: 49). Incidentally, Powell, who was apparently fond of neologisms, also coined the term "Amerind," as a cover term for the red man. This new term signalled the end of the potential stereoscopy of the referent of the term "American" (see above pp. 74ff.), which had existed during the opening decades of the century. Powell's coining of "Amerind" suggests that the unalloyed "American" had come to settle exclusively on the white man.

The Bureau was not interested in "mainstreaming" Indians. Rather, it was interested in studying their cultures, which had been affected by contact with the whites, and in recording it before it was entirely lost. As for the intellectual content of the Bureau's research program, it can be found in the work of Lewis Henry Morgan (1818–81), which Powell adapted. Morgan was a "cultural evolutionist" and life-long student of the Iroquois, whose first book, *League of the Ho-dé-no-sau-nee, or Iroquois* (1851), was hailed by Powell to be "the first scientific account of an Indian tribe ever given to the world" (quoted in Malefijt 1977: 147). Morgan is well known for having elaborated, along with Edward Burnett Tylor (1832–1917), the pancultural evolutionist scheme comprising seven stages: lower savagery, middle savagery, upper savagery, lower barbarism, middle barbarism, upper barbarism, then, finally, civilization. All aspects of culture were of interest to Morgan: dances, games, religion, material culture, government, and family organization, as well as language, and he believed that all aspects of sociopolitical organization were interrelated with one another and tied to technological developments and economic pursuits. He thereby implicitly recognized cultures as functional wholes. With this emphasis on culture, Morgan was not Darwinian and was attempting to define man outside of biology, as was Powell.

Morgan's lines of thinking appealed to Powell, who saw as the goal of efforts at ethnic classification the means "of measuring the susceptibility of the various tribes to civilization [and] to education." Morgan's index of cultural development would provide a way to arrange "amical" and "harmonious" Indian groups on the reservations, even though the groups might be linguistically, and otherwise, unrelated (Darnell 1970a: 45–56). Although Powell's ideas did not quite pan out in practice, his research program did carve out a place for "linguistic anthropology." It was Powell's goal to place the American Indian within the evolutionary development of mankind as a whole, and by the end of the century, it was established that linguistic anthropology "should deal with the history and evolution of language itself and with the classification of people for their comparative study by anthropologists'' (Darnell 1970a: 47).

Although Powell was engaged in gathering as much data about the American Indians as possible, he saw to it that the Bureau devoted a considerable share of its attention to the study of the Amerind languages. When the Bureau was founded, Powell brought with him over six hundred linguistic vocabularies, which he had acquired from the Smithsonian (Darnell 1970a: 60). Manuscripts were added to this collection in later years, and they were the most valuable property of the Bureau. Data-gathering was the Bureau's most important function, although Powell was limited by congressional appropriations and never had a full-time scientific staff that exceeded fifteen members (Darnell 1970b: 89). Although admittedly small, the funding of the Bureau ''has been taken by historians of anthropology as the beginning of professional anthropology in America'' (Darnell 1970b: 89).

One of those Bureau linguists, Albert Gatschet (1832–1907) was, like Gallatin before him, a native (francophone) Swiss. Gatschet studied linguistics both in Switzerland and Berlin, specializing in Greek. He joined the Bureau in 1879 and produced, among other things, an exhaustive study of *The Klamath Indians of Southwestern Oregon* in 1890. Gatschet's work did not earn him, however, a place in Boas's 1911 *Handbook*, for, although Gatschet had a great deal of descriptive material, Boas did not think ''Gatschet knew how to write an 'analytical' grammar of the extent and detail required for the *Handbook*'' (Darnell 1970a: 287).

Gatschet is interesting in that he provides a definite link to the French Americanists, for he collaborated on American Indian languages with Lucien Adam (1833–1918) and Raoul de la Grasserie (1839–1914). Adam was active in the Société des Américanistes and advocated as early as 1879 the banishment of all hypotheses linking the American Indians to the ancient Etruscans or the Phoenicians (or any other chance people, say, the Basques), which, he claimed, were ''rêveries'' of the eighteenth century (Toumi 1984: 369). This pronouncement, however, did not prevent de Charencey from proposing a Basque–Algonquian connection in 1902, or Rivet from trying to link the Americans to the Australians in 1925. More pertinently with respect to the American side of the story, Adam took direct issue with Daniel Brinton on the subject of the American Indians' supposed propensity to ''holophrasm.''

Adam saw, as early as the 1880's, that transcriptions of non-written languages might build in the idea of polysynthesis in their orthographic conventions. That is, what Brinton saw as "visibly synthetic" in his transcription of the phrase from the Bribri language of Panama: *je-be su-eng*, Adam saw as a function of Brinton's orthographic practice of hyphenation. Echoing Heckewelder's and Duponceau's early arguments about how a speaker of Delaware might view the irregularities in the English lexicon, Adam argues that a Bribri linguist might well be tempted to write the French phrase "I see you" *je te vois* as *je-te-vois* (see Andresen 1984b). Boas's arguments against Brinton's conception of holophrasis are entirely similar to Adam's (see pp. 217–18).

The French connection aside, the Bureau produced in the closing decades of the nineteenth century a kind of "bulk linguistics." As for the quality of the Bureau data, it is a part of the "folk history" of linguistic anthropology that the nineteenth century was a period of data accumulation, and rather poor data at that. However, if we rely for a moment on Edward Sapir's opinion, we see a different perspective. In the first issue of the *International Journal of American Linguistics*, Sapir reviews the "Linguistic Publications of the Bureau of American Ethnology." He acknowledges that in quality, linguistic publications of the Bureau have run a very long gamut, extending all the way from "distressing amateurishness" to work of "as high a standard of phonetic finish and morphological insight as one could hope to find anywhere in descriptive linguistic material" (1917: 78). Sapir also acknowledges the precise difficulties – mostly phonetic – in these studies, but he is willing to state that "in spite of the difficulties . . . the general level of quality in the linguistic publications of the Bureau must be admitted to be high" (1917: 79).

The quality was apparently good enough to produce Powell's classificatory achievement in *Linguistic Families of North America north of Mexico* which appeared in 1890. This classification remains "the conservative baseline for Amerindian linguistics" (Darnell 1970b: 95) and "has stood the test of time remarkably well" (Haas 1967: 253).

Like Gallatin, Powell based his classification on lexical evidence, and on considerably *more* lexical evidence than Gallatin. While Powell recognized that both lexicon and grammar change, he believed that grammar changed even more rapidly than lexicon, such that it was necessary for classificatory purposes to concentrate on the words of a language. "Grammatic structure is but a phase or accident of growth," Powell explained in 1890, "and not a primordial element of language. The roots of a language are its most permanent characteristic." By contrast, the "grammatic structure or plan of a language" – here echoing Duponceau – "is forever changing, and in this respect the language may become entirely transformed" (quoted in Haas 1969b: 252). Powell's decision to privilege lexicon over grammar for classificatory purposes differs slightly from Gallatin's reasons. Whereas for Gallatin, words changed faster than grammar because new words were an index of progress, something added external to language, Powell sees language change as a language-internal process. For Powell, "new words are formed by combination, and . . . these new words change by attrition to secure economy of utterance" – here sounding like Whitney – "and also by assimilation (analogy) for economy of thought" (quoted in Haas 1969b: 251; Powell's parentheses).

Still, for Powell, language change is not entirely an internal process. Powell writes:

> In primitive society, language grows in two ways, on the one hand there is a steady enrichment and differentiation due to the coining of expressions for new ideas; on the other hand there is a spasmodic enrichment and modification, both in terms and in grammatic structure, produced by the shock of contact.
>
> (quoted in Darnell 1970a: 75)

The enrichments in both lexical and structural forms that result from language-external developments such as progress and the "shock of contact" are then subjected to a simplification resulting from the major language-internal process identified above: "the natural tendency toward economy in expression."

Powell sees, across the North American continent, a directionality in these processes of language change. The direction is toward unification and mutual intelligibility. Powell infers that the history of the American Indian languages has been one of linguistic integration, from multiplicity to unity. Out of the large number of distinct and original tongues in North America, the history of the peoples has been chiefly one of linguistic integration. Whitney had argued for a similar directionality, namely that "human speech is now, upon the whole, tending toward a condition of less diversity with every century; but," Whitney adds – and here is a crucial "but" – "this is only owing to the vastly increased efficiency at present of those external influences which counteract the inherent tendency of language to diversity" (1887 [1867]: 181). Thus, Whitney sets himself in direct opposition to "those authors" namely, Ernest Renan and Max Mueller, who, "affirm that the *natural tendency* of language is from diversity to uniformity" (1887 [1867]: 177; emphasis mine). Whitney is patently against the position "that dialects are, *in the regular order of things*, antecedent to language; that human speech began its existence in a state of infinite dialectic division, which has been, from the first, undergoing coalescence and reduction" (1887 [1867]: 177; emphasis mine). Whitney quotes Mueller to the effect that "As there were families, clans, confederacies, and tribes before there was a nation, so there were dialects before there was a language" (1887 [1867]: 180). Whitney continues by pointing out the fallacy involved in Mueller's comparison, to whit for Whitney, that families, clans and tribes are *not* the ultimate elements in the history of humanity, that they did not spring up independently, each out of the soil on which it stands. For Whitney, dialects do not precede language. A unity always precedes differentiation, and the diversifying force of the individual (or the individual community) is always subordinate to the unifying force of the group (or greater community) (1887 [1867]: 176-7).

Whitney's political conception of language is absolute, wherein the concept of *political unity* is a constant: wherever there is a dialect differentiation, there has been first a unified group which spoke the language. The implication here is that a political unity might be as small as only a limited number of families or, if one attempts to follow back the fate of our race, it might even have been a single pair, which then expanded by natural increase and scattered (1887 [1867]: 180-1). The point is that the "true view of the relation of dialects and language" is and always has been "that growth and divarication of dialects accompany the spread and disconnection of communities, and that assimilation of dialects accompanies the coalescence of communities" (1887 [1867]: 181). If the same tongue is now spreading over wide territories, such as English, this is only due to more effective means of checking, annulling, and reversing the tendency to differentiation (see above p. 166). Insistence on language as "an institution founded in man's social nature, wrought out for the satisfaction of his social wants" remains stable in Whitney's conception of language and in Whitney's conception of language through history. For Whitney, however, the concept of political unity is not only a constant, it is also a given.

When the political conception of language is dismantled at the end of the nineteenth century, the concept of political unity, and in particular "nation," will be taken up by Brinton as an element of linguistic anthropology.

Daniel Garrison Brinton (1837–99)

A full-length study of Brinton, "the fearless critic of Phila-delphia," exists in the form of Regna Darnell's Master's thesis, "Daniel Garrison Brinton: An Intellectual Biography" (1967). Darnell has further integrated Brinton's work into a larger frame-work in her PhD dissertation "The Development of American Anthropology 1879–1920" (1970a), which emphasizes the profes-sionalization and institutional history of American anthropology.

For Darnell, Brinton is a kind of "transitional" figure in anthropology. Brinton was formally trained as a medical doctor, was a practicing physician in West Chester, Pennsylvania, and served as a surgeon in the Federal army during the Civil War. He also happened to be named Professor of Ethnology and Archaeo-logy in the Academy of Natural Sciences of Philadelphia in 1884. He went on to hold the first academic professorship in anthropo-logy in the United States, although honorary (i.e. without salary), by being named Professor of Archaeology and Linguistics at the University of Pennsylvania in 1886 (see Darnell 1970b, 1971).

Brinton's academic appointment was not an unqualified success, for he attracted no students (see Darnell 1967: 66; and Darnell 1970b). At the same time, he was fully committed to the idea of academic anthropology, and he was in contact with Boas in the early stages of the latter's academic career, in that Brinton was among those to congratulate Boas on his first appointment, at Clark in 1889 (Darnell 1967: 75–6). The correspondence between Brinton and Boas shows that, in Boas's early days at least, Boas found it politic to defer to the older and more established Brinton on certain matters. With Boas coming to shape academic anthropology in the early twentieth century and Powell leading government anthropology in the late nineteenth century, Brinton has been squeezed out of the historical picture. Although he enjoyed considerable prestige among anthropologists of his day, Brinton suffered, at the same time, a paradoxical isolation from the developing science of anthropology (Darnell 1967: 2).

Brinton aptly closes the nineteenth century by affiliating not with academic institutions but with scientific societies. His primary association was with the American Philosophical Society, to which he was elected in 1869, and after which date he began his long series of publications in the *Proceedings* of the society. He was later elected to the American Association for the Advancement of Science (established in 1848), of which he was elected president in 1894, thus sharing the honor of the position with both Morgan (elected president in 1880) and Powell (elected president in 1888).[6] In Darnell's studies, Brinton is shown to have been fully integrated into the social network of anthropologists of his time, both national and international. He was a member of the anthropological societies of Berlin and Vienna, the ethnographical societies of Paris and Florence, and of the International Congress of Americanists, of which he was twice vice-president and once president. He also served as president of the Numismatic and Antiquarian Society of Philadelphia as well as of the American Folklore Society. The memorial meeting held by the American Philosophical Society for Brinton demonstrates the degree of his integration and influence in the late nineteenth-century American scientific community. Twenty-three societies were represented, including the American Oriental Society and the Modern Language Association.

Brinton's life and work is also integrated into the present history of American linguistics from four points of view.

1 Brinton was in competition with Powell to produce a definitive classification of the American Indian languages. Unlike Powell, he based his classification on grammar, and Powell's classification has proved the more enduring. Brinton's *American Race* of 1891 was, however, the first systematic classification of the aboriginal languages of both North and South America.

Although Powell's and Brinton's conclusions were similar in

most cases, their methods differed sharply. Brinton favored morphological criteria and wide genetic connections, whereas Powell used lexical criteria for conservative estimates of genetic relationship. Brinton's primary emphasis was on the least-known stocks, i.e. those of South America. His aim was to fill in broad outlines of a linguistic survey rather than to refine the existing genetic classification. Brinton adopted Gallatin's work for the Eastern United States virtually unchanged (Darnell 1967: 145ff.). Since Brinton read German fluently (he had studied for a year in Heidelberg, Paris, and Vienna after receiving his medical degree in 1861), he was drawn to the German studies of the American languages south of the United States, most notably Buschmann's studies of Nahuatl and, of course, Wilhelm von Humboldt's general writings, which included observations on "Mexican" also used by Whitney, namely the ubiquitous *ni-naca-que* "I flesh, eat" (quoted above p. 153). Brinton did not, however, accept Buschmann's classifications wholesale, and coined the term Uto-Aztecan for a particular stock of languages in Mexico. The term is still with us today, although not Brinton's particular grouping.

2   Mention of the Germans brings us to Brinton's intellectual pedigree. Brinton openly and repeatedly refers to "the labors of Wilhelm von Humboldt, as expanded by Professor Steinthal" for his intellectual parentage and acknowledges his own effort as an attempt "to popularize a profounder philosophic analysis of [the American] tongues than has heretofore appeared in works on the subject" (1890: 306). Brinton deplored his countrymen's lack of interest in Humboldt, and in 1885 he translated an unpublished 1822 essay of Humboldt's on the structure of the American Indian verb, and published it in the *Proceedings* of the American Philosophical Society. No mention is made there of John Pickering, or of Pickering's objections to Humboldt's 1822 *Ueber das Entstehen der grammatischen Formen und ihren Einfluss auf die Ideen-Entwicklung*, which Pickering placed in the 1830 edition of the *Encyclopedia Americana* (see above p. 109).

Brinton, as Boas after him, stands in the midst of a long line of German thought that goes back to Herder, extends through Humboldt and Steinthal, and is played out in Wundt. Contrary to Brinton's statements, however, neither Humboldt nor Steinthal was unknown in the United States before Brinton's time. Rather, they were unappreciated. After all, Whitney, all the while acknowledging Germany as the home of Indo-European philology, did not hesitate to single the Germans out as being exceptionally careless of what he called the questions of linguistic philosophy. Whitney was vigorously opposed to the idea of language as a natural organism, growing by its own forces and its own laws, with which men cannot interfere. He was opposed to what he called the "sentimental" and "metaphysical" view of language, which tended toward an admiring contemplation of language in its comprehensive relation to the human mind and to human progress; and, when writing on German linguistic philosophy, Whitney tended to use phrases such as "false profundity" and "exaggerated and illusory opinions." Thus, it would be more accurate to say that Brinton was not the first to discover German linguistic philosophy, but he was the first to legitimize it in American Indian studies, which no longer belonged – as the arcs of development were sorting themselves out by Brinton's time – to the "science of language" or to "general linguistics," but rather to "linguistic anthropology." If we refer back to the beginning of the nineteenth century and Duponceau's three-way division for the "science of language," what he called philology – namely, phonology, etymology, and ideology – we see that by the end of the nineteenth century phonology and etymology belonged to "linguistics," while ideology (German-style) belonged to "anthropology."

With Brinton, then, the Humboldtian concept of "inner form," or *innere Sprachform*, surfaces full force in certain quarters of American thought about language. When Brinton writes that "the science of linguistics . . . deals not with languages, but with *language*" (1890: 315), he confronts the familiar problem of how to account for the similarity and diversity in human cultures and human expression that may easily be traced all the way back to eighteenth-century France. The French tradition had attempted a solution to the problem by separating the subject matter of *grammaire générale* (i.e. "l'esprit humain") from that of *langue* (i.e. "nation"). Brinton will join the two subject matters. Brinton subscribes to the idea of a psychic unity for the human race. It is precisely that concept of psychic unity that made it imperative for Brinton to explain the existence of profound differences among groups of peoples. For an explanation of those differences, Brinton relied on the particular spin that the Germans gave to the problem of cultural diversity, namely an absolutistic evolutionary framework which emphasized the subjective and psychological, the *innere Sprachform*, the "logical" basis of genetic classification. The concept of "nation" would also belong in the same absolutistic evolutionary framework.

Brinton never focused in his writings on any one particular American Indian culture or language. Rather, he was always striving for the pancultural, the universalist statement. He wanted to explain the organization of *the* human mind rather than the organization of *a* human culture (Darnell 1967: 103). Here again, "nation" would not explain the differences among peoples, except in an evolutionary framework.

Language was, of course, the key to inner form, and although Brinton did not focus exclusively on language, when he did write on the subject, it was almost invariably on the American Indian languages. In his collection, *Essays of an Americanist* (1890), is reprinted in his 1885 article, "American Languages, and Why We Should Study Them," in which he writes that the American languages "offer an entertaining field to the psychologist." The psychological interest derives from "their transparency . . . the clearness with which they retain the primitive forms of their radicals" (1890: 312). Brinton does make reference to the *n–l–r* alternation in the "different dialects of Delaware" (1890: 315). Like everyone before him, Brinton does not approach the American languages as material for "purely" (i.e. "scientific") linguistic investigation. Rather, they provide the stuff of psychological generalizations.

Brinton attempted to "combat" the prejudice that the American languages were barbarous. He praised the flexibility and richness provided in the American languages by the processes of polysynthesis and incorporation, which "are unconscious efforts to carry out a certain theory of speech which has aptly enough been termed *holophrasis*, or the putting the whole of a phrase into a single word" (1890: 322).

Turning from the structure of these languages to their vocabularies, Brinton also attempts to correct the widespread notion that "they are scanty in extent and deficient in the means to express lofty or abstract ideas" (1890: 325). Of their vocabularies, however:

It would be very unfair to compare the dictionary of an Indian language with the last edition of Webster's Unabridged. But take the English dictionaries of the latter half of the sixteenth century, before Spenser and Shakespeare wrote, and compare them with the Mexican vocabulary of Molina, which contains about 13,000 words, or with the Maya vocabulary of the convent of Motul, which presents over 20,000, both prepared at that date, and your procedure will be just, and you will find it not disadvantageous to the American side of the question.

(1890: 325)

Although Brinton grants the American Indians (note: not those within the borders of the United States) more ways to express "lofty and abstract ideas," his basic periodization with respect to English (and, by extension, to other "Aryan" languages) is not so very different than that of Gallatin's (see above pp. 111–12). That is, Brinton is subscribing to a kind of linguistic progress, indexed in sheer numbers of vocabulary items, that postdates the Renaissance.

Even granting the American Indians a certain measure of commensurability with the European languages, Brinton is not about to jeopardize the superior position of the "Aryan" languages in the evolutionary hierarchy. Appealing once again to the profundity of Wilhelm von Humboldt, Brinton explains that it is the "quality, not merely the quantity, of words [which is] the decisive measure of verbal wealth" (1890: 338), such that many "savage languages" have twenty words signifying to eat particular things but no word meaning "to eat" in general. For instance, "the Eskimo language has different words for fishing for each kind of fish, but no word 'to fish,' in a general sense." Thus, Brinton finds that "such apparent richness is, in fact, actual poverty" (1890: 338). He then proceeds to rate the languages of the world on the Humboldtian classificatory model, which has four stages: isolating, agglutinative, incorporative, and inflective. Each classification might have a "higher" and a "lower" grade of the process within the grouping. Brinton demonstrates, for instance, the "higher" grade of incorporation through the Mexican sentence *ni-naca-qua*, meaning "I flesh, eat" (1890: 341).

3 Brinton wanted a unified discipline of anthropology, which derived from his concept of the psychic unity of mankind (Darnell

1967: 88). This concept allowed Brinton to postulate the unity of the human species as an object of study by a science of man. It provided evidence "far weightier than any mere anatomy can furnish" because it dealt with "the resources of the soul." The unity was one of cognitive process rather than of actual content, and the content differed widely among various groups. For Brinton, "mankind was one not because it was everywhere the same, but because the differences represented different stages of the same process" (Darnell 1967: 90). The concept of psychic unity committed Brinton to the idea that "like effects have like causes," and to the idea that cultural similarities are due to parallel developments in an evolutionary framework and not due, for instance, to something like cultural diffusion.

Because of the postulated psychic unity of mankind, the origin of language was a meaningless question to the extent that language was a universal human trait which either existed or did not exist. From Humboldt, Brinton borrowed the assumption that the first stage of language could never be fully reconstructed, and again following Humboldt, Brinton saw language as an organismic system which could exist only in its entirety (Darnell 1967: 92). From this follows the importance of the entire structure of the language at the moment it is forged. He thus locks language into race and builds in the superiority of one race over another on structural grounds.

4 In 1894, the year of Whitney's death, was published Brinton's presidential address to the International Congress of Anthropologists, entitled "The 'Nation' as an Element in Anthropology."

When Brinton writes that "the first object of Nationality is unity" (1894: 24) and that "linguistic unity is the indispensable basis of national unity" (1894: 26), he is not only aptly summarizing American thought about language that extends back to Webster, but also marking the transition of the concept of "nation" from language study proper to anthropology. Consistent with the rest of his views, the advent of "nation" is a progressive one and exists at the "higher" stage of cultural evolution. "The unit of the primitive horde," Brinton writes, "is the family," with its "cohesive principle" being "purity of descent" (1894: 21). Next comes the tribe, then the nation, with an intervening step in the federation, in which "several tribes agree to forget their jealousies and unite in defense or offense" (1894: 24). However, federations are not as highly evolved as nations, for "federations of tribes never go so far as to attempt to establish linguistic or dialect unity. Only accidentally does one tongue partly encroach upon another one in this stage of society" (1894: 25). In a nation, however, neither the preservation of physical (familial) type nor tribal language is of consequence, for "the Nation breaks down the walls of narrow tribal animosities; it increases the number of those whose patriotic interests are in common, and thus widens the area of duty and the conceptions of ethics" (1894: 29).

Brinton's concept of nation is remarkably like the theoretical American conception of nation in that "the individual is indeed the true purpose of the state" (1894: 31), in which is provided "personal liberty," "personal happiness," and "maximum happiness." However, Brinton states that the United States does not yet fully recognize that "linguistic unity is the indispensable basis of national unity" (1894: 26). That is, it is within Brinton's own memory that the Acts of Assembly of his own state (Pennsylvania) were issued in two languages (unspecified as to which two), thus "encouraging a long-existing linguistic discrepancy between the citizens of that commonwealth" (1894: 26).

Brinton looks even beyond national unity to international unity. For Brinton, the basis of international unity will, of course, be an international language. Indeed, Brinton supported the scientific value of *Volapük* in his reports as chairman of the committee on "International Language," sponsored by the American Philosophical Society. Just as the "time is not far off," Brinton writes, "when one system of weights, measures and coinage, one division of time, one code of international law, one mode of quarantine and sanitation, one costume, will prevail throughout the civilized world," there must also come "a unification of speech" (1888: 5). Brinton begins with the observation that "the Aryan stock is now and has been for two thousand years the standard-bearer of the civilization of the world," and thus he does not hesitate to advance the idea that the universal language should be "based upon the general linguistic principles of that stock" (1888: 5). He specifies the phonetics, the lexicon, and the grammar of *Volapük*, firmly believing that the growth of internationalism, which would necessarily bring human unity in its wake, was the solution to the world's problems. Thus, beneficial effects of unity held for the most civilized nations as for the least. "When, as is the case with one of the present European empires [Germany?]," Brinton writes, "we hear of thirty-six different languages being current under one rule, we may be sure there is no real coherence in the nation" (1894: 26).

Brinton's ideas supporting *Volapük*, or any artificial international language, did not survive the nineteenth century. However, another of his ideas concerning the political aspects of language, the one concerning spelling reform, was apparently accepted. That is, Brinton was fanatically opposed to spelling reform. For Brinton, reformed spelling would destroy the individuality of words, would efface their associations, and would obliterate their history. The past history of a language and its literature were the valuable heritage of the student, and in any case, mental culture was supposed to require hard work (Darnell 1967: 136). From Franklin through Whitney, various proposals for spelling reform had been proposed, either with an eye to promoting the literacy so necessary to the production of an informed voting public, or with an eye to facilitating the spread of English as a world language. Brinton closes the chapter on spelling reform at the very moment that English, not *Volapük*, is poised to become the international language of the twentieth century.

5

THE SEARCH FOR
AUTONOMY: 1900–24

DISCONTINUITIES

When we turn the page to twentieth-century language studies, we meet with a distinct sense of discontinuity from the nineteenth century. Readers today are accustomed to thinking of Boasian relativism and Saussurean structuralism as radical departures from nineteenth-century strategies and approaches to language and linguistics.

Our received history certainly offers this horizon of retrospection for the discipline. When it came time to "up-date" those nineteenth-century histories written by Benfey, von Raumer, Thomsen, and Pedersen, twentieth-century linguists opted for an "additive" view of history. Leonard Bloomfield takes this tack when he offers a brief overview of the development of the discipline in the opening pages of *Language* (1933: 14–20). Here he chooses not to recast the established histories of the nineteenth century, which identify "core" linguistics with Indo-European studies in Germany. Rather, Bloomfield accepts them whole, regarding them as the "first chapter" in the history of the discipline – an important first chapter to be sure, but one now closed. To that first chapter about the "great stream" of nineteenth-century Indo-European studies, Bloomfield need only *add* the second chapter, the one about the "accelerating current" of general linguistic study, the current which he wished to help define. For Bloomfield, the subject matter of the first chapter, "language history," neatly distinguished itself from the subject matter of the second chapter, "language structure." Even the most recent histories, whatever they are writing for or against, tend to rehearse this division.[1]

The temptation to view the twentieth century as separate,

perhaps even *autonomous* in some ways, from the nineteenth is almost irresistible. First, there is the mystique of the round number cut-off date of 1900. Second, and in a rather satisfying way, a history of the discipline which posits a separation of the nineteenth century from the twentieth makes for an easy and elegant recapitulation of a theoretical division which is supposed to hold within the twentieth-century configuration of the discipline itself, namely: diachrony versus synchrony – that is, if one wishes to equate *la linguistique diachronique* with "historical linguistics," as Bloomfield (1923) seemed to want to do.[2] In addition to the aesthetics of isomorphism, it is just plain convenient, when writing a history, to find a starting point which is not too distant. Then, too, developments in other human sciences lend support to the sense of twentieth-century departure. The year 1900 appears on the title page of "The Interpretation of Dreams," the work which that dominating twentieth-century figure, Sigmund Freud (1856–1939), regarded as his masterpiece. Freud's exploration of the unplumbed depths of the unconscious provided a great new territory into which the equally new-found structures of language could be mapped.

For the United States in particular, there is the sense that American linguistics comes "into its own" in the twentieth century. Although this sense has been the direct product of the historical gap in American linguistics which it has been my task to fill, the sense of twentieth-century American rupture can nevertheless can be supported. World War I (1914–18) could justifiably be identified as a turning point. American reaction against Germany during the war freed American linguists to work on non-Indo-European languages. Even before his studies of Algonquian, Bloomfield had turned first to Tagalog, spoken in the American colony of the Phillipines, i.e. the language of a group dominated by anglophones which was not Amerindian.[3]

World War I understandably produced consequences in Europe which affected American linguistics. In France, the war signalled the end of the tradition of anthropological linguistics in French institutions; and that end coincided with the rise of Boas, Sapir, and Bloomfield, whose studies would eclipse all previous ethno-linguistics, both European and American.[4] With the disarray in Germany as a result of the war and the death of ethnolinguistics in France, the next "moment" in European language studies, as is well known, was heralded by the first edition of the *Cours de linguistique générale* (1916) by Ferdinand de Saussure (1857-1913). It is of interest that Bloomfield, in his 1923 review of the second edition of the *Cours* (1922), downplays the sense that Saussure's *Cours* represented a radical departure from what had come before in Europe. In this review and others of Bloomfield's programmatic writings of the 1920s, he consistently valorizes a distinctly American version of linguistics (see below).

Then there was Henry Louis Mencken (1880-1956). The year after the War To End All Wars ended, Mencken brought out *The American Language*, which he subtitled, with great foresight, *A Preliminary Inquiry into the Development of English in the United States*. In the Preface, Mencken underscores the innovative nature of his idea to investigate the differences between the English of England and the English of America. Fascinated by the subject, he declares that he discovered, upon search, that no work existed describing and accounting for the differences and that, in fact, "the whole literature of the subject was astonishingly meagre and unsatisfactory" (1919: v). With that, he announced his departure from the (nineteenth-century) study of English, American and British, which was born out by all the subsequent editions of the work, making it, in itself, a kind of twentieth-century institution.

Mencken's leading-with-the-chin Americanism against Old School grammarians will find echo in the slightly pugnacious attitude of post-World War I American linguists toward their European counterparts. Mencken, for instance, declares it quite beyond his understanding that "to examine and exhibit *the constantly growing differences between English and American*" should be considered an "anti-social act," as it is by "certain American pedants." Mencken chides those same pedants for their "somewhat childish effort to gain the approval of Englishmen," explaining the effort as "a belated efflorescence of the colonial spirit, often commingled with fashionable aspiration" (1919: vi-vii; emphasis mine). It is difficult to respond adequately to Mencken's pronouncements. He is sounding here – as he well knows, even in this first edition – exactly like the Noah Webster of over a century previous and without any shadow of a sense that what he is saying is *not* new. It cannot be that Mencken thinks that the idea of examining "the constantly growing differences between English and American" could be anything other than the oldest of old hat.

It must be rather that he thinks that the idea of casting off the colonial shackles of linguistic usage has some feeling of permanent freshness built into it. His attitude perfectly encodes the historically well-entrenched American denial of the past, even in the very act of writing about it. With Mencken is reinforced the paradox, peculiar to American language studies that (and I have stated it before) not having a history has so far been part of the history of American linguistics.

In a distinctly neo-Websterian move, Mencken writes *as if* the predicted division between English and American had already occurred. He claims that the exigencies of his vocation (as editor of newspapers, magazines, and books, as well as book critic) has made him ''almost completely *bilingual*'' (1919: vii; emphasis mine). His example of bilingualism is the following sentence: ''I can write English, as in this clause, quite as readily as American, as in this here one.'' However, unlike the Webster of 1789, the Mencken of 1919 is a man of compromise, wishing to find a ''compromise dialect'' between English and American ''which embodies the common material of both'' thus making it ''free from offense on both sides of the water.'' A potential example of this judicious and balanced compromise is perhaps found in Mencken's observation a few lines previous that: ''In some ways, as in intonation, English usage is plainly better than American. In others, as in spelling, American usage is as plainly better than English'' (1919: vii). The phrase ''plainly better'' is not explained but assumed to be obvious. I assume, as well, that Mencken means for the two Englishes to put their heads together and work out this ''compromise dialect'' in the manner of the Brinton-supported *Volapük*. Curiously, though, not many pages later in the first chapter, ''By Way of Introduction,'' Mencken criticizes any grammarian for having described and argued for an American language which was ''seldom the actual tongue of the folks about him, but often a sort of Volapük made up of one part faulty reporting and nine parts academic theorizing'' (1919: 7). The ''nine parts academic theorizing'' seems to be the key here: Mencken did not suffer from being an academic, neither did his spiritual great-great-great grandfather, Webster.

To give Mencken his due, his neo-Websterian zeal and enthusiasm for his subject is made palatable with a good deal of what Webster lacked, namely humor; and Mencken's first edition, which was subsequently greatly changed at the suggestions of (tolerable) academics, does provide a history of the American language (almost against itself), though it is certainly not the first. The first chapter, in particular, provides evidence of how lively a topic remained that of Americanisms, even in the first quarter of the twentieth century, and it still offers a good study of the history of the entire issue of English versus American in the nineteenth century. Although the first edition does not include reference to Whitney, subsequent editions do, and Mencken reserves some praise for George Marsh and his *Lectures on the English Language* of 1860, a source from which Whitney also drew. In distancing himself, however, from such fuddy-duddy nineteenth-century figures, Mencken seemed to capture the spirit of the American "new blood" that resulted from Old World immigration that hit high tide at the turn of the twentieth century.

The second-generation German-American Mencken was not alone in heralding this American fresh start. To begin at the beginning of my periodization for this chapter, the sense of discontinuity from the past and fresh departure for American linguistics is given a particular spin by Franz Boas. On the one hand, Boas consciously and deliberately disassociated himself from the Americanists who came before him, most pointedly Brinton. It is a rather delicious paradox that "Papa Franz," the patriarch of American twentieth-century linguistics, also disclaimed any "Americanness" for himself. Roman Jakobson has fondly recalled, recounting his early meetings with Boas, that Boas "with his keen sense of humor, used to say . . . 'Jakobson *ist ein seltsamer Mann!* [Jakobson is a strange man!] He thinks that I am an American linguist!'" (1979: 164). He used Boas's disclaimer, however, to argue that Boas strongly believed in the international character of linguistics and of any genuine science.

Boas certainly would have believed in the international character of linguistics, for he was German-born and arrived in the United States when he was already a grown man of twenty-eight. However, while Boas wished to transcend the narrow and superficial limits of nationalist interests in science, he was, on the other hand, very much a product of science as it was conceived and produced in Germany in the mid-nineteenth century. It is merely a further facet of the paradox for the history of American linguistics that a man so thoroughly shaped by nineteenth-century

Germany came to be identified with this twentieth-century American sense of departure.

CONTINUITIES

Franz Boas (1858–1942)

A study entitled "Influences During the Formative Years" provides excellent insight into those forces which shaped Boas's scientific approach. In this study, which appears in a volume of *American Anthropologist* commemorating the centenary of Boas's birth, Kluckhohn and Prufer point out, with respect to that birthdate, that Boas was born in the same year as Durkheim and Simmel. The next year saw the birth of Henri Bergson, John Dewey, and Havelock Ellis. Freud was born in 1856, and Max Weber in 1864. Kluckhohn and Prufer note that there "clusters within an eight-year span the birthdates of a surprising proportion of those who have had a tremendous impact upon 20th century thought about man in society" (1959: 4). Elaborating on this theme of dates, the year 1859 alone saw the publications of Darwin's *Origin of the Species*, Marx's *Critique of Political Economy*, Virchow's *Cellular Pathology*, and Mill's *Essay on Nature*, among others. To cut Boas off from the masters and mentors of the historical time and place where he was formed would be to ignore the personal and intellectual tradition which Boas himself claimed as his own.

In his obituary for Rudolf von Virchow (1821–1902), Boas identifies in effect, through commentary on Virchow's life, both his own scientific approach and his politics. Virchow was a physician, a pathologist, and a liberal political leader. He was the first eminent nineteenth-century German to argue for the intrinsic equality of the races, and his publications on this subject created a stir in the Second Reich (Kluckhohn and Prufer 1959: 21–2). Boas's writings against the degraded social position of Afro-Americans in American society certainly reflect this line of thinking (see p. 258, note 5). Virchow was also an unceasing opponent of anti-Semitism in Germany, the unpleasant effects of which Boas undoubtedly suffered in his formative years (Kluckhohn and Prufer 1959: 10–11). Although I have run across no information about how much better Boas found the climate for Jews in

America in general and at Columbia in particular, it is known that one of Boas's students, namely Edward Sapir, apparently encountered anti-Semitic feeling at Yale in the 1930s (Hymes and Fought 1981 [1975]: 905; Anderson 1985: 219). I am not competent to comment on the history of possible anti-Semitism in American academic institutions, but I have long entertained the suspicion that Boas's desire to dissociate himself from existing American institutional frameworks might have derived from a desire to dissociate himself from the strongly Anglo-Saxon (which does not, of course, necessarily imply anti-Semitic) temper of American higher education. William Dwight Whitney and his brand of northeastern academic mandarinism was still casting a long shadow when Boas first arrived in the United States in 1887.

Most importantly, Virchow's cautious approach to the classification of data under the point of view of general theories was fully adopted by Boas. Boas wrote that Virchow regarded such general theories as "dangerous" and "that the sound progress of science requires of us to be clear at every moment, what elements in the system of science are hypothetical and what are the limits of that knowledge which is obtained by exact observation" (1902: 443). Boas's attention to the particular, e.g. his intensive study of the Kwakiutl over a period of half a century, set him distinctly apart from, say, his American colleague Daniel Brinton, who was committed to grand schemes and universal parallelisms without much intensive attention to any one particular culture. Kluckhohn and Prufer identify Boas's attachment to Virchow-style science as the "isolative" approach, one not concerned with phenomena in their totality (1959: 11; 20–5).

To this "isolative" approach, Kluckhohn and Prufer contrast the "embracive" approach of Boas's line of thinking, which is best represented by the geographer, Alexander von Humboldt. Humboldt was an empiricist, and yet his outlook stressed the holistic or "embracive," and phenomenological. The figure of Alexander von Humboldt is deeply set in Boas's intellectual background. Boas spoke of this Humboldt in "awe" (Kluckhohn and Prufer 1959: 11), while Virchow dated the modern age of scholarship from the return of Alexander von Humboldt to Prussia in 1827, followed by the death of Hegel in 1831 (Herbst: 1965: 57). With the end of Hegel and the coming of Humboldt, the philosophic age was over, and the scientific age had arrived.

For Boas, the geographic and the linguistic coincided early in his career. His first geographical researches, those in Baffinland in 1883, included the study of the indigenous Eskimo language. However, while Boas openly referred to the science of Alexander von Humboldt, there is no reference in Boas's writings to the work of Alexander's brother, the linguist Wilhelm (Kluckhohn and Prufer 1959: 13). This absence of mention might well have been due to the fact that Brinton had already cornered the American market on Wilhelm von Humboldt and that Boas saw no profit in allying himself to Brinton's intellectual source.

On the relationship of Boas and Brinton, Darnell has provided ample documentation of the cordial relationship they enjoyed (1967: 75–87). At the same time, Boas's research methods were very different from Brinton's, and Boas was against the evolutionary theory common among the American anthropologists of the generation before him. Early on in his American career, that is already in the 1890s, Boas was trying to change the direction of ethnological inquiry from the direction Brinton had given it (Darnell 1967: 86). Boas's intellectual achievement is remarkable, but equally remarkable is the way that he managed to establish his place in the academic framework of twentieth-century American anthropology (see Darnell 1970a: 235–64). Since Boas's *Handbook* was an avowed continuation of Powell's 1891 classification, it can be said that part of the sense of departure that Boas established at the turn of the twentieth century was precisely in the academic institutionalization of the profession of "anthropology." Significantly, Boas's effort was concurrent with the institutionalization of "linguistics" at Johns Hopkins. Although the two disciplines were separately conceived, they converged significantly in their integration of German thought into their disciplinary foundations.

Before leaving Germany, Boas had formally studied physics and geography, making him by inclination and training a *Naturwissenschaftler*. True to the distinctions of the German science of his day, Boas understood his researches in ethnology to belong to the *Geisteswissenschaften*, or, as he phrased it in his "Introduction" to the *Handbook*: "ethnology is understood as the science dealing with the mental phenomena of the life of the peoples of the world" – here the "mental phenomena" correspond to *Geist* – and he continued that "human language, one of the most important manifestations of mental life, would seem to belong naturally to

213

this field" (1911: 63; quoted also in Hymes and Fought 1981 [1975]: 983). The only linguist Boas met in his student years in Germany was Steinthal, but at that time Boas was not yet actively interested in language and afterwards regretted never having attended Steinthal's lectures (Jakobson 1944: 188). He also, later in life, admitted one of his sources of inspiration to have been Steinthal, which again would set him in line with Brinton and very far apart from Whitney. However, Boas does not mention Steinthal's name in his 1911 "Introduction." He does, however, mention Max Mueller, another of the figures to whom Whitney was so vigorously opposed.

Boas did meet Wilhelm Wundt (1832–1920) in his student years (Kluckhohn and Prufer 1959: 11). Although Boas subscribed to a version of Wundt's folk psychology, or *Voelkerpsychologie*, he did not accept Wundt's line between folk and civilized (Hymes and Fought 1981 [1975]: 983). Following in the tradition of Humboldt and Steinthal, Boas and his turn-of-the-twentieth-century ethnology contained a universalist thesis with particularistic implications, associated with language typology. As Hymes and Fought see it: "Boas not only considered that some features are universal to languages, but also that all languages reflect the history and culture, and more particularly, the psychological makeup, of the community of which they have been a part" (1981 [1975]: 983). Boas sought functional and not substantive universals and understood *Geist* to capture the implications of "mental phenomena" or "mental life," which had not only psychological implications but, more importantly, ethnological implications in that each particular culture and language had its own distinctive mental configurations, as expressions of the group. Wundt was also to influence the early Leonard Bloomfield in the latter's 1914 *Introduction*.

Boas's 1911 "Introduction" reads as a summary of Boas's thought. Covering some eighty pages, it is relatively short and to the point. Boas's succinct argumentation, along with his lack of overt reference to predecessors, give the "Introduction" a flavor of fresh departure. At the same time, however, it can be read as a summary of all major nineteenth-century issues. I do not intend to expose here a thorough analysis of Boas's thought. I intend only to weave him into his historical time and place by comparing his opinions, on four points, to the opinions expressed by the most influential person in American language studies to immediately precede him, namely William Dwight Whitney. In this comparison, Whitney and Boas do not seem as discontinuous, one from the other, as might be at first supposed.

1 Like Whitney, Boas dissociated language and culture and race. Toward the beginning of his "Introduction," Boas states: "The assumption that type, language, and culture were originally closely correlated would entail the further assumption that these three traits developed approximately at the same period, and that they developed conjointly for a considerable length of time" (1911: 13).

Boas then offers the opinion that "This assumption does not seem by any means plausible." He reasons that "the differentiation of the more important subdivision of the great races antedates the formation of the existing linguistic families," and then makes an appeal to the institutional nature of language seconded by the uniformitarian principle, both espoused by Whitney, that

> At any rate, the biological differentiation and the formation of speech were, at this early period, subject to the same causes that are acting upon them now, and our whole experience shows that these causes act much more rapidly on language than on the human body.
>
> (1911: 13)

Boas is led to the inescapable conclusion that "In this consideration lies the principal reason for the theory of lack of correlation of type and language, even during the period of formation of types and of linguistic families" (1911: 13).

Like Whitney, who proposed that the absolute numbers of languages in the world was diminishing due to purely extralinguistic factors (see above pp. 195–7), Boas also seemed to think that

> As far as our historical evidence goes, there is no reason to believe that the number of distinct languages has at any time been less than it is now. On the contrary, all our evidence goes to show that the number of apparently unrelated languages has been much greater in earlier times than at present.
>
> (1911: 12)

However, Boas does not cast his argument in terms of ever-expanding political groupings, as does Whitney. Being an anthropologist, Boas places biological considerations first: "I believe," he argues, "that it may be safely said that all over the world the biological unit is much larger than the linguistic unit." That is to say, that

> groups of men who are so closely related in bodily appearance that we must consider them as representatives of the same variety of mankind, embrace a much larger number of individuals than the number of men speaking languages which we know to be genetically related.
>
> (1911: 12)

Boas does not offer any reason for the fact that "the number of apparently unrelated languages has been much greater in earlier times than at present." In general, it would seem that Boas would follow more closely Whitney's reasoning on the issue of dialect coalescence and reduction, rather than, say, Mueller's (see above p. 196).

2 On alternating sounds, Boas's arguments parallel some of Whitney's opinions. Boas is famous for having pointed out that "The alternation of the sounds [in an English-speaker's perception of particular North Pacific Indian] is clearly an effect of perception through the medium of a foreign system of phonetics, not that of a greater variability of pronunciation than the one that is characteristic of our own sounds" (1911: 18).

As early as 1861, Whitney had accused German scholars, and in particular Lepsius, of falling prey to phonetic features peculiar to German when attempting to describe the phonetic alphabet. In his article, "On Lepsius's Standard Alphabet," Whitney writes for the case of describing voiced and voiceless obstruents (s/z, f/z, p/b, etc.), that

> the really eminent physiologist Johannes Mueller can see no difference between a *p* and a *b* except a difference in regard to the force of utterance; and the noted grammarian Becker can find nothing better to say of them that the one, the soft, is naturally fitted to stand at the beginning of a syllable, and the other, the hard, at its end: that is to say, that *but* is a correct and normal compound of sounds, while *tub* is something topsy-turvy, an infraction of the order of nature, and ought not, we

suppose, to be uttered – as, by most Germans, it cannot be.
(1861: 229)

Whitney, well aware in this passage of the potential interference of the linguist's native language, opined: "This defect is something rather characteristically German."

The importance of cultivating an *Indian ear* to properly distinguish Indian sounds goes back, of course, to Heckewelder (see above p. 95). Boas recognized the methodological importance of this insight for the entire description of the languages contained in his *Handbook* when he stated that

No attempt has been made to compare the forms of the Indians' grammars with the grammars of English, Latin, or even among themselves: but in each case the psychological groupings which are given depend entirely upon the inner form of each language.
(1911: 81)

That is to say, that "the grammar has been treated as though *an intelligent Indian* was going to develop the forms of his own thoughts by an analysis of his own form of speech" (1911: 81; emphasis mine).

3   On the question of holophrasm, Whitney got tangled, but was willing to readjust through his reading of Trumbull (see above pp. 177–8). Nevertheless, Boas seems to make a radical break with the past when he trenchantly observes that

Thus it happens that each language, from the point of view of another language, may be arbitrary in its classifications; that what appears as a single simple idea in one language may be characterized by a series of distinct phonetic groups in another.
(1911: 26)

Boas concludes:

The tendency of a language to express a complex idea by a single term has been styled 'holophrasis,' and it appears therefore that every language may be holophrastic from the point of view of another language. Holophrasis can hardly be taken as a fundamental characteristic of primitive languages.
(1911: 26)

Boas does not mention Francis Lieber, who coined the term "holophrasis," nor Lieber's context (see above pp. 118–19). Neither does Boas mention Lucien Adam, who earlier had been critical of Brinton's idea that certain Indian languages were "visibly synthetic" and with a propensity to "holophrasm." Adam saw this "visibility" rather as a product of the orthographic convention of hyphenation (see above pp. 193–4). Here Boas's thought seems to cap certain ideas about holophrasis that were in circulation rather than to break new ground.

There is a limit to how much one can completely reconcile Whitney's and Boas's approaches. Certainly, Whitney's orientation differed from Boas's: Whitney's specialty was Sanskrit; Boas's was Kwakiutl. Whitney privileged written records; Boas did not. However, there do seem to be distinct points of convergence and continuity, the study of which might illuminate and give substance to any subsequent study of the history of American linguistics.

4   Where Whitney and Boas diverged most radically was in their approaches to un/consciousness and linguistic behavior. For Whitney, language behavior was a product of human will, and continuously subject to the centrifugal force of idiosyncratic variation, which could be, just as continuously, checked by an opposing centripetal (ultimately, political) force (see above pp. 166–7). "Consciousness" and "mastery" figure highly in Whitney's account of language and language use, in a line harkening back to Condillac and the Enlightenment, onto which is superimposed an added dimension of consciousness inscribed in the very tradition of language studies. This "super"-consciousness of language, i.e. the activity of thinking of speech, of talking about it and observing it, could, in Whitney's view, sometimes form a part of a nation's peculiar character (see above p. 163), as it did for the heritage of nineteenth-century America.

On this score, Boas's approach is different. For Boas, the "reality" of language lay in the unconscious processes expressed in the grammatical and phonemic patterns in a language. These patterns most specifically do not rise into individual consciousness, and consequently, they are not interfered with by the individual. This unconsciousness, in turn, secures the rigid and imperative character of the grammatical and phonemic patterns (Jakobson 1944: 189). Boas's most often-quoted statement on the unconscious character of grammatical patterns occurs, again, in his "Introduction":

> It would seem that the essential difference between linguistic phenomena and other ethnological phenomena is, that the linguistic classifications never rise into consciousness, while in other ethnological phenomena, although the same unconscious origin prevails, these often rise into consciousness, and thus give rise to secondary reasoning and to reinterpretations.
>
> (1911: 67)

Boas identifies grammar as the singling out, as the classification and expression of various aspects of the experience of the group that *must* be expressed. The individual has no choice. By the turn of the twentieth century, then, the dismantling of the political conception of language, with its assumption of individual freedom, was complete in both arcs of development: both in "linguistic science" and "linguistic anthropology."

Furthermore, in the line of Humboldt–Steinthal–Wundt, Boas identifies the "natural unit of expression" to be "the sentence; that is to say, a group of articulate sounds which convey a complete idea" (1911: 27). Whitney, holding to the Anglo-French tradition of sign theory, states that "the history of language reposes on that of words. Language is made up of signs for thought, which, though in one sense parts of a whole, are in another and more essential sense isolated and independent entities" (1887 [1867]: 54). Whitney, on the other hand, still gives precedence to the part – the word – over the whole. For Whitney, then, ". . . etymology, the historical study of individual words, is the foundation and substructure of all investigation of language" (1887 [1867]: 54–5; also partially quoted above p. 159).

At the same time, however, Boas, like Whitney, still understands "explanation" as primarily historical, making whatever it is the linguist finds worthy and of interest in language study to be a product of individual and language/culture-specific historical processes. Studies such as Hymes and Fought (1981 [1975]) and Anderson (1985: 194–216), which put Boas in his historical framework, note that Boasian grammars "itemize" but "do not structure." That is, Boas would have denied some "autonomous," internal structure or system in language or, at least, would have regarded such a structure abstracted away from its historical grounding to be unnecessary and, quite possibly, incomplete.

Leonard Bloomfield (1887–1949)

The transition from Boas to Leonard Bloomfield is a smooth one here. Furthermore, the transition from Whitney to Boas, even the continuity between the two is well exemplified in Bloomfield's first text, *An Introduction to the Study of Language* (1914), which draws explicitly on both Whitney and Boas. Bloomfield wrote this work while he was an instructor in German at the University of Illinois (1913–21), during which period he spent a year in Germany (1913–14) studying with Leskien, Brugmann, and Oldenberg at the Universities of Leipzig and Goettingen. For the purposes of a larger history of American linguistics, it is clearly Bloomfield's 1933 *Language* which is his historical legacy. However, for the purposes of this present book, I wish to focus on the 1914 *Introduction* to demonstrate how, even drawing on Whitney, it writes the traditional interests of nineteenth-century English studies in America out of the discipline of ''linguistic science'' (see also Andresen 1987a).

In the 1914 *Introduction*, Bloomfield's acquaintance with Boas's work is obvious. Not only does Bloomfield cite Boas's *Handbook* in a long list of books entered under the heading ''How to study linguistics'' (1914: 317), Bloomfield also opens his fifth chapter, entitled ''Morphology,'' with the observation that ''The morphological classes of a language represent communal associative habits: they express the associative connections which the national mental life of a people has made between the types of experience which the language expresses in words.'' Then Bloomfield essentially paraphrases Boas's famous statement, quoted immediately above:

> The classifications of language are, in fact, the clearest expressions of the associations made by the community as a whole. They are, accordingly, of great ethnologic significance. This significance is increased by the fact that they are far less subject to reflection than other communal activities (such as religion) . . .

However, Bloomfield makes an observation that seems more typical of Whitney than of Boas when he adds: "... and are never, in any but the most highly cultured communities, modified by such reflection" (1914: 120). With this rider, Bloomfield might have had in mind Whitney's belief, referred to immediately above, that the activity of thinking of speech, of talking about it and observing it, can sometimes form a part of a nation's character. For Whitney, "where speech is most unconsciously employed . . . there its changes are rifest," while, by way of contrast, "any introduction of the element of reflection is conservative in its effect" (1887 [1867]: 148). Thus, for Whitney, a people who reflect on their speech, who are *conscious* of it, will alter it but slowly (see above p. 163). However, Bloomfield does not, in the *Introduction*, elaborate, as does Whitney, on the consequences of any "modifications by reflection" in "these highly cultured communities."

Bloomfield's debt to Whitney in this 1914 *Introduction* is even more prominent than Bloomfield's acknowledgement of Boas's work. In the very first paragraph of the Preface, Bloomfield states his desire to follow in the path opened up by fellow American William Dwight Whitney in *Language and the Study of Language* (1867) and *The Life and Growth of Language* (1875) (1914: v). Despite this prominent reference, little scholarly attention has been given to the connection between Bloomfield and Whitney. This lack, of course, is entirely symptomatic of the fact that a history of American linguistics is not supposed to exist.

Instead, more attention has been focused on what Bloomfield, still in the Preface, states as his purpose, namely to incorporate the progress made in the science of language since Whitney's time. This progress was made, in Bloomfield's opinion, primarily by Wilhelm Wundt. It is, indeed, the Wundtian orientation of Bloomfield's *Introduction* that has attracted the attention from scholars: Chapter III, "The Mental Basis of Language," the passage on word order (186–8), and the passage on the relationship of linguistics to psychology (322–3). This Wundtian orientation is then usually contrasted to Bloomfield's later, radical change to the behaviorist psychology of his colleague at Ohio State, Albert P. Weiss (1879–1931). With respect to the relationship of linguistics to psychology and Wundt's *Voelkerpsychologie*, it is apparent that even in 1914, Bloomfield was against confounding the discipline of psychology with linguistics, for he stated that "perhaps the student of a mental science could and ideally should refrain from any running psychologic interpretation" (1914: 322); quoted also in Hymes and Fought 1975: 983, note 21). The key here is that "mental" meant for Bloomfield, as it did for Boas and, for that matter, Wundt, *Geist*: the mental configurations of particular cultures and languages.

Bloomfield's Wundtian orientation certainly has deserved the attention it has gotten, for it shows how thoroughly the German orientation had penetrated American language studies. However, it is of interest here not in and of itself but rather because it marks the major rupture with Whitney's approach. Now, Whitney had acknowledged the pre-eminence of the German philology of his day, he taught German privately to supplement his salary at Yale and even wrote two German readers (1870, 1876), two German grammars (1869, 1885), and a Germany dictionary (1887). Nevertheless, Whitney maintained, as we have seen, a strong English-language orientation in his work. It is precisely Bloomfield's German-language orientation in the *Introduction* that sharply distinguishes his attempt at *general linguistics* from Whitney's. At issue is not the several long pedagogical passages on points of German grammar that appear in Bloomfield (1914: 143, 147, 180), nor even the entire chapter he devotes to the teaching of spoken foreign languages (Chapter IX), which have no real counterpart in Whitney's two *Languages*. Rather, what is absent in Bloomfield but present in Whitney is the social and political consciousness of language, and this absence would mark Bloomfield's work off from Whitney's in the following three ways.

1 Whitney, but not Bloomfield, subscribed to the Manifest Destiny of the English language that had begun with Noah Webster. In his *Introduction*, in a passage on the subject of the English language in America, Bloomfield states the fulfilment of Webster's and Whitney's prophecies in matter-of-fact terms: "Our continent, north of Mexico, once harbored a few million Indians speaking over a hundred, perhaps several hundreds, of mutually unintelligible languages; today this area contains more than a hundred million inhabitants, nearly all of whom speak English" (1914: 262). This passage appears in the sections on the "Increase in uniformity" and "Decrease in uniformity" in language and

does not portray this circumstance as desirable (as did Whitney) or undesirable. Bloomfield ends the passage by mentioning that the differentiation among the global varieties of English will probably never rise to the point of unintelligibility (1914: 265), thereby concurring with Whitney, but without any of Whitney's argumentation about the unifying effect of the written language.

Over a decade after his *Introduction*, Bloomfield did become interested in the idea of standard language and the social implications of certain types of language use. In a 1927 article entitled "Literate and Illiterate Speech," Bloomfield chose to investigate the distinction between "good" and "bad" in a community with no written language, namely the Menomini of Wisconsin. Sounding like Whitney, Bloomfield writes at one point: "Now, as civilization progresses, the population grows denser, means of communication improve, and petty political boundaries lose their importance" (1927: 434). At another, Bloomfield, again like Whitney, recognizes the inherent variability of language in any one community: "but so far in the history of mankind complete standardization seems nowhere to have taken place" (1927: 435). Still, the focus of Bloomfield's study is the Menomini community and not the social and political consequences for the future of American English.

2 The above example demonstrates that Bloomfield was, in the long run, less interested in American English as a theoretical and research pursuit than in those languages which American English had displaced, i.e. the American Indian languages. By contrast, Whitney was interested in (physically) displacing the American Indian languages. Whitney devoted his energies to writing such works as *Essentials of English Grammar* and to helping to establish the Spelling Reform Association and the American Dialect Society.

Here, again, Bloomfield followed Boas's, not Whitney's, lead out of the hierarchical and evolutionist nineteenth century and into the relativist twentieth century. But was it only that the revaluation of the American Indian languages within linguistic anthropology needed to be "paid for" at the expense of American English studies? Or were there other reasons why Bloomfield should have ignored the social and political issues surrounding American English that had been at the foundations of Whitney's thought? Several answers have already suggested themselves in this chapter.

First, by 1914, it could be said that the major thrust of American expansionism (in North America) had been completed, so that the spread of English across the continent was no longer at issue. Then, too, Mencken's post-World War I (re-)assertion of American English independence from British English could be interpreted as an expression of a "coming of age" confidence for speakers of American English. Added to which, the three arcs of development had already separated in the academy, and the concerns of American Indian languages and those of American English were thought to be separate anyway.

At the same time, however, the fact that Mencken pursued his study of American English outside of the academy indicates how important were German scholarship and German-language-oriented issues inside the academy. By adhering to Wundt, Bloomfield wiped the slate clean of Whitney's American English consciousness. No longer do we find in Bloomfield's *Introduction* such politically charged statements as were to be found in Whitney: "Aristocracy and exclusiveness tend to final overthrow, in language as in politics" (1887 [1867]: 150). No longer does Bloomfield speak of language as a *res-publica*, or "thing of the people," where the linguistic act is compared to voting or suffrage. Bloomfield is, of course, aware of the social character of language, but his treatment of it is not prominent. He devotes only one separate paragraph to the "social character of language" (1914: 17) in the first chapter. He speaks of that "social character" throughout the *Introduction* exclusively in terms of *habit*, typically a mechanized and unconscious habit: "And as, moreover, the individual, from childhood, practises his speech until the details of it are mechanized and unconscious, he is rarely aware of the specific characteristics, such as the phonetic or the grammatical, which are involved in it" (1914: 17).

Whitney's interest in American English went hand-in-hand with his interest in the social and political setting for language and language change, in languages-in-contact, and in dialect variation. Bloomfield's lack of interest in American English led him away from these approaches and to more internal (perhaps psycho-culturally motivated) structural explanations for language and language change.[5]

3 Whitney, but not Bloomfield, embraces sign theory. Sign

theory belongs more to franco-anglophone thought of the eighteenth century than to nineteenth-century German thought, which Bloomfield was transmitting. Where Whitney speaks of language as a "system of arbitrary signs for thought," even a "congeries of signs," Bloomfield is apt to formulate, by way of contrast, that

> language is not . . . a system of unalterably fixed and indivisible elements. It is rather a complex set of associations and experiences in groups, each of which is accompanied by a habitual sound-utterance, – and all these associations are, like all others, certain of displacement in the course of time.
>
> (1914: 70)

Whitney adhered to the idea that words as signs of ideas were the "social contracts" in miniature, which the person born into the community inherited but which the individual was free to assemble at will. Bloomfield, on the other hand, and in a Wundtian and Boasian framework, took the sentence to be the primary unit of analysis throughout his 1914 *Introduction* (110–19), and this approach resurfaces explicitly in his 1923 review of Saussure:

> In detail, I should differ from de Saussure chiefly in basing my analysis on the sentence rather than on the word; by following the latter custom de Saussure gets a rather complicated result in certain matters of word-composition and syntax.
>
> (1923: 319)

Equally interesting in this respect is Bloomfield's criticism of Sapir's treatment of the sentence in Bloomfield's 1922 review of Sapir's *Language*. For his definition of the sentence, Bloomfield criticizes Sapir for falling back on "the irrelevant subject-and-predicate notion of logic" and refers the reader instead to Meillet's "real" definition in terms of linguistics (in Hockett 1970: 93).

In any event, what Bloomfield is accomplishing in his 1914 *Introduction* is the carving out of some "autonomous" (independent from society) level in language, which would eventually serve as the focus of "general linguistics." For Whitney, nothing in language could conceivably be "autonomous."

For all these seeming discontinuities from Whitney's approach, a remarkable continuity with Whitney's work exists in Bloomfield's 1914 database. After all, it has always been Whitney's use of "real

live data" that was supposed to have marked off the real beginnings of "general linguistics." However, the telling contrast
between the two approaches to "general linguistics" is found in
the way Bloomfield chose to "recycle" Whitney's example of the
etymology of the word *mint*. In Chapter 3, I argued that Whitney's
very choice of the word *mint* to illustrate his point that "historical
circumstances" and "mental associations" always interpenetrated
illustrated most pertinently Whitney's fundamentally *non-
autonomous* view of language. In this example of *mint*, Whitney
refuses, in effect, to abstract the concept of *value* away from
language use (see above pp. 161–2). However, in his *Introduction*,
Bloomfield strips Whitney's example of its theoretical implications
and incorporates it blandly in his chapter on semantic change. He
"demotes" it, as it were, to a list of common words which have
derived from proper names: "the word *money* meant originally the
'mint,'" Bloomfield writes, "which was named in Rome from the
close-by temple of Juno *Moneta*, this last being perhaps the family
name of some Roman clan for whom the temple was named"
(1914: 247–8).

It is hardly surprising to discover that Bloomfield should have
borrowed this example, and others, from Whitney's rich data from
the Indo-European languages. What is surprising is to discover the
extent to which Bloomfield used as well Whitney's examples from
the aboriginal American languages. Remember that Bloomfield did
not begin his work on "exotic" languages until after 1914. To
take but one example: Bloomfield used on four different occasions
Whitney's example (taken, in turn, from Humboldt) of the
"Mexican" grammatical feature of incorporation (*Einverleibung*) in
the phrase "I flesh-eat" *nina-kakwa* (1914: 98, 167, 179, and 253).
An exhaustive study of the database similarities between Whitney
(1867, 1875) and Bloomfield (1914) goes beyond the limits of this
present study. With regard to the history of American linguistics,
the point here is that Bloomfield's database ties him directly into
the whole of the history of American linguistics, not only into
Whitney but also into Pickering and Duponceau.

Edward Sapir (1884–1939)

Edward Sapir neatly returns us to the very beginning of our story,
that is, to the list of negative comparisons between the state of

American language studies in 1769 *vis-à-vis* that of European language studies (see above pp. 22–30). More specifically, Sapir returns us to Johann Herder's *Ueber den Ursprung der Sprache* of 1770, which comes to haunt twentieth-century American linguistics by way of Sapir's Master's essay. Sapir wrote this essay as a graduate student in Germanics and Semitics at Columbia University, just before he began his doctoral studies there with Boas. By birth (at Lauenberg, Pomerania) and inclination, Sapir was well inclined to the Germanic cast of American higher education that fully marked the turn of the twentieth century.

Sapir's Master's essay, first published in 1907, is deeply steeped in the thought and literature of the German-speaking world. In Sapir's account of Herder's *Preisschrift*, the subtle, high-minded German *Romantiker* prevailed handily over the English and French Enlightenment thinkers, those "naturalists" with their "crude", mechanistic psychology [which] makes their speculations often seem rather infantile today" (1984 [1907]: 360). Condillac, for instance, "probably the most profound of the *philosophes*" was also the most "ingenious," yet "not truly convincing." For Sapir, the great difficulty that Herder found with Condillac's *Essai* was "the failure to draw a sharp line between the instinct of the animals and the higher mental powers of man" (1984 [1907]: 361).

In drawing the Condillac–Herder cleavage, Sapir immediately brings into play, for this present history of American linguistics, those issues whose consequences were played out on both sides of the Atlantic during the course of the nineteenth century in a series of oppositions: *grammaire particulière*/*grammaire générale*, political/ mechanical, conscious/unconscious, philology (or, alternatively, cultural anthropology)/linguistics, all of which were cross-cut by the theoretical division between *Geist/Natur*. Sapir, of course, aligns himself with the second half of each opposition in the Germanic tradition of Herder–Humboldt–Steinthal–Wundt, then well-established in American anthropology's approaches to language, first through Brinton, then through Boas. For Sapir, however, language glowed with more inner radiance than it did for his mentor, Boas. The word that comes to mind in this context is "mystic," precisely because commentators on Sapir's work, over the last sixty years, have tended to explain why Sapir's approach to language is *not* mystic, often in connection with the idea of "Drift" as elaborated in his *Language* of 1921.[6] However one wishes to characterize Sapir's approach to language, one can say that he viewed it, from his Master's essay onward, as supremely "special," and that its "specialness" resided on the "inside," as was so clearly expressed in his 1925 article "Sound Patterns in Language."

To return to the young Sapir's opinion, it was Herder to whom modern linguistics was most indebted for having done away, in his 1770 *Preisschrift*, with "the conception of divine interference [in the origin of language], and the introduction of the idea of slow, but gradual and necessary, development from rude beginnings" (1984 [1907]: 356). With Herder, then, it became apparent how the crude conception of the "invention" of language "had to give way more and more to that of the unconscious, or . . . largely subconscious, development of speech by virtue of man's psychic powers" (1984 [1907]: 356). To indicate how forward-thinking was Herder in this respect (as well as to disparage those who held positions on language quite opposite to the Herderian orientation), Sapir argues that "Even long after Herder had demonstrated the untenableness of the orthodox theory, many scholars still clung to a view which made God, as Goethe put it, 'a kind of omnipotent schoolmaster.'" The word "schoolmaster" ties perfectly into Sapir's next observation: "I note, by way of illustration, that our Noah Webster still considered it [divine origin of language] the most probable explanation" (1984 [1907]: 359). With this not quite accurate judgment, we might consider Webster's fate sealed with respect to twentieth-century American linguistics. It is no wonder that, several decades later, Kemp Malone chose to publish his study of Webster, "A Linguistic Patriot," in the first issue of *American Speech* and not in the first issue of *Language*, where it would have competed with Sapir's "Sound Patterns" (see Preface).[7]

Then, too, we might note here that one's belief in the "ultimate" origins of language is not diagnostic of any one approach to language in its day-to-day functioning. One could argue for the thoroughly institutional character of language and still either defer the question of whether or not a deity exists, or even "fall back" on an explanation of the divine origin of language. In Sapir's aside on Webster, just as in his reference to Whitney (see above p. 140), what Sapir might have been dismissing was Webster's and Whitney's thoroughly political conception of language – but this is mere speculation on the slim evidence of two rather oblique comments. Similarly, whether one conceives of language politically or mechanically does not necessarily correlate with opposing views on the biology of language. Just as Whitney had argued against equating the ability to speak with biological functions, like the circulation of the blood or even learning to walk (1887 [1867]: 399), so Sapir opens the first chapter of *Language* by distinguishing inherent, biological functions, like walking, from non-instinctive, acquired, "cultural" functions, like speech (1921: 3–4). Where Whitney and Sapir differ is in where they "place" the "reality" of speech (note that both refer to it as "speech"): Whitney locates the reality of language external to the individual, out in the "marketplace"; Sapir locates it within, in the psyche, in the special domain of human reason.

As sympathetic as was Sapir to the Herderian conception of human reason, he was certainly not entirely uncritical of the eighteenth-century German, particularly with respect to Herder's view on so-called primitive languages. Sapir's arguments against Herder are reminiscent of Duponceau's and Pickering's objections to Humboldt. Namely, Sapir gently criticizes Herder's idea that "primitive" languages have no grammar: "Herder thought of grammar, as was very natural in the eighteenth century, as something which was, with increasing civilization, brought to bear on language from without" (1984 [1907]: 376). However, Sapir points out that typically "original" languages possess "*truly* grammatical features of incredible complexity, as in the case of the Eskimo verb or Bantu noun" (1984 [1907]: 376). Sapir also argues against the "oft-asserted and oft-repeated statement of the incredibly rapid change of the languages of primitive tribes" by noting that it "is founded on the untrustworthy reports of linguistically inefficient missionaries." Indeed, Sapir continues, "the most startling cases of linguistic conservatism are found among certain primitive peoples, such as the Eskimos" (1984 [1907]: 380). These passages have led to the hypothesis that Sapir must have encountered Boas *before* writing his Master's essay, which Murray (1985) proposes and subsequently confirms (1986).

More overt coincidences between Sapir's writings and Boas's can be found in Sapir's later work. Like Boas, Sapir dissociates race, language, and culture (1921: 212–18), as did Bloomfield earlier (1914: 271), which latter did not need to choose between

Boas (1911: 5–14) and Whitney on the issue, for Whitney had also dissociated them (1887 [1867]: 372, 376). The dissociation is consistent with a belief in the fundamentally institutional character of language.

However, when it came to the concept of "nation," Sapir's treatment is necessarily and predictably different from Whitney's or even Brinton's. In arguing for the separation of language and culture, Sapir writes:

> Particularly in more primitive levels, where the secondarily unifying power of the "national" ideal does not arise to disturb the flow of what we might call natural distributions, it is easy to show that language and culture are not intrinsically associated.
>
> (1921: 213)

That is to say, for Sapir, "nation" is a "secondarily unifying power" (for Whitney and Brinton it would have been primary), which opposes itself to "natural distributions," suggesting a nation/nature dichotomy, added to which "the 'national' ideal" is, apparently for Sapir, principally that: an ideal, rather than the reality it was for Whitney and Brinton. In the footnote after the quote-marked word "national," Sapir tells us that: "A 'nationality' [again quote-marked] is a major, sentimentally unified, group. The historical factors that lead to the feeling of national unity are various – political, cultural, linguistic, geographic, sometimes specifically religious." So, again, for Sapir, "nationality" is something *interior* to the individual, a sentiment, a feeling, and not something *exterior* to the individual, an act, a communal act, say, the act of voting or ratification. Sapir does continue in the footnote: "In an area dominated by the national sentiment there is a tendency for language and culture to become uniform and specific, so that linguistic and cultural boundaries at least tend to coincide" (1921: 312, note 10). Again, the wording points inward, to "an area dominated by the national *sentiment*," and not outward, to an area dominated by such-and-such laws voted upon in such-and-such elections and enacted by such-and-such governing bodies.

Sapir's emphasis on inner feeling and particularly on *innere Sprachform* played a direct role in his historical work, particularly in his classification of the American Indian languages. In this respect, Sapir continues Brinton's classificatory efforts based on grammar rather than lexicon (see above p. 199). Sapir's emphasis on the inner structure of a language also motivated his typological classificatory framework which, according to Anderson, "is much more complex, and accordingly more delicate than any of the traditional nineteenth-century schemes . . . [and] serves a fundamentally synchronic, descriptive purpose." Because of this, "it is intended . . . to describe what the structure of a language is, rather than how far along a presumed evolutionary scale it has progressed" (1985: 226). Anderson relates Sapir's interest in typology to his notion of "Drift" as well as to his historical work, and Anderson's discussion need not be repeated here (1985: 226–7).

It would be illuminating here to relate Sapir's interest in typology along with his highly intuitional genetic classifications (not suspected in, say, Goddard 1914) to his gift for poetry, but such an exploration will have to await a future study. Suffice it to say in this brief sketch of Sapir's place in the history of American linguistics that he has been the most poetic of American linguists, and as such has proven to be the most quotable. Indeed, he has been widely quoted, and his 1921 *Language* contains a number of phrases and passages which have become proverbial: "All grammars leak" (1921: 38); "Single Algonkin words are like tiny imagist poems" (1921: 228); "Every language is itself a collective art of expression" (1921: 225); "When it comes to linguistic form, Plato walks with the Macedonian swineherd, Confucius with the head-hunting savage of Assam" (1921: 219); "In watching my Nootka interpreter write his language, I often had the curious feeling that he was transcribing an ideal flow of phonetic elements which he heard, inadequately from a purely objective standpoint, as the intention of the actual rumble of speech" (1921: 56, note 16). From his 1929 article "The Status of Linguistics as a Science" comes the passage on linguistic relativism that is the most widely known and which has made of Sapir the most legitimate eponym of this hypothesis:

> The fact of the matter is that the "real world" is to a large extent unconsciously built up on the language habits of the group. No two languages are ever sufficiently similar to be considered as representing the same social reality. The worlds in

which different societies live are distinct worlds, not merely the same world with different labels attached.

(quoted in 1949: 162)

It is not a coincidence that in his very next paragraph, Sapir comments that: "The understanding of a simple poem, for instance, involves not merely an understanding of the single words in their average significance, but a full comprehension of the whole life of the community as it is mirrored in the words, or as it is suggested by their overtones" (quoted in 1949: 162).

Whatever the relationship between Sapir, his mentalism, his poetry, his typologizing, and even his relationship to the Wundtian-turned-Weissian Leonard Bloomfield, it can be noted that Sapir might have had some effect, after all, on Bloomfield's sensibilities. In Bloomfield's intellectual testament, his own *Language*, Bloomfield himself indulged in a rare, if restrained, flight into imagery making. He closes his chapter on "Semantic Change" with a reference to the stormy Romantic poet, Wordsworth, using a poetic metaphor from Wordsworth to comment on the "picturesque saying" that "language is a book of faded metaphors." Bloomfield forges an image of his own when he reverses that saying by pronouncing that "poetry is rather a blazoned book of language" (1933: 443).[8]

In a detailed analysis of Sapir's conception of phonological structure and his descriptive practice in phonology, Anderson notes that for Sapir the full system of the phonemic pattern in a language is not given by phonetic factors alone (1985: 231), and that Sapir desired to avoid positing underlying forms which would violate generalizations about surface structure forms (1985: 249). If I understand Anderson's account correctly, it looks as if Sapir is not positing some autonomous phonological component in language anymore than he would posit some aspect of language that was autonomous either from the culture or from the individual. Rather, it was, for Sapir, the reverse. As Anderson points out: "For Sapir, the fundamental problem of linguistics was thus not the construction of a 'theory of grammar' but the elucidation of the relationship between language on the one hand and culture and personality on the other" (1985: 228). However much Sapir's feeling for language depended on his sense of "inner feeling," he viewed language structure as being determined culturally, in an *external* and *contingent* fashion and not as a result of innate, *internal*, i.e. biological, or otherwise *exigent* factors (see Anderson 1985: 228).

Now, Anderson identifies that the appropriate object of study in linguistics is actually *grammar* (1985: 7), with a focus on rule-governed regularity, and not *languages*, with a focus on representations. In accounting for Sapir's particular views on phonology, which correlate with his focus on language (not grammar) viewed culturally, and in a historical and contingent (non-biological) fashion, Anderson offers this explanation:

> In the social and political context of the 1920s and 1930s (and subsequently), this stress on environment rather than heredity as a determinant of human cognitive functions and attitudes was generally felt to be an important contribution of the social sciences, useful in supporting 'liberal' positions on desirable social change.
>
> (1985: 223)

In other words, Anderson explains Sapir's theory of language, in part, by situating it in its own historically contingent social and political framework. I heartily approve. The next move would be to put the focus on *grammar* in its historically contingent social and political framework – something Newmeyer in *The Politics of Linguistics* (1986) was not quite able to do. All theories and approaches – not just some – operate in some social and political context or another, and not just when a particular theory seems to promote some perceived social "good." Linguistic theory is not more insulated today from time and place than it was in the 1920s and 1930s, in the 1870s, in the 1820s, or in the 1770s.

Louise Pound (1872–1958)

The "crinoline curtain" that has hung over the history of American linguistics (and the sciences in general) lifts with Louise Pound. She also ties in Mencken's *American Language* to the rest of the American academic linguistic scene by having helped him with subsequent editions of this work and by having maintained a life-long correspondence with him. Mencken readily acknowledged her generous help in the various Prefaces of *The American Language*.

In terms of her educational pedigree, Louise Pound is, furthermore, thoroughly integrated into the general history of American linguistics. Nebraska born and bred, she first received her linguistic instruction at the University of Nebraska in the late 1880s and early 1890s from a well-educated faculty assembled in Lincoln. She had as teachers C.E. Bennett, who became head of Classics at Cornell, and August Hjalmer Edgren, a Yale PhD and student of William Dwight Whitney, who later became rector of the University of Gothenburg, Sweden (Eble 1987). She received her Master's from the University of Nebraska in 1895, and then went to the University of Chicago in 1897 and 1898 for further graduate work. There she took a course from George Hempl (the *grease/greasy* man), who had studied for three years at Goettingen, Tuebingen, Strassburg, Jena, and Berlin, taking his doctorate at Jena in 1889. She herself then spent the year 1899–1900 at the University of Heidelberg, where she studied with Johannes Hoops, editor of *Englische Studien*. She received her PhD within that year.

Upon her return to the United States, she became an adjunct Professor at Nebraska in 1900, joined the Dialect Society in 1901, and became editor of *American Speech* in 1925, along with Kemp Malone of Johns Hopkins and A.G. Kennedy of Stanford. Pound was particularly active in the Dialect Society, for which she provided an interesting and valuable "A Historical Sketch." In this piece, Pound states that, without doubt, the establishment of *American Speech* was influenced by the existence of the Dialect Society (1952: 27); and although Mencken's *The American Language* of 1919 can hardly be claimed to have been inspired by the Dialect Society, Mencken did make much use of its publications in subsequent editions and in later years became a member – reluctantly, one might assume, from Pound's study (1952: 27). Again, the academic and the non-academic intersect here, especially at the meeting where Mencken appeared on one of the Dialect Society's programs, "an event that attracted an unusually large attendance for that meeting" (1952: 27).

As one of her co-editors of *American Speech*, Arthur Kennedy has written in the "Foreword" to *The Selected Writings of Louise Pound* that "Not many decades ago the English philologist devoted his attention chiefly to Early English; today, he is willing to give equally serious attention to the language of his own day." For this shift in attention, Kennedy opines that "in large measure . . . Louise Pound has helped to make this possible" (in Pound 1949: xi). A glance over the range of subjects Pound chose to write about confirms that she, in the grand tradition of American linguistics, chose to view language in a radically non-autonomous manner. Further study of Pound's view of language and her impact on the development of certain trends in twentieth-century American linguistics is only to be encouraged.[9]

AUTONOMY ENVISIONED

This far-from-exhaustive overview of the work of Boas, Bloomfield, Sapir, and Pound has been presented primarily in the service of understanding the kinds of theoretical and disciplinary autonomy that American linguists were searching for in the early 1920s. I suspect, however, that it is anachronistic to collocate the actual term "autonomy" with the time-frame of "the early 1920s." I have not yet come across any linguist of the period using that specific word.[10] Nevertheless, if that orientation which one (i.e. any given reader of this history or perhaps only myself) would now identify as "autonomous linguistics" does indeed exist, then I would argue that the possibilities of that "autonomy" were certainly envisioned by the mid-1920s. Although I would also argue that this search for – perhaps "groping toward" is a better phrase here, for it does not invest the historical direction with intentionality – autonomy was a group effort, the possibilities of that autonomy were most programmatically sketched out by Leonard Bloomfield.

Now, a discussion of the concept of "autonomy" with regard to twentieth-century linguistics takes us down as many winding and intertwining paths as would, say, a discussion of the concept of *arbitraire* in eighteenth-century language studies. To frame the entire discussion, let me first argue *against* the idea that a programmatic elaboration of theoretical and disciplinary autonomy conceived of by any one linguist (say, Bloomfield) *preceded* the overt manifestations of theoretical and disciplinary autonomy, e.g. the establishment of the Linguistic Society of America in 1924, as a group separate from either the Modern Language Association or the American Philological Association. Instead, I would say that these overt manifestations – i.e. the establishment of the Linguistic Society of America or the writing of a specific document, e.g. Bloomfield's "Set of Postulates for the Science of Language" (1926) – *sum up* a disciplinary trend rather than begin one.

That trend can be traced back to the 1880s and 1890s and the epistemological aftermath of the *Lautgesetz* controversy, when it was determined what the object of "linguistic science" should be, namely the regularities found in language. Let us remember that the American Philological Association was established *before* the 1880s and under the aegis of William Dwight Whitney, whose conception of language was not sympathetic to Neogrammarianism.

Before Bloomfield's organizational efforts and written pronouncements of the mid-1920s, the discipline of linguistics was *already* in the process of sorting itself out – as we have seen in Chapters 4 and 5. The arcs of development had separated without any one particular person announcing that they had separated or that there were even any arcs *to* separate. In the half-century before the establishment of the Linguistic Society of America, a variety of departments devoted to various aspects of language and language study were being established in academic institutions and proliferating on the American scene, positions were being created and filled, course work was being drawn up and taught, and all the while journals were being founded and editorial policies decided. A significant practical framework was already in place by 1924, such that the founding of two separate journals, such as *Language* and *American Speech*, captured a distinction between the interests of two already separate groups. Of course, these groups partially overlapped: for instance, the first editors of *American Speech*, Louise Pound, Kemp Malone, and Arthur Kennedy were foundation members of the Linguistic Society of America.

To play on the insight of Hymes and Fought, who realize that "A true history of linguistics . . . should not proceed as if linguistics were never done, but only stated and organized" (1981 [1975]: 919), I would say that after several decades of linguistics "getting done," it *then* gets "stated and organized."

An indication of the kinds of autonomy being sought by American linguists in the period immediately preceding the establishment of the Linguistic Society of America can be extracted from a very short piece written by Bloomfield: to wit, his 1923 review of the second edition of Saussure's *Cours*. The interest of this review was first suggested to me by Joseph (1987a). I hope to add to Joseph's analysis by anchoring Bloomfield's review in the context of this present history of American linguistics.

In this review of Saussure, Bloomfield sketches out a triple passage to autonomy for American linguistics:

1 Bloomfield is carving out a place for American linguistics, a national autonomy, one separate from the European "yoke." He downplays the sense that Saussure's *Cours* represented a radical departure (in Europe) from what had come before (in Europe). "The value of the *Cours*," Bloomfield opines, "lies in its clear and rigorous demonstration of fundamental principles. Most of what the author says has long been 'in the air' and has been here and there fragmentarily expressed; the systematization is his own" (1923: 318). Among those ideas already known that the *Cours* has merely systematized, Bloomfield mentions: "It is known that the historical change in language goes on in a surprisingly mechanical way, independent of any needs, desires, or fears of the speakers" (1923: 318; also quoted in Joseph 1987a). In other words, Saussure belongs more or less to the line of "mechanical linguists," the Neogrammarians, and cannot, therefore, be thought to be innovative. Given that and Saussure's psychology, which does not go "beyond the crudest popular notions" (1923: 318), Bloomfield is creating a place for his own "true" innovative contribution: the integration of the home-grown American Weissian behaviorism to linguistics. Whatever else can be said about the sense of radical departure effected by Saussure that was inherited by the late twentieth century, it does not come by way of Bloomfield.

Sapir was also given to disparagement of European linguists and the valorization of American linguists. On the subject of the quality of the publications of the Bureau of American Ethnology, Sapir flatly refuses to make any direct comparison of American Indian linguistic work with that of most Indo-Germanic philologists. The latter deal with written records whose accuracy is beyond personal control, while the former must take full responsibility for all field records. "There is therefore no use contrasting the breathless finesse of a German *Lautschieber*," Sapir writes, not without irony, "with the relatively rough and ready carrying-on of the majority of Indian linguists." But Sapir does not leave the matter there. He continues:

Anyway, most of us have a shrewd suspicion that many a renowned denizen of the German universities, impressive in his balancing of imponderable phonologic nuances, would find himself sadly up a tree when confronted with the live problems of an intricate Indian language that he was forced to study by pure induction.

(1917: 79)

The French fare no better at Sapir's hands. Not many years later, in reviewing Meillet and Cohen's *Les Langues du monde*, Sapir observes that "It was cruel to assign the vast field of American Indian languages to a single specialist. No one person living today could even begin to get his bearings on it, let alone do justice to it." Sapir suggests that "it might have been necessary for the editors to go outside of France" to secure the co-operation of at least one other specialist, but they did not do so. He concludes, again not without heavy irony:

> If it was the intention of the editors to show how well an essentially international task could be carried out with the splendid resources of French scholarship alone, all we can say is that they must be congratulated on coming as near solving an impossible task as it was reasonably possible to do.

(1925b: 375)

The disparagement of European studies of American Indian languages and the valorization of American studies of American Indian languages at the expense of European approaches to language is a tradition at least as old as is the study of American Indian languages in America.

2 In his review of Saussure, Bloomfield, echoing Sapir's comments above, does not miss the opportunity to jab at the Europeans' lack of field work. This lack is intertwined, in this review, with Bloomfield's commitment to the linguist as teacher of foreign languages, which is distinguished from the European linguists' corresponding lack of commitment to the teaching of foreign languages. By 1923, Bloomfield had already worked on Tagalog through an informant. In 1923, Bloomfield was also employed by the Department of German and Linguistics at Ohio State, where some of his duties included the teaching of German, and was so employed for most of his academic career, that is, until 1940 and his appointment as Sterling Professor of Linguistics at Yale.

Bloomfield criticizes Saussure not only for his lack of any

"psychology beyond the crudest popular notions," but also for his phonetics, which "are an abstraction from French and Swiss-German which will not stand even the test of an application to English" (1923: 318). He concludes the passage with the remark that

> Needless to say, a person who goes out to write down an unknown language or one who undertakes to teach people a foreign language, must have a knowledge of phonetics, just as he must possess tact, patience, and many other virtues . . .
>
> (1923: 318)

The next clause, however, mitigates what he has just written: ". . . in principle, however, these things are all on a par, and do not form part of linguistic theory."

Here Bloomfield is distinguishing between the linguist as theorist and the linguist as teacher of foreign languages, a distinction which did not exist for Whitney, whose political conception of language and commitment to the idea of linguist as general member of society did not find a tension between the theoretical and pedagogic activities. For Whitney, the pedagogical was political, the political was pedagogical, and the whole of his activity coherently mirrored his conception of language. Of course, when the political time came (World War II) for Bloomfield to engage in political action of a linguistic sort, he did contribute actively through the Intensive Language Program. However, he perceived something of a schism between his teaching and his theorizing, a schism for which his theorizing itself is responsible.

Sapir's teaching career does not seem less problematic than Bloomfield's. From 1910 to 1925, he was Chief of the Division of Anthropology within the Geological Survey of Canada (see Darnell 1984 and Murray 1981 for discussion of Sapir's Canadian years). According to the Sapir–Kroeber correspondence, beginning in 1921, Sapir wished to leave Ottawa, owing to the intellectual isolation there (Golla 1984: 364, note 1). Kroeber states the situation baldly: "There is no doubt you [Sapir] should leave Ottawa. The means of getting away is likely to be less certain. There aren't many Universities with a professorship of linguistics. I doubt whether we [at the University of California, Berkeley] shall ever have an opening for you" (January 17, 1921). Kroeber expressed a similar regret a few months later (April 29, 1921). The correspondence ends in 1925 with Kroeber's assurance that Sapir will hear from him by the time he is settled in Chicago.

Let us remember that Sapir was housed first in the Department of Anthropology and Linguistics. Again, when he was appointed at Yale in 1931, he was Sterling Professor of Anthropology and Linguistics. That is, linguistics as a discipline was not yet institutionally "autonomous," but Bloomfield is certainly suggesting already in 1923 that it could be or should be.

3   In his review of Saussure, Bloomfield notes that Saussure distinguishes sharply between "synchronic" and "diachronic" linguistics (1923: 318), but then Bloomfield turns around and equates "historical linguistics" with *la linguistique diachronique* (1923: 319) – a move Saussure was determined *not* to make (see Harris 1987: 87ff. for a minute analysis of Saussure's distinction). Whatever the reasons for Bloomfield's misunderstanding of Saussure's distinction, it did serve the purpose of making the study of "historical Indo-European grammar (the great achievement of the past century) . . . merely a single province [of linguistic study]" (1923: 319). The more Bloomfield could dissociate the nineteenth century from the twentieth and traditional French and German linguistics from American linguistics, the better rhetorical position he stood in to form the Linguistic Society of America.

As Roman Jakobson tells the story, the formation of the Linguistic Society of America had more to do with new developments in Eastern Europe than Old World traditions in Western Europe, namely with the Moscow Linguistic Circle and the Prague Linguistic Circle (1979: 161–2). Already in 1923, we see that Bloomfield was distancing himself from France and Saussure. After all, the French had established their Société de Linguistique over a half-century earlier (1865), and so their model could no longer be considered the most forward-looking or progressive.

Although the "foreign policy" interests of the Linguistic Society of America were to shift from Paris to Prague in the 1930s, the affiliations of the foundation members of the Linguistic Society of America in 1924 sum up, in effect, American linguistic activity in the period immediately preceding 1924, revealing the strong Western European orientation which Bloomfield, among others, was ultimately reacting against. Of the 264 foundation members listed in the first issue of *Language*, only 204 included their specialties, and 60 did not indicate a university address, among them Sapir and Goddard. There is a total of twenty-five women in the list. Among those foundation members who were academically employed (sixteen of the twenty-five women), about two-thirds came from fields traditionally linked with nineteenth-century German scholarship: Germanic and/or Indo-European philology (40), Greek and Latin (44), and English, with its heavy German-language orientation (48). Romance Languages also had strong representation (39), as well as Semitic (12). The other third was made up of a composite of anthropology (12), psychology (4), phonetics (2), Oriental languages (3), and philosophy (2).[11]

Bloomfield envisioned a triple autonomy for American linguistics, the science of language: an autonomy from European approaches; an institutional, disciplinary autonomy (teaching duties, departmental affiliations, separate society, separate journal); and an autonomy from the historical development of the field, i.e. the nineteenth-century German conception of historical linguistics.

All these autonomies for the disciplinary pursuit of linguistics were predicated on a prior autonomy, that of *language* from "something else." That "something else" was identified, above, by Bloomfield, again in his review of Saussure. To the implicit question "From what is language [here, historical change] independent?" Bloomfield answered: from "any needs, desires, or fears of the speakers" (1923: 318). Sixty years later and in the same vein, Frederic Newmeyer was moved to write on the subject of autonomous linguists and *their* beliefs that "all autonomous linguists share the belief that a language can be analyzed successfully without taking into consideration the society or beliefs of its speakers" (quoted above p. 31). My story is now complete: my end of 1924 no longer points backward to 1769, for Noah Webster and William Dwight Whitney are here definitively factored out, but forward to 1989.

The next chapter in American linguistics, then, is that of "autonomous linguistics." Hymes and Fought have succinctly told that story. Contrary to the epoch-making claims of transformational–generative grammarians, Hymes and Fought see more continuities than ruptures between structuralism and transformationalism, when they write either from the point of view of autonomy as a theoretical premise, that

We do in fact think that if the fundamental premise of structuralism is seen as the study of language as an autonomous system, a system central to the understanding of the history and use of language, but to be analyzed independently of history and use first, then the ways in which Chomsky's work continues preceding structuralism and completes it seem more decisive than the ways in which it does not.

Or from the point of view of autonomy as a goal, that

Or, if we see in the history of structuralism a complex development, with specific complexities at any one time, and the autonomy of linguistic form as an initial impulse and goal gradually arrived at, then again the unfolding and deepening of that impulse and goal would seem to culminate, so far as we can now see, in Chomsky's work.

In either case, they continue:

All of the preceding steps in the exploration of autonomous linguistic form are given a place in a single system, and the autonomy of that system from history and use is rationalized, indeed, given the noblest significance possible, by interpreting it in terms of the human mind, of the distinctive powers of human nature.

(1981 [1975]: 922)

In light of the above summary, in light of the preceding history of American linguistics, and in light of a variety of new approaches and perspectives to emerge on language in the early 1980s and to converge in the late 1980s, a series of questions might be profitably asked anew: In what sense is linguistics autonomous? In what sense is language (or, then, *grammar*) autonomous? In what sense does one – or can one – *successfully* analyze a language without taking into account the society or beliefs of its speakers? And if one does challenge this autonomy and its predicted success, does one at the same time threaten the hard-won integrity of the discipline of linguistics?

CONCLUSION: AMERICAN LINGUISTICS CIRCA 1990

The historical record of linguistics has long been for me a source for thinking about language. The historiographic approach has consistently provided me with a way of thinking about language, that is with a way of examining present ideas, claims, concerns, premises, and/or approaches to language by comparing them to the ways other thinkers in other times and at other places have thought and theorized about language. The historiographic approach is, in this sense, a "comparative method" of linguistic theories whose (admittedly elusive) goal is some understanding of the phenomenon of language by studying the various frames that have been fitted (and have failed to fit) over this "object" language in the past. The historiographic approach has required of me a long apprenticeship, to be sure, and has been one that has been anything but obvious in the context of "doing" linguistics in the United States during the last several decades.

This is not a lament. With the help of a congenial and international group of historiographers, I have persisted in finding that the historical record of linguistics in general and of American linguistics in particular yields a rich source for thinking about language. So that there is no mistake about what this "thinking about language" might entail, I have not approached the historical record in gleeful anticipation of finding the "first" person to have said something or to have advanced some theory, nor even to discover "lost" ancestors of the type: the "first" structuralist or the "first" transformationalist. Neither have I conceived of the historiographer's primary job *necessarily* to be the uncovering of previously "known" facts about language that have since been "forgotten," thus making of the historiographer the guardian of a (n ever-growing) pool of information designed to prevent "the reinvention of the wheel." However, if one wished to make a more elegant case for the study of linguistic history as "preventive medicine," one could certainly claim a need for its study on the grounds that the historical record of linguistics has become too rich to insure that all productive, interesting, and/or useful approaches, insights, and/or theories about language could be adequately transmitted by any one school of thought or approach to language or, then, even, by any one history.

Neither is the historiographer a referee on the sidelines, only watching and not doing linguistics, whose job it is, in a contest of competing theories, to determine the winner. Nor, by the same token, does the historiographer feel it incumbent upon her to demonstrate an "underlying" unity to all divergent approaches or to reconcile contradictory positions, to reassure other (not historiographically inclined) linguists that the noisy, fractious field of linguistics and the linguists in it are, and always have been, one big, happy family.

However, with respect to reconciling seemingly divergent points of view, I will take this opportunity to suggest that the approach taken in John Haiman's edited volume *Iconicity in Syntax* of 1985 (a way of thinking about language I find particularly satisfying; see Andresen 1987b) and Whitney's "Phusei or thesei – Natural or Conventional?" paper of 1875 (another way of thinking about language I find satisfying) are not as incompatible as they might at first appear. In his Introduction, Haiman alludes to Whitney's paper as "one of the most uncompromising attacks on iconicity" (1985: 2) – a statement which seems to set Whitney's work against Haiman's.[1] Yet, in his article, Whitney is arguing for the arbitrariness of the sign primarily as a way of arguing against the (nineteenth-century) association of language and race; and he is pointedly attacking "that great apostle of the phusei theory, Steinthal" (1971 [1875]: 120) and the latter's idea that society is "merely" the medium "in which the heaven-implanted germs of speech can develop themselves," which, for Steinthal, made language an "instinctive human product" (1971 [1875]: 121). Whitney, like Haiman and others, was against the idea of any (let us say, anachronistically) *autonomous* approach to language that would cut language and the study of language off from use, from history, or from its social setting. Viewing language as a radically institutional product of the sociopolitical and historical "workings out" and classifications of the group, Whitney (as opposed to Steinthal, or even Max Mueller) did not see the particular language input (again, speaking here anachronistically) as the variable "trigger" to the universal grammar "hard-wired" in the autonomous and innate language faculty of the individual.

Instead of insisting on a reconciliation between the iconic approach and Whitney's sociopolitical approach, however, let us see them rather as complementary. In fact, that is exactly how Traugott (herself a contributor to the Haiman volume) sees it in her article "On Regularity in Semantic Change" (1985). There she argues that "the philological/sociohistorical view of semantic change . . . developed in the nineteenth century" (1985: 158) and her own cognitive approach "must ideally complement each other in any full theory of semantic change" (1985: 168). Her article points the way to understanding regularity in semantic change – an area previously considered exempt from lawfulness.[2] She concludes by arguing for the idea that experience, general cognition, and semantic structures interpenetrate to a greater degree than is allowed in modularist approaches, and against the idea that what is non-modular is intractable (i.e. "non-scientific") (1985: 169–70).

While on the subject of widening the contexts for understanding language and the study of language, I note that even the entire phusei–thesei debate itself can be interpreted in a wider historical and political context. As Roy Harris, in *The Language-Makers* (1980), suggested, the ancient debate over natural nomenclaturism and the modern debate over linguistic innateness are "explicable only in light of their immediate political, social and academic background" (1980: 185). Both debates are woven into the webs of moral and political responsibilities of their times. Harris writes:

> In ancient Greece the responsibilities were those attendant upon a new form of social organisation: democracy. Today, the responsibilities are also those conferred by the potentialities of power. But the power in question is no longer confined within the political framework of the community.
>
> (1980: 186; also quoted, in part, in Auroux 1986b: 23)

In establishing the origins of the modern debate in terms of a nineteenth-century Darwin–(Max) Mueller confrontation, Harris notes: "It throws an interesting light on modern intellectual history that whereas Darwin's views about evolution as a whole triumphed, it was Mueller's views about the uniqueness of language which survived" (1980: 171). He then concludes, however, in light of recent studies of the non-uniqueness of human abilities in the animal kingdom:

> If we wish to understand why belief in man's monopoly of language, having survived the Darwinian revolution, eventually came under attack when it did, the answer must be sought in the social, political and intellectual climate that has developed in the West since 1945.
>
> (1980: 186)

I also note that the century-long glorification of "Language as the Rubicon which no brute will dare to cross" has something to do with the fact that Mueller's views on language triumphed, while Whitney's did not, which is not divorced from our understanding of the past history of linguistic theory and debate. Neither, then, is the "rediscovery" of the ethological concept of language independent of our historical rethinking. In any case, Harris does not seem to me to be wrong in his contextualization of the issue in the framework of reflection on the "morality of wielding world power."

Lastly, with respect to what the historiographer does and does not do (and as is clear from the foregoing two paragraphs), the historiographer (namely, myself) is not neutral with respect to where her interests, sympathies, and tastes lie in the current marketplace of academic linguistic ideas. Nor does it follow that in finding an approach interesting or sympathetic – e.g. Whitney's – does she find *all* of it interesting or sympathetic.

So what does a historiographer such as myself do? The same thing as other linguists: think, investigate, gather information, and write about language. However, if the historiographic approach has a particular function (i.e. can be of some use to other linguists or to anyone else), that function might best be described as "therapeutic," where the historiographic investigation functions as a "biofeedback mechanism" for linguists. That is to say that our past is not "just history," and that many problems in language studies uncritically inherited from the past and now institutionalized act as intellectual straitjackets unless we find a way of reconceptualizing those problems and reshaping our institutional practices. I argue that present problems and practices are products of our past, and that we are influenced by historical trends and ideas all the time, even though (or, perhaps, particularly because) the study of our linguistic past is considered to be a waste of time – or, more pertinently with respect to American linguistics – our past has generally been considered *not to exist*.

Now, with this rather grand claim for the "therapeutic" value of historiography, does it not follow that the historiographer, by knowing this past, should be able to have the "inside edge" on all our problems, and, thereby, be able to forecast the future? Not necessarily. However, being so immersed in historical perspectives, she is certainly more tempted, perhaps, to prognosticate than others. I see no reason to resist the temptation.

To return to the questions I posed at the end of Chapter 5 which turn on the concept of autonomy, I do not see a bright future for the approach to language which presupposes the autonomy of syntax or phonology and whose theory of mind is modular. Rather, I do see a bright future for those approaches which integrate the study of language into use, society, history, and general cognition. I do see a bright future for those approaches to language which do not draw data from introspection. I do see a bright future for those approaches to language which have not isolated, *a priori*, the "adult grammar of the native speaker" as the interesting "object" of investigation but which, instead, integrate new findings in human biology, evolution, the brain, and studies of language origin, both phylogenetic and ontogenetic. A good theory of language will be like any theory respecting human behavior: it must be a *biological* theory, consistent with evolution, consistent with an individual's development, and, like any good theory, testable at many levels.

This is hardly prophecy, however. I feel as though, in some sense, many linguists have already closed the chapter on our autonomous moment – a moment that extends back through the last hundred years, in my historical estimation, to Neogrammarianism, the moment when, as our received history tells us, linguistics finally became "scientific," that is when it was determined that a language changes in a surprisingly regular fashion that is somehow impervious to the knowledge, beliefs, goals, or intentions of its speakers. In the last one hundred years, the investigation of the regularities has moved from that of "sound laws admit of no exceptions" to those phonological and morphological regularities of structuralism to the rule-governed syntactic structures of transformationalism and on to the regularities of semantic change, where the study of language spills out over (and again) into the realms of the knowledge, beliefs, goals, and intentions of its speakers.

This is *in no way* to disparage the achievements of the last one hundred years, or the last thirty years, of linguistics. Nevertheless, I believe that many linguists have already turned away from rationalist and autonomous interpretations of the syntactic regularities of the last thirty years and have returned to the study of language as human behavior in both the cognitive and social settings. As most linguists born before 1970 know, "behaviorism" has been until recently – and perhaps still is – something of a dirty word in linguistic circles. However, those studies I find satisfying now are the ones that depart from an enriched and enhanced sense of behaviorism to be found in the work, for instance, of Studdert-Kennedy and others, who devote an entire volume, *The Psychobiology of Language* (1983), to an investigation and critique of the linguist's description of language as an autonomous cognitive system.

Since this is my conclusion, I will take the liberty of turning straight to Studdert-Kennedy's conclusion on the question of the autonomy of language. Autonomy for the linguist, Studdert-Kennedy writes, "refers to the fact that the formal apparatus of primitive terms and relations needed to describe the two subsystems [here: syntax and phonology] are distinct and, indeed, incommensurable with respect both to one another and to other modes of cognition." However,

> as soon as we consider how such formally distinct processes might be instantiated in the nervous system, the sharp distinctions begin to blur. . . . this does not mean that separable subsystems within language do not exist; it means only that they are not readily isolated in practice. This serves to emphasize that all studies of brain activity in language function will be of dubious value until we can increase our knowledge of neural circuitry . . . . Systems are conceptually recalcitrant because, by definition, they consist of parts that are both separable and connected. In other words, full autonomy of language, or its subsystems, is neurologically implausible.
>
> (1983: 224)

The task for the biologist, then, is to derive the properties of language from the properties of its components. That is, the biologist's "task is to understand how language as a system emerged from some novel combination of more primitive, non-linguistic mechanisms" (1983: 225). Where do we look for understanding? To the individual, for

> the unit of natural selection is the individual, not the gene, or even the gene complex. Moreover, the unit is the individual in relation to other individuals – very obviously so in the case of interlocking patterns of social behavior, such as language.
>
> (1983: 3)

Studies in glossogenetics suggest that language was not planned and produced from scratch by a guiding intelligence (God, Reason, or any other mental "leap"), but is rather the outcome of trial-and-error, step-by-step "tinkering."

Evolution, too, seems to be primarily a matter of "tinkering," of using what is there, adjusting and readjusting those elements to produce new objects of increasing complexity. If we accept this, then we must also acknowledge several puzzles in language whose answers do not seem to be coming from within linguistic theory as it is presently conceived.

1 The almost overwhelming problem of how to account for complex syntactic structures seems to have an amazingly simple answer in the study of Simon "The Architecture of Complexity" (1962) (referred to in Sampson 1980: 240). A complex organization, be it social, biological, physical, or symbolic, has a greater chance of being put together over time if it is hierarchically organized. Simon argues that "complex systems will evolve from simple systems much more rapidly if there are stable intermediate forms than if there are not" (1962: 473), where the stable intermediary forms are "subassemblies" which are hierarchically organized and which possess a special property, "near decomposability," which allows for interactions among the subsystems. Simon's proposal, which I have hardly explained here, seems worth working into the other two puzzles I outline next.

2 It does not seem likely that we can understand meaning through introspection. In evolutionary perspective, meaning might arise in the case of an animal needing to move appropriately, needing to recognize things as prey, or as food, or as nest-building

material. This seems consistent with the concept of Evolutionarily Stable Strategies outlined in Parker (1984). An Evolutionarily Stable Strategy is a competitive optimum adopted by most members of a population, which is not designed to deal with some fixed condition, such as the onset of winter, but which rather depends critically on the types and frequencies of the other strategies adopted by the other members of the population. Language as an Evolutionarily Stable Strategy depends strongly on the strategies played by other individuals, with meaning arising as a pay-off for needing to know where the good berries are or how to keep warm.

3 The most vexing problem confronting those linguists not transformationally–generatively inclined has been in the arena of language acquisition. Generative theory has hammered home the point about the extreme rapidity and accuracy with which children all over the world learn their first language especially in the presence of defective stimuli. This argument supports the idea of an innate language faculty. In a recent review, (again) Sampson points to the promise of Parallel Distributed Processing as an empirical approach which demonstrates that "the rule-governed nature of linguistic behavior need not involve rules at all" (1987: 873). These studies have shown that the knowledge of the past-tense network of English, for instance, "is derived entirely from the external inputs. No inductive leap from data to theory ever occurs" (1987: 877).

It is satisfying to me to have new studies which counter the accepted (generative) account of, say, David Lightfoot in *The Language Lottery*, who consistently returns to the point of the "impoverished input conditions" of language learners and concludes that "an account of language acquisition should not depict children only as good mimics, slaves to their accidental experiences, reproducing only what they have heard and knowing only those things for which there is direct evidence in their experience" (1983: 208).[3]

If (as I am arguing here) the autonomous approach to language has outlived its usefulness, if it is actually *not needed* for explanation, is it not then the case that the present disciplinary nature of linguistic practice is threatened? Yes. The most extreme expression of the consequences of this threat is found, once again, in

Sampson, who concludes his *Schools of Linguistics* with the observation that:

> The true general theory of language is that there is no general theory of language; the only features common to all human languages are predictable consequences of principles belonging to other, established disciplines, so that there is no room in the intellectual arena for an independent theoretical subject called "general linguistics."

(1980: 241)

If Sampson is right, should we not then panic and/or despair? Not at all. In any case, Sampson's statement might have seemed more radical, and therefore, threatening, in 1980 than in 1990. Revision is now taking place across many of those "established disciplines" Sampson refers to as well as in the discipline of linguistics, which was never a theoretical or practical whole in the first place. For instance, Ladefoged and Halle have recently called for a "large-scale revision" of the International Phonetic Alphabet which, they note, is nearly one hundred years old. The revision is certainly inconvenient, but they argue convincingly for the need to undertake such a revision (1988). Likewise for the charting and recharting of the branches and subbranches of the Indo-European languages found in every textbook of the last hundred years (see Introduction, p. 14) – and for many other aspects of disciplinary theory and practice.

At the same time, and emerging out of the field of literary studies (which is experiencing its own revision), come the rich and linguistically well-informed critiques of judgment and value and language and communication in the work of Bourdieu (1982, 1984 [1979]) and Smith (1988). From Bourdieu we derive a concept of culture that is the mediating link between ruling-class interests and everyday life, which takes its shape from his notion of cultural capital as the different sets of linguistic and cultural competencies that individuals inherit by way of the class-located boundaries of their family. His thorough politicization of culture, linguistic practices, and even schooling make it difficult to imagine a future pragmatics which ignores his theories, or a concept of language which does not recognize it as instrumental to the playing out of relations of power, or even the teaching of linguistics in the classroom which does not recognize its social and political responsibilities.

251

For her part, Smith has mounted, among other arguments, an effective post-structuralist critique of truth value which calls into question the inherited ("essentialist" or "foundationalist") notions of "communication" that extend back (in my history) to Locke and forward to Grice and are encoded in Whitney's belief in "mutual intelligence, which is the great object of speech" (1971 [1875]: 118). For Smith, there is *no* "communication" in the sense either of the *"making common* of something (for example, 'knowledge') that was previously the possession of one party or in the sense of a *transferral or transmission of the same* (information, feelings, beliefs, and so on) from one to the other" (1988: 109). Smith is, quite rightly, critical of Grice and Habermas and "speech-act theorists generally" who do not recognize that listeners are also agents or that listeners' actions and reactions are more than just listening and understanding (1988: 204–5, note 31).

In light of the above pages, the unsatisfying aspects of, say, Whitney's thought can be easily identified: 1) although he was committed to the political conception of language, his "idealist" model of communication obscured the particular power that he personally wielded as a typical nineteenth-century white, Anglo-Saxon, American male. He was certainly aware of that power and deliberately wrote from that position. For him, however, it was somehow "natural"; 2) the particular dimension of the political conception of language from Webster to Whitney with its explicit doctrine of Manifest Destiny for the English language is – to say the very least – politically inappropriate in the second half of the twentieth century. I will only refer here to Harris's acknowledgement of the problems and responsibilities of wielding world power; and I will leave it to another historian entirely to determine whether the doctrine of Manifest Destiny for the English language was also politically inappropriate for the nineteenth century.

I return to my initial statement of this Conclusion, that the historical record of linguistics has consistently provided me with a source for thinking about language. For me, this record has served not only as the source of our present theories and practices; it is also the source of ideas "already thought up" against which one can imagine that which has not "already been thought up." Scanning the historical record, I see a parade of images and metaphors designed to capture the particularity of the "object" language. In condensed version, I perceive for the eighteenth century a static model of language and mind as mechanism. In the nineteenth century, the triumphant metaphor was of language conceived as a dynamic organism. In the twentieth, Saussure taught us that language was not concrete *substance* but rather *forme*, and reconceived the object of linguistic science to be static *langue*. Chomsky later recast *langue* into a dynamic competence. The investigation subsequently focused on (adult) grammar with language acquisition viewed non-problematically, or at least, succinctly, with the assumption of innate "hard-wiring," whose specifics would be spelled out in the course of the elaboration of the grammar.

Perhaps "language" is not any of these "things" at all (not even a formal thing or a rule-governed abstract grammar) but rather a reflection of *verbal eventings*, that is to say, then, a *behavior*, a social behavioral *strategy*, consistent with other animal and behavioral strategies, whose instantiation is not fundamentally different from the communication strategies discussed in "Animal Signals: Mind-Reading and Manipulation" (Krebs and Dawkins 1984).[4] Nor is language acquisition conceived of differently – if one wishes to close the historical circle – than in the strongly empiricist account provided in Condillac's 1746 *Essai*, albeit without the rationalist underpinnings or goal of enlightenment or idealist model of communication.

In its instantiation, acquisition, and maintenance, this behavioral strategy could be seen, in Smith's terminology, as the result of the *differentially consequential interactions* of the verbal agents:

> that is, an interaction in which each party acts in relation to the other differently – in different, asymmetric ways and in accord with different specific motives – and also with different consequences for each. It is inevitable that there will be disparities between what is "transmitted" and what is "received" in any exchange simply by virtue of the different states and circumstances of the "sender" and "receiver," including what will always be the differences – sometimes quite significant ones – produced by their inevitably different life-histories as verbal creatures.

> (1988: 109)

I note, in addition, that *regularities*, or predictabilities, are nevertheless produced as results of these differentially consequential interactions, and those regularities have produced "objects" we call English or Swahili or Papua, with all of the attendant, hierarchically organized subregularities. "Language," then, becomes the regularized product of the differentially consequential results of the intersections of verbally interacting members of some, and the same, community; however, the regularization or the standardization that results is a consequence and not a premise, i.e. it is not "built into" the preprogram for the product. The regularities are results of the intersections of all the previous effective social interactions: those intersections that have worked for an individual verbal agent interacting with other verbal agents who have their own experiential history of what verbal strategies have worked for them.

My ideas in the Conclusion are eclectic and the deliberately idiosyncratic results of my own "tinkerings." Whether or not they are "voted for" or "seconded" by anyone else is going to be the product of the "shaking-down" and regularizing process of my own speaking community of linguists over time.

My approach to the historical record is not nostalgic. There is no sense of a wishful return to a prelapsarian state of language studies – say, the one that came before the mean, old "exceptionless sound-law" Neogrammarians – when the recognition of the political dimensions of language made language theory "better" or "more accurate" or even when linguists were more "unified." (They certainly were not more unified "in the good old days.") Nor, then, is my historiographic approach a vision that "the best is yet to come." It is not even an affirmation that "we're on the right track now." (Investigators always think they are on the right track. Otherwise, they would not be on it.) Whatever else a historiographer does and does not do, she does claim that it is the case that the future path is securely, even *inescapably*, forged by our past and by our view of that past.

NOTES

PREFACE: AMERICAN LINGUISTICS CIRCA 1925

1 For an excellent account of "what happens next" in American linguistics after 1925, I refer the reader to *American Structuralism* (1981 [1975]) by Dell Hymes and John Fought. Another excellent historiographic study proves to be Stephen Anderson's *Phonology in the Twentieth Century. Theories of Rules and Representations* (1985), which is both narrower in scope in that it focuses exclusively on phonology and wider in scope in that it incorporates international trends. For the more recent period and with a very different way of writing history, there is also Frederick Newmeyer's *Linguistic Theory in America. The First Twenty-five Years of Transformational Generative Grammar* (1986 [1980]).

2 See Joseph (1987a) for a finely nuanced appreciation of Bloomfield's Saussureanism.

3 Hymes and Fought identify the crystalization of an "American" approach to linguistics in the late 1930s and early 1940s (1981 [1975]: 910–12, 1019). Among all the many good reasons Joseph (1987a) cites for Bloomfield's rather sly criticisms of Saussure, Joseph does not mention Bloomfield's desire to reject European-style linguistics in order to valorize his "American" approach, nor Bloomfield's stated connection to Whitney's work and approach (see also Chapters 3 and 5).

4 Frederick Newmeyer's recent book *The Politics of Linguistics* [1986], which is, in effect, the history of and apology for autonomous linguistics, would have benefited from an improved sense of "political." Newmeyer is apparently unwilling to see the politics of his own position, which is that of classical rationalism. Thus, he repeatedly fails to recognize that the history he is writing of autonomous linguistics is itself political, thereby lending either irony or confusion to his very title. For a critique of Newmeyer that cuts through the confusion, see Smout (forthcoming).

5 Sapir writes: "In their recently published work on 'The Meaning of Meaning' Messrs. Ogden and Richards have done philosophy a signal service in indicating how readily the most hard-headed thinkers have allowed themselves to be cajoled by the formal slant of their habitual mode of expression" (1925a: 154).

It is interesting to note that Ogden and Richards had, in their first chapter of *The Meaning of Meaning*, under the heading "The Ethnologists," referred to Sapir's 1921 *Language* as "one of the ablest and most interesting of recent linguistic studies." They noted, however, that with a poorly defined use of the term "concept" on Sapir's part, Sapir "is unable in this work – which is, however, only a preliminary to his [never written] *Language as Symbol and as Expression* – to make even the distinctions which are essential inside symbolic language" (Ogden and Richards: 1930 [1923]: 7–8, note 1).

It is perhaps this passage in Ogden and Richards that prompts Sapir, in his *American Mercury* article, to write the very next line after the one quoted above:

> Perhaps the best way to get behind our thought processes and to eliminate from them all the accidents or irrelevances due to their linguistic garb is to plunge into the study of exotic modes of expression. At any rate, I know of no better way to kill spurious "entities."
> (1925a: 154)

Joseph (1987a) focuses precisely on this problem of "concept" in Ogden and Richards and Bloomfield's objections to it. An analysis of Ogden and Richard's triangular diagram of meaning, and its relationship first to Saussure, then to Sapir, then to Bloomfield, goes well beyond the bounds of the present study.

INTRODUCTORY ESSAY: THE GOALS OF LINGUISTIC HISTORIOGRAPHY

1 However, for a critical review of Greenberg, see Lyle Campbell's 1988 review article.

2 Opening the Preface to *Sociolinguistics. Proceedings of the UCLA Sociolinguistics Conference, 1964* (1966), the editor, William Bright, credits an early use of the term "sociolinguistics" to a 1952 article by H.C. Currie, "A Projection of Socio-linguistics: The Relationship of Speech to Social Status," *Southern Speech Journal* 18: 28–37.

3 The origin and development of American Sign Language reconfirms a strong French influence that existed in America in the early decades of the nineteenth century. The story might unofficially begin with Condillac's postulation of "le langage des gestes" in his *Essai sur l'origine des connaissances humaines* (1746). The story officially begins with the Abbé de l'Epée who introduced the use of sign in France in the 1750s. Laurent Clerc brought the French sign system to the United States in 1817 and then passed it on to Thomas Gallaudet. Thomas's son, Edward, helped transform the Columbia Institution for the Instruction of the Deaf and the Dumb and the Blind into Gallaudet College in 1864.

For an account of the political events on the campus of Gallaudet College in March, 1988, see Oliver Sacks "The Revolution of the

Deaf," *The New York Review of Books*, XXXV, No. 9, June 2, 1988, pp. 23–8.

The interest in sign language in relationship to the American Indians has an equally long and fascinating history, beginning with Heckewelder ([1881], see Chapter 2) and his observation that "The Indians do not gesticulate more when they speak than other nations do" (128) and culminating, in a certain sense, with D.G. Mallery's *Sign Language Among North American Indians Compared with That of Other Peoples and Deaf-Mutes*, Washington: Government Bureau of Printing, 1881.

An important relay in the intertwined interests between sign language, the signs of language, deaf–mutes, and the history of American linguistics is Francis Lieber's "Paper on the Vocal Sounds of Laura Bridgman" (first published in the Smithsonian Contribution to Knowledge, Washington, December, 1850). A study of the relationship between this mid to late nineteenth-century interest in the deaf, their communication and general speech phenomena with the work of the Scottish-born Alexander Graham Bell (1847–1922) remains to be done. Bell came to the United States in 1870 and, early in 1873, he was appointed professor of vocal physiology and the mechanics of speech in the School of Oratory of Boston University. As Konrad Koerner has pointed out, both Bell and Thomas Edison (1847–1931) were close contemporaries to the *Junggrammatiker* and both had impacts on the development of phonetics and hence on linguistics (1977: 336, note 4). See E.F.K. Koerner, "1876 as a Turning Point in the History of Linguistics."

4 Jakobson displays his uncanny feel for the history of American linguistics in this thumbnail sketch:

> Perhaps the most inventive and versatile among American thinkers was Charles Sanders Peirce (1839–1914), so great that no university found a place for him. His first, perspicacious attempt at a classification of signs – "On a New List of Categories" – appeared in the *Proceedings of the American Academy of Arts and Sciences*, 1867, and forty years later, summing up his "life long study of the nature of signs," the author stated: "I am, as far as I know, a pioneer, or rather a backwoodsman, in the work of clearing and opening up what I call *semiotic*, that is, the doctrine of the essential nature and fundamental varieties of possible semiosis, and I find the field too vast, the labor too great, for a first-comer."
>
> (1965: 22)

The image Peirce fashions for himself as an American pioneer was certainly consistent with his time, and Jakobson is shrewd enough to have recognized the importance of Peirce's difficulties in finding institutional support in the second half of the nineteenth century. I cannot help but wonder why it took a Russian Formalist to rediscover Peirce, and I sense that American linguists' early failure to have appreciated Peirce is related to their same impulse to separate Sapir's poetry from the rest of his writings on language. To relate the two would certainly have seemed natural, and even have been encouraged, in the context of, say, the Prague Linguistic Circle of the 1920s and 1930s. For a brief allusion to Sapir's ties to the Prague Circle, see, again, Jakobson, (1979: 162).

To insist on the franco-american connection with respect to signs and sign theory, I refer the reader to a recent study allying Peirce's work to that of the French *Idéologue* Maine de Biran (1766–1824): Achim Eschbach (1986), "Notes sur la *Note sur l'influence des signes* de Maine de Biran." In *Les Idéologues. Sémiotique, théories et politiques linguistiques pendant la Révolution française*, ed. W. Busse and J. Trabant, 59–72. Amsterdam: John Benjamins.

5 I wish to thank Guy Bailey for having provided me with a copy of Harrison (1884). Although Harrison is (as one would expect for the time) given to making statements about "the Negro" that "much of his talk is baby-talk" or that "the slang which is an ingrained part of his being [is] as deep-dyed as his skin" (1884: 233), Harrison still provides valuable information both on elements of Black English as well as on population numbers, estimating between 6 and 7 million Blacks in the South (1884: 232).

From 1619, when twenty Africans were first deposited at Jamestown, Virginia, to the present, Afro-Americans have been an integral and problematic part of American history in general and, thus, of this specific history of American linguistics, from Jefferson to Boas. Since I do not intend to cover the topic here I refer the reader to Boas's early twentieth-century pieces (1974a [1906], 1974b [1906], 1974c [1909]) for strong arguments against nineteenth-century theories of race and strong arguments for understanding the degraded position of the Afro-American as the result of social, and not hereditary, conditions.

1 IN THE BEGINNING (1769–1815): THE POLITICAL CONCEPTION OF LANGUAGE

1 The German reads: "Haben die Menschen, ihren naturfaehigkeiten ueberlassen, sich Sprache erfinden koennen? und auf welchem Wege waeren sie am fueglichsten dazu gelangt?" The question, however, was originally posed by the Berlin Academy in French: "En supposant les hommes abandonnés à leurs facultés naturelles, sont ils en état d'inventer le langage? et par quels moyens parviendront-ils d'eux-mêmes à cette invention?"

2 Auroux and Boes (1981) provide an excellent discussion of these *vocabularia comparativa*. This article investigates, in general, *les programmes de recherches* of the various vocabularies and, in particular, the program established by Court de Gébelin in his *Monde Primitif* (1773–82). Court de Gébelin's project has ties to the history of American linguistics, namely through P.S. Duponceau, one of the most influential early American linguists, who was secretary to Court de Gébelin in 1776–7.

3 I have gleaned the contents of Jefferson's library from various sources, most notably from Hauer (1983) who relies primarily on Millicent

Sowerby (1952–9), *Catalogue of the Library of Thomas Jefferson*, 5 vols, (Washington, DC: Library of Congress); and Baugh (1940). In addition, I used the 1829 *Catalogue. President Jefferson's Library*, by Nathaniel Poor (Washington: Gales & Seaton).

4 In his presidential address to the first meeting of the American Oriental Society in 1842 (printed in the first volume of the *Journal of the American Oriental Society*) (1849), John Pickering makes this very point. In rather modestly heroic terms, Pickering compares language studies in the young America to the conditions under which Sir William Jones pursued the study of Sanskrit in India at the mid to end of the eighteenth century. Pickering cites Jones's remarks in the Preface to the first volume of *Asiatic Researches* to the effect that "a mere man of letters, retired from the world and allotting his whole time to philosophical or literary pursuits" was an unknown character among the British residents in Calcutta, where every individual needed to be first *a man of business* in the civil or military state, and thus constantly occupied, either in the affairs of government, in the administration of justice, in some department of revenue or commerce, or in one of the liberal professions. Jones remarks then that very few hours could be reserved for any study that had no immediate connection with *business*, even by "those who are most habituated to mental application."

Pickering then laments, mildly:

> To these remarks we may, in our own case, add the disadvantages incident to all young nations, where the same individual is obliged to know and practise different branches of the same art of business, which, in older and larger states, are divided among several persons.
> (1849a [1842]: 3)

For a discussion of this point, see Chapter 3, pp. 124–5.

5 Auroux writes of "des espèces de lois, venues d'on ne sait où, qui transcendent les actes de parole et imposent leurs normes ou changent automatiquement la langue."

6 Auroux identifies that *langue* "n'est ni conçue comme le résultat d'agents immanents et mystérieux, ni comme une abstraction produite par l'approche scientifique, mais comme une réalité construite par des agents humains définis."

7 Beauzée's definition for *langue* is: "l'ensemble des usages propres à une nation pour exprimer ses pensées par la voix."

8 Auroux concludes that: "le sujet de grammaire générale c'est l'esprit humain, la raison pareillement distribuée en chaque homme," while "le sujet de la langue c'est la nation."

9 For a discussion of the first uses in English of the term "standard" applied to language which go back to the early eighteenth century, see Joseph (1987b: 3–7).

Joseph's welcome and thorough study of the "life cycle" of a standard language was made known to me after I had completed the entire manuscript of this present book. His study of the general phenomenon of the concept and development of the "standard language" is global in scope. Although Joseph refers very little to the particular variety of the American English standard, his findings clearly have much to offer my arguments in this first chapter. However, an integration of Joseph's work into my own will have to await the future.

10 Father Michael Denis (1729–1800) is regularly given credit for the first use of the word *Linguistik* in any language in his *Einleitung in die Buecherkunde*. Denis uses the word synonymously with *Sprachenkunde*, which is only a general label for the classification of books concerning vocabularies, alphabets, grammars, and dictionaries. The second time the word is used is by Vater in *Mithridates*, which also utilizes *allgemeine Sprachenkunde* in its title. Thus begins a very complicated history of the use of the German terms *Linguistik, Sprachenkunde, Philologie*, and *Sprachwissenschaft*, which does not become any less complicated in either French or English, especially when one adds such adjectives as "comparative" or "historical" or yet "historical–comparative." The story is only further complicated by the intertwining stories of the development of language studies in France, Germany, England, and America.

George Bolling recognized the difficulties in his article, "Linguistics and Philology" (1929), when commenting on the confusion in the English usage alone. Although his article is instructive, his statement that "We [the Americans] began with a British heritage [in the usage of the term 'philology']" (30) is manifestly false and symptomatic of the general amnesia Americans have always had for the history of American linguistics. We will return to this general problem in Chapter 2 where it is clear that American linguists, such as Pickering and Duponceau, were very conscious that they were breaking new ground in their approach to Philology. Pickering, in particular, is aware that he is *not* following British example.

11 Benfey writes: "Reich war dieses Jahrhundert an geographischen Entdeckungen und das schon sehr erstarkte *linguistische Interesse* bewirkte, dass man den Sprachen der neu entdeckten Gebiete sogleich eine nicht unerhebliche Aufmerksamkeit zuwendete."

12 See here Andresen (1983) for a discussion of the substantialist conception of language in the eighteenth-century French tradition. In short:

> the substantialist conception of signs and language necessarily pervades the way that signs and words are talked about and manifests itself particularly in the metaphors that are chosen to describe language in the eighteenth century. That is not to suggest, however, that the eighteenth century formulated the idea of a metalanguage; it did not, and the lack of one may be ascribed to the conception of language as a substance. The *grammaries générales* envision the substance of signs specifically in terms of material: words are the cloaks of ideas; they are "swatches" of material that envelop ideas. The verb *revêtir*, which had currency throughout the seventeenth and eighteenth centuries, indicates this basic function of signs . . . . This expression of materiality through the verb *revêtir*

survives in the French tradition at least until the *Idéologues* and Destutt de Tracy at the end of the eighteenth century. All the *grammariens* refer either implicitly or explicitly to the substantiality of words and language.

(1983: 272–3)

13 Volney writes: "Il ne suffit pas de savoir le grec et le latin pour raisonner sur la philosophie du language, pour bâtir de ces théories que l'on appelle des grammaries universelles."

14 Franklin's benevolent dealings with the Indians have been commented upon widely, especially the incident in 1763 when he single-handedly raised a militia to avert an Indian massacre at the hands of white settlers in Western Pennsylvania. An interesting book by Bruce E. Johansen, *Forgotten Founders: Benjamin Franklin, the Iroquois, and the Rationale for the American Revolution* (Ipswich, MA: Gambit, 1982) goes farther and suggests that many of those aspects of the American Constitution we are accustomed to thinking of as original with the Founding Fathers were borrowed by Franklin from the Iroquois. Johansen argues that it was Canassatego, a mid-eighteenth-century leader of the Iroquois, who was the first to suggest a union of the thirteen colonies on the basis of the Five Nation Confederacy of the Seneca, Mohawk, Onondaga, Oneida and Cayuga. Johansen also points out that Locke, who never came to the New World, had been influenced by the example of the North American tribal governments. Locke quotes a book published in French in 1636 that described the system by which the Huron Indians of Canada elected their kings, who governed by "consent and persuasion [rather] than by force and compulsion, the public good being the measure of their authority."

Of Jefferson's dealing with the Indians, a recent study from an Indian point of view shows Jefferson to have come to the Cherokee with overt gestures of friendship and good will but with covert and duplicitous actions which ultimately hurt the Cherokee. See the 1979 reprinting of "Thomas Jefferson's Advice to the Cherokees [1809]" in *Journal of Cherokee Studies* 4.2: 64–6.

2 FROM PHILADELPHIA TO THE FIELD: 1815–42

1 The *Journal of Cherokee Studies* has several articles discussing the role of Andrew Jackson and the Cherokee Removal. See in particular "'Forcibly If We Must': The Georgia Case for Cherokee Removal, 1802–1832" by Carl Vipperman, *Journal of Cherokee Studies* 3.2: 103–9 (1978).

A rare pamphlet by Jeremiah Evarts (1781–1831) entitled "Present Crisis in the Condition of the American Indians" of 1830 (to be found in the Duke University Rare Book Room) is an impassioned protest by a white man against the treatment of the Cherokee. He plainly defends the Indians in Lockean and Jeffersonian terms:

The Cherokees are human beings, endowed by their Creator with the
same natural rights as other men. They are in peaceable possession
of a territory which they have always regarded as their own. This
territory was in possession of their ancestors, through an unknown
series of generations, and has come down to them with a title
absolutely unincumbered in every respect. It is not pretended, that the
Cherokees have ever alienated their country, or that the whites have
ever been in possession of it.

(1830: 7)

Evarts is critical of Jefferson, whom he quotes as saying that the people
of the United States should "feel power, and forget right" (1830: 5).
He is unfailingly critical of the hypocrisy of the various treaties
negotiated by the United States with the Cherokee and of Jackson's
duplicity in dealing with the Indians.

It is difficult to find figures pertaining to the Indian population was
in the seventeenth and eighteenth centuries and, thus, to determine
exactly how negatively they were affected by territorial expansion by the
whites. Evarts gives some estimates: "It is computed, that there are
within our national limits more than 300,000 Indians; some say
500,000; and, in the southwestern States, the tribes whose immediate
removal is in contemplation, have an aggregate population of more than
60,000" (1830: 4).

Duke History Professor, Peter Wood (personal communication), has
estimated that the Indian population of the South dropped from 80 per
cent of the total population in 1685 to a scant 3 per cent in 1790.
During that same period, he claims, the white population had more
than tripled, reaching 62 per cent, and the black population jumped
from 1 per cent to 35 per cent of the total population. Wood also points
out that the primary factor responsible for the decline of Indian population was disease. Thousands of Indians were wiped out when they were
exposed for the first time to small-pox, measles, and diptheria brought
to America by European settlers. Of course, warfare, slavery, and
exportation played their parts in killing the Indians.

2 Benfey writes:

Mit dem Jahre 1819 trat auf dem Gebiete der germniaschen
Philologie, vor allem dem *sprachwissenschaftlichen Theile* derselben ein
Wendepunkt ein, welcher nicht bloss fuer sie eine vollstaendige
Umgestaltung herbeifuehrte, sondern auch fuer die Sprachwissen-
schaft ueberhaupt von allertiefster Bedeutung war.

(emphasis mine)

3 Duponceau was also just as likely to write a *Dissertation on the Nature and
Character of the Chinese System of Writing* (1838), while Pickering wrote *On
the Pronunciation of the Greek Language* (1818) and *A Comprehensive Lexicon
of the Greek Language* (1826), which was not superceded until Liddell-
Scott (Rousseau 1981: 73). Pursuing these works would take me far
beyond the limits I have prescribed for myself.

4 Like the word *lengthy*, the word *Yankee* and its etymology seem to spur comment from everyone, myself included. Webster drew scorn, first, for his 1810 etymology where he derived *Yankee* from Persian (*Janghe* or *Jenghe*, signifying a *warlike man*, a *swift horse*) and then for his 1828 etymology, which he derived from *Yengeese*, "a corrupt pronunciation of the word *English* by the native Indians of America." In a different move, Mencken proposes a Dutch derivation, something on the order of *Jan* plus *Kees* (1963: 122). A more recent re-assertion of the Indian derivation can be found in J.L. Dillard's *All-American English* (1975: 114–15), a work that is entertaining, controversial, and avowedly anti-Mencken. Simpson, too, revives the Indian etymology, citing Cooper's etymology of 1823 (1986: 172–3). Evidence for both the Indian and the Dutch derivations can be found as far back as the late seventeenth century.

It should be noted that Webster's (and Cooper's) etymologies are based on the reliable source of Heckewelder:

> *Yengees*. [The Lenni-Lennape] now exclusively applied to the people of New England, who, indeed, appeared to have adopted it, and were, as they still are, generally through the country called *Yankees*, which is evidently the same name with a trifling alteration. They say they know the *Yengees*, and can distinguish them by their dress and personal appearance, and that they were considered as less cruel than the Virginians or *long knives*. The proper English they call *Saggenash*.
> (1881 [1819]: 143)

It is not only Webster who picks up on Heckewelder's etymology. So precise a linguist as Pickering cites it in his review of Heckewelder (1819: 167).

I, too, prefer the etymology of *Yankee* from the Indian *Yengeese* for the sole reason that it doubles the stereoscopy I am arguing for between the white settler and the red aborigine. *Yankee* encapsulates the metaphoric vision that embraces the American Indian and the European settler in one complex image, for the word is a microcosm of early American linguistic trade: the Indian took the English word for "English" and gave it back to them (Indian-giving in reverse), aptly through the "back door" of slang.

5 The original German reads:

> je weiter aufwaerts er klimmen kann, desto schoener und vollkomm-ner duenkt ihn die leibliche gestalt der sprache, je naeher ihrer jetzigen fassung er tritt, desto weher thut ihm jene macht und gewandtheit der form in abnahme und verfall zu finden.

6 The *Encyclopédie* sentence reads: "La langue de ces sauvages est gutturale et très-pauvre, parce qu'ils n'ont connoissance que d'un très-petit nombre de choses."

7 Sagard-Théodat writes:

> Nos Hurons, & generallement toutes les autres Nations, ont la mesme instabilité de langage, & changent tellement leurs mots, qu'à

succession de temps l'ancien Huron est presque tout autre que celuy du présent, & change encore, selon que i'ay peu coniecturer & apprendre en leur parlant: car l'esprit se subtilise, & vieillissant corrige les choses, & les met dans leur perfection.

8 Bréboeuf writes:

Toutes les lettres labiales leur manquent; c'est volontiers la cause qu'ils ont tous les lévres ouuertes de si mauuaise grace, & qu'à peine les entend-t'on quand ils siflent, ou qu'ils parlent bas. Comme ils n'ont presque ny vertu, ny Religion, ny science aucune, ou police, aussi n'ont-ils aucuns mots simples propres à signifier tout ce qui est est.

9 Herder writes:

De la Condamine sagt von einer kleinen Nation am Amazonenfluss, ein Theil von ihren Woertern koenne nicht, auch nicht einmal sehr unvollstaendig, geschrieben werden. Man muesste wenigstens neune oder zehn Sylben gebrauchen, wo sie in der Aussprache kaum drei auszusprechen scheinen.

10 Herder writes:

Die Huronen haben jedesmal ein doppeltes Verbum fuer eine beseelte und unbeseelte Sache: so dass Sehen bei "einen Stein sehen" und Sehen bei "einen Menschen sehen!" immer zween verschiedne Ausdruecke sind – man verfolge das durch die ganze Natur – welch ein Reichthum!

11 Just as Huron was the model of Indian language, the article "Caraibe" in the *Encyclopédie* serves as the mid-eighteenth-century model of Indian savagery: they were anthropophagous, naked, their children crawled on all fours, they were polygamous and the women gave birth without pain. These Jesuits considered this last aspect of savagery as the "proof" of the innocence of the savages: they were exempt from the punishment inflicted on Eve. The word *cannibal* comes from a form of the word *caraibe*.

12 Rousseau writes: "Les sauvages d'Amérique ne parlent presque jamais hors de chez eux; chacun garde le silence dans sa cabane, il parle par signes à sa famille; et ces signes sont peu fréquens."

13 Lepsius writes:

Auch der verdienstvolle *John Pickering* nahm in seinem *Essay on a uniform orthography for the Indian languages of North America*. Mem, of the Amer. Acad. of arts and sciences (auch besonders abgedruckt. Cambridge. 1820) das *Vocalsystem* von *Jones* an, brachte aber die *consonantische* Umschrift eher zurueck als vorwaerts.

The statement is found as footnote 4 on pp. 10 and 11 of the German 1855 edition. Curiously, the 1863 English edition of Lepsius omits this footnote, so that no reference to Pickering at all occurs in English.

14 I wish to thank Hans-Ulrich Boas of the University of Goettingen for having made available to me a xerox of the German translation of Pickering's work.

15 In Pickering's 1844 presidential address to the American Oriental Society, he writes of a Polynesian language in the Sandwich Islands:

> The Vocabulary was collected, in the year 1811, by the late Wm. P. Richardson, Esq. of Salem, and is made the subject of a particular notice and acknowledgement by the late eminent philologist Baron William von Humboldt (to whom it was communicated about twenty years ago) in his great work entitled Ueber die Kawi-Sprache auf der Insel Java, (on the Kawi, or Original Language of the Island of Java,) 3 vols. 4to. Berlin, 1836–9: See vol. ii, p. 297. Professor Vater gives no specimen of this language in the Mithridates.
>
> (1849b [1844]: 52, note; see also Chapter 3)

16 Hippolyte Taine (1828–93), for instance, identifies the one-word stage, "holophrasis," as the first stage in language acquisition in his 1876 article "Note sur l'acquisition du langage chez les enfants et dans l'espèce humaine," *Revue philosophique* 1: 5–23. Taine cites everywhere Max Mueller. Taine expresses a Monboddo-type ladder ("échelle"), and he puts "le singe . . . sur la même échelle que l'homme, mais à beaucoup d'échelons au-dessous, sans que jamais l'exemple ou l'éducation puisse le faire monter jusqu'à l'échelon où arrive un Australien, le dernier des hommes" (22). The bottom rung is apparently occupied no longer by the American Indians but by the Australians.

3 THE INSTITUTIONALIZATION OF AMERICAN LINGUISTICS: 1842–94

1 See Franklin (1984) for a recent study of Marsh's life, work, and general impact on mid-to-late nineteenth-century American scholarship. In terms of career, Marsh resembles Pickering and Duponceau in that he was a part-time scholar, lawyer, businessman, congressional representative and diplomat. Unlike Pickering or Duponceau, however, he limited his linguistic horizons exclusively to the English language. His most important contributions to the history of English studies in the United States were two lecture series, the first in 1858–9 at Columbia College, published as *Lectures on the English Language*, and the second delivered at the Lowell Institute in 1860–1, published as *The Origin and History of the English Language and of the Early Literature It Embodies*.

See below, p. 154, for a further allusion to Marsh's work in the context of Whitney's. An investigation of the points of contact between Whitney and Marsh and their relationship to the general development of nineteenth-century English studies remains to be done.

2 Condillac makes the following division in the opening paragraph of

Section Seconde of his *Essai sur l'origine des connaissances humaines* which is entitled "L'Analyse et la génération des opérations de l'ame": "On peut distinguer les opérations de l'ame en deux espèces, selon qu'on les rapporte plus particulièrement à l'entendement ou à la volonté. *L'objet de cet essai indique que je me propose de ne les considérer que par le rapport qu'elles ont à l'entendement*" (p. 114, 1973 edition, text established and annotated by Charles Porset. Auvers-sur-Oise: Galilée).

Although Condillac, in separating *entendement* (reason) from *volonté* (will) is not making here a distinction between the "physical" and the "moral" sciences in the nineteenth-century German style, it is interesting to note that *volonté* first got factored out of (classical rationalist) language discussion in the eighteenth century.

3 Jakobson quotes Saussure: "L'Américain Whitney, que je révère, n'a jamais dit un seul mot, sur les mêmes sujets [i.e. the theory and method of linguistic science], qui ne fût juste, mais comme tous les autres [linguists past and present], il ne songe pas que la langue ait besoin d'une systématique" (1971: xxxvii). This same sentence is quoted in Koerner (1973: 80) and Anderson (1985: 196).

4 In his Preface, Powell refers to J.D. Whitney and not to W.D. Whitney. This could be a typographic error. In "The Development of American Anthropology 1879–1920: From the Bureau of American Ethnology to Franz Boas," Regna Darnell writes that Powell's "alphabet, originally devised by William Dwight Whitney of Yale, became a cause of considerable consternation in the Bureau" because of its rigidity (1970a: 65). It certainly makes sense that William and not Josiah should have been the author of the alphabet. Still, Josiah and Powell were known to one another, and Josiah could have had a hand in the alphabet project. However, Darnell cites correspondence between Powell and Gatschet referring unambiguously to William the Orientalist and not to Josiah the Geologist to the effect that "Professor Whitney is an excellent Orientalist, but knowing nothing of the phonetics of American languages he could not be expected to draw up an alphabet setting at rest *all* requirements in this line" (1970: 66). Nevertheless, Powell's 1880 *Introduction* refers to J.D. Whitney, hence my confusion.

5 Newton never said it, nor Galileo, nor Freud. The historian of science I. Bernard Cohen scoured the annals of discovery for scientists who announced that their own work was revolutionary, but he could produce only this short list of sixteen: Symmer, Marat, Lavoisier, von Liebig, Hamilton, Darwin, Virchow, Cantor, Einstein, Minkowski, von Laue, Wegener, Compton, Just, Watson and Benoit Mandelbrot. I believe, however, that Stephen Jay Gould would take Darwin's name off this list.

6 It is of interest to note that Deborah Tannen uses the phrase "ratifying listenership" to describe certain types of dialogue interactions in a recent article "Repetition in Conversation: Toward a Poetics of Talk." I am not arguing that Tannen's use of "ratification" is the same as Whitney's, only that there is a significant terminological convergence between Whitney's "political" conception of language and Tannen's

sociolinguistic orientation. In my Conclusion, I mention the unsatisfying aspects of Whitney's "political" conception (see p. 252).

7 See Joan Leopold "Duponceau, Humboldt et Pott: La Place structurale des concepts de polysynthèse et d'"incorporation."" (1984). Leopold writes that it was Humboldt and not Pott who developed the term and the idea of "incorporation." For Humboldt, incorporation referred to the phenomenon where the object of the verb is found in the same word as the verbal root. One of the examples that Humboldt gives is the Nahuatl word *ni-naca-qua* for "I-flesh-eat" (69).

8 The present study is not the place to undertake an examination of the sources of influence on Saussure, nor even an extended comparison of Whitney and Saussure. By stating that Whitney is a relay between Saussure and the French eighteenth century, I do not mean to discount the influence of a linguist such as Michel Bréal and his *Essai de sémantique* of 1897 who understood that the Ideologues, those inheritors of Condillac, were closer to the truth than anyone imagined when they said that words were signs. Bréal writes:

> Nos pères de l'école de Condillac, ces idéologues qui ont servi de cible pendant cinquante ans à une certaine critique, étaient plus près de la vérité quand ils disaient, selon leur manière simple et honnête, que les mots sont des signes.
> (quoted in Auroux, Désirat, and Hordé 1982; also in Andresen 1988a)

9 I have long been interested in the relationship between the particular examples used by a writer to illustrate particular arguments about language, for I do believe that, in many cases, they are not chosen at random but are indexes of the author's entire conception of language. See Andresen (1981) for a particular exposition of this point with regard to the way Charles de Brosses uses his examples, which is similar to the way I am arguing that Whitney chooses his.

4 THE ARCS OF DEVELOPMENT SEPARATE: 1875–1900

1 I am indebted to Sylvain Auroux for the concepts of "exigences théoriques" and "contingences historiques." These concepts are used and elaborated primarily in Auroux's *La sémiotique des Encyclopédistes. Essai d'épistémologie historique des sciences du langage* (1979a). See Andresen for a review: "*Arbitraire* and *contingence* in the Semiotics of the Eighteenth Century" (1984a).

Auroux also makes use of the terms *arbitraire* and *contingence* in his study of "La querelle des lois phonétiques" where he states that:

> On a toujours reconnu au langage un *double statut*; d'un côté une régularité et une nécessité (qui permettent de formuler des règles, des lois, des catégories générales), de l'autre, un arbitraire et une contingence, qui se manifestent soit dans la variabilité des actes de

parole, soit dans la mutabilité historique des langues.

(1979b: 8)

2 The fourth edition of *Language Files. Materials for An Introduction to Language*, prepared by the Department of Linguistics at The Ohio State University uses as the first "key word" for File 135 "Regional Variation" the word *greasy* (1987: 351).

3 In 1925 Bloomfield postulated the reconstruction of [çk] for Proto-Central-Algonquian: *meçkusiwa* "he is red," which looked aberrant at the time. Bloomfield claimed that the symbol *[ç] had a purely abstract value, and was merely a place-holder indicated by the rest of the Proto-Central-Algonquian sound system, representing reconstructed [ck], [ck], [hk], and [hk], in Fox, Ojibwa, Plains Cree, and Menomini, respectively. Three years later, Bloomfield (1928), after having had the opportunity to examine a variety of Cree spoken in Manitoba, presented the form *mihtkusiw* "he is red" with the combination [hkt] found in no other word. Thus, he justified the reconstruction *[çk]. See also Sapir (1931).

4 Meillet and Cohen write:

> On peut se demander par exemple si les langues américaines, encore mal connues pour la plupart et peu étudiées au point de vue comparatif, se prêteront jamais à l'établissement de grammaires comparées précises et complètes; les sondages faits jusqu'ici promettent peu.

5 Rivet writes that the lack of regular phonetic correspondence

> montre que la notation n'a pas été faite avec toute la rigueur désirable, à moins que l'on admette que ces langues n'obéissent pas à des règles aussi strictes que, par example, les langues indo-européennes, hypothèse qui ne semble pas devoir être écartée *a priori*.

6 The American Association for the Advancement of Science was founded in Philadelphia in September of 1848. It was the first permanently successful effort to establish in the United States a truly national scientific society embracing all the sciences.

It was not, however, the first effort to bring such a society into being. In 1816, John Quincy Adams, John C. Calhoun, Daniel Webster, Edward Everett, Henry Clay, and other national leaders launched the Columbian Institute for the Promotion of Arts and Sciences. The word "Columbian" confirms our sense that the word "American" had not yet come to settle on the (Euro-)American white man in the second decade of the nineteenth century (see above pp. 76, 191–2, 262, note 4). In any case, the diverse and ambitious objectives of the Columbian Institute proved to be too much for the founders who were occupied with many other activities. By 1825, the Institute had become inactive, and in 1840 it "passed into" the National Institution for the Promotion of Science. Earlier, there had been proposals to found a society on the model of the British Association for the Advancement of Science (established 1831), but when this resolution was put before the American Philosophical Society, the proposal was decided to be "inexpedient."

5 THE SEARCH FOR AUTONOMY: 1900–24

1 For instance, Stephen Anderson writes: "Conventional wisdom holds that the distinctive content of twentieth-century linguistics can in large part be traced back to the work of the Genevan linguist Ferdinand de Saussure" (1985: 27).

Writing against the claims of transformational–generative grammar, writing against even the existence of such a field as "general linguistics," Geoffrey Sampson nevertheless also subscribes to a version of this "conventional wisdom." When he writes that "the years around 1900 happen to have marked an important turning-point in the history of modern linguistics" (1980: 13), he is announcing, in effect, that he will be replowing familiar historical ground; and although Sampson makes it clear that linguistics did not begin in the twentieth century, his first chapter "Prelude: The Nineteenth Century" merely repeats what I am calling the "received history of linguistics." See Geoffrey Sampson (1980).

Although Sapir and Bloomfield approach language differently, they had a similar view of the history of the discipline, namely this same "received history." Sapir wrote in his 1929 "Linguistics as a Science": "Linguistics may be said to have begun its scientific career with the comparative study of the Indo-European languages" (1949: 160).

Even Deborah Cameron in her *Feminism and Linguistic Theory*, an approach to which I am sympathetic, uncritically repeats, rather than recasts, the received history of linguistics. Cameron orients her overview of linguistics in the twentieth century around Saussure, identifying the "scientific study of language" to be "a specifically modern development" (1985: 10) and continues on through the expected "moments": American structuralism, transformationalism, linguistic anthropology. It is not my intention here to disparage Cameron's book, which is clearly written and contributes in interesting ways to the "politics of variation" and to the understanding of "silence, alienation and oppression" engendered by sexist language. It is rather my intention to point out how widespread is the acceptance of the received history of linguistics, even in expositions where it would be to most advantage to have a *different* history to refer to.

2 On this point see Joseph (1987a) and Harris (1987: 89) and below, in the section entitled "Autonomy Envisioned" (pp. 235–42).

3 In 1912, Arizona became the forty-eighth state, the last in the continental United States. Even before the completion of the continental expansion, Americans had had their sights fixed even farther westward. As a by-product of the Spanish-American War of 1898, the Philippines, formerly a Spanish colony, had become an American colony by 1901. The connection between the Philippines as an American colony and Bloomfield's work on Tagalog was suggested to me by Stephen Murray (personal communication). The "Preface" to Bloomfield's *Tagalog Texts with Grammatical Analysis* (1917) is published in Hockett (1970: 78–81).

4 For a particular exposition of the fate of linguistic anthropology in

France at the time of World War I, see Sylvain Auroux, *Linguistique et anthropologie en France (1600–1900)*, Collection Travaux d'Histoire des Théories Linguistiques, n. 1, série VIII, Université Paris 7, 1982.

5 See, however, William Moulton "Bloomfield as Dialectologist" in Hall (1987: 139–54). Bloomfield's interest in dialectology was, admittedly, weak, and earned him a place in Labov's group of "asocial" linguists (see above p. 143).

6 Robert Lowie, in his review of Sapir's 1921 *Language*, writes: "Dr. Sapir discovers a definite 'drift' – a tendency, moreover, that may persist in languages long after their separation from the parental stock . . . though certainly there is no mystic agency that impels speech towards a predetermined goal" (in Koerner 1984: 44).

Anderson, on Sapir's Drift, writes: "Often presented as something quite mystical, the most straightforward way to interpret Sapir's notion of linguistic drift is simply as the claim that change is motivated by structural factors" (1985: 227).

This charge of Sapirian "mysticism" may have originated with Bloomfield. Hockett writes of what Charles Voegelin has told him of the relationship between Bloomfield and Sapir:

Each had a deep respect for the other, but with certain reservations. Sapir admired Bloomfield's ability patiently to excerpt data and to file and collate slips until the patterns of the language emerged, but spoke deprecatingly of Bloomfield's sophomoric psychology. Bloomfield was dazzled by Sapir's virtuosity and perhaps a bit jealous of it, but in matters outside language referred to Sapir as a "medicine man."

(1970: 539–40)

7 This is not to suggest that Malone and Sapir were in any sort of competition. The arcs of development had firmly separated by 1925 – or, rather, the separation that had already begun in the 1870s was now codified by the appearance of separate journals. What Sapir was responding to in his "Sound Patterns" was not an American issue anyway. According to Uhlenbeck, Sapir was responding specifically to the German phonetician, Panconcelli-Calzia, director of the then well-known phonetic laboratory in Hamburg, who claimed that the only scientific approach to the study of speech sounds was experimental phonetics. Sapir, by contrast, argued that the nature of speech sounds could not be properly understood in purely phonetic terms (Uhlenbeck 1979: 122–3).

8 This association of poetry and language theory is not idle. In his recent book *The Language Parallax. Linguistic Relativism and Poetic Indeterminacy*, after quoting the line from Bloomfield that "Poetry is the blazoned book of language," Paul Friedrich adds: "And language implies . . . *rough drafts* for poetry" (1986: 33). I would further add that language implies rough draft for linguistic theories. See my review of Friedrich's book in *Language and Society* (1988b).

9 It is my belief that Jane Hill, Professor of Anthropology at the

University of Arizona, Tucson, is currently at work editing a volume for Professor Koerner's series on the work of women linguists in the twentieth century. She may, in fact, be beginning with Louise Pound.

10 It would be interesting to know when and where the first occurrence of the phrase "autonomous linguistics" appears. However, that first occurrence would not actually be as important as the *second* appearance of the phrase, that is, the place where the term was, quite literally, *seconded*, or "voted for" by another linguist.

If I calque one of Whitney's passage (quoted above p. 146), I get a satisfying description of linguistic theory as group effort. The italics mark my changes in Whitney's phrasing:

> The whole process of *language-theory-making* and *language-theory-changing*, in all its different departments, is composed of single acts, performed by *individual linguists*; yet each act is determined, not alone by the needs of the particular case, but also by the general usages of the *community of linguists* as acting in and represented by the *individual linguist*; so that, in its initiation as well as its acceptance and ratification, it is virtually the act of the *community of linguists*, as truly conventional as if *linguists* held a meeting for its discussion and decision, *which they often, in fact, do.*

11 Lack of funding has prevented me from pursuing the kind of archival work – e.g. a study of the records of the Linguistic Society of America housed in Philadelphia at the American Philosophical Society – that would yield a richer and more interesting account of the establishment of the Linguistic Society of America.

CONCLUSION: AMERICAN LINGUISTICS CIRCA 1990

1 The context for Haiman's statement about Whitney is this:

> Bolinger's paper deals with intonation, whose status has always been exceptional in discussions of the arbitrariness of the linguistic sign. Even Whitney, whose classic article on thesei or phusei is one of the most uncompromising attacks on iconicity (1875), conceded in this article that intonation was both iconic and universally so.
>
> (1985: 2)

Haiman is presumably referring to the place in the article where Whitney writes: "The capacity of tone to serve as the immediate expression of feeling, intelligible to all human beings without explanation and without training, is beyond dispute" (1971 [1875]: 118–19). The page before, Whitney also makes a reference to the phusei of onomatopoeia and concedes that "these imitative signs are by no means all primitive; the disposition toward their use also leads to their production from time to time, or, in the history of manifold change in the form of words, *acts as a shaping force*" (1971 [1875]: 117; emphasis mine). A few lines later, Whitney makes a parallel between tone and gesture in "ordinary speech."

Where Whitney differs, perhaps, from contemporary iconists, is in his belief that the iconic character of onomatopoeia, intonation, or gesture is "by no means essential to their usefulness as signs, but is rather ornamental, giving them an added attraction" (1971 [1875]: 117). The distinction between what is "essential" and what is "ornamental" is predicated on his belief of the function of language:

> Its office [of onomatopoeia] is not unlike that belonging to tone and gesture in our ordinary speech – impressive, decorative, artistic, but not indispensable in order to *mutual intelligence, which is the great object of speech,* and is fully attained by the use of signs respecting which we only know that others have formed with them the same associations as ourselves, and will, when we use them, think what we are thinking and desiring them to think.
>
> (1971 [1875]: 118; emphasis mine)

Here, Whitney is placing himself in line with (what I am calling) the Locke-Condillac tradition of communication: the idea that the essence of communication is the making common of our thoughts, or, the transferral or transmission of our thoughts to the other, where communication is viewed as *essentially* co-operative, rational, and well-intentioned behavior. That which goes along with the expression of this message, then – intonation, onomatopoeia, gesture – is "not indispensable" and, therefore, "ornamental."

2 For an example of the idea that semantic description cannot, by definition, be scientific, I have chosen (almost but not entirely) at random the following passage from Sampson. While he concedes that "phonetics and phonology seem to be one aspect of human behaviour which is rather clearly describable in terms of statements that predict the nonoccurrence of logically possible combinations," he observes that "semantic description, on the other hand, cannot be scientific, because our semantic behaviour is an example *par excellence* of the unregimented, unpredictable working of the conscious human mind" (1980: 236; quoted also in Auroux 1986b: 22).

3 Lightfoot, in *The Language Lottery: Toward a Biology of Grammars* (1983), certainly heads in the direction whose future I am predicting to be bright. He incorporates into his arguments, where possible, his readings in biology and evolution, and he makes his theoretical position and his methodological premises entirely clear. All of these moves are to his credit. However, the thorough-going rationalism of his stance leads him to suggest at various times throughout his argument that those (let us say, empiricists) not holding his position believe that cognitive capacities are not, or, at least are not significantly, shaped by genetic (does he mean, biological?) factors. Speaking for myself as one who does not believe in a rationalist conception of the mind, it seems nevertheless impossible to me that cognitive capacities (or any human capacity) are *not* biologically shaped. The question is one of *at what level of specificity?* It is deeply biological that the brain as a general-purpose perceiving

and thinking organ is *not* inherently marked for a prescribed function or meaning. It is deeply biological that, through experiences, connections are made and "maps" are drawn in brain regions, even those for vision and touch. It simply cannot be a charge laid *against* empiricists (or, more specifically, the theory of the brain proposed by, say, Gerald Edelman) that they ignore biology if they do not believe that the world is in any way "labelled," that is, that they do not believe that the world has enough information in it to instruct the brain, making the world a bit like a computer tape, while the brain, then, acts as a computer to interpret that information. It is still completely *biological* that the brain has no program, that individual groups of cells do not have any *a priori* fixed purpose, and that particular cells in the brain's centers are not inherently marked for a prescribed function or meaning.

What seems to me to be at issue, rather, is the question: Why do we need a theory of *mind* at all? At best, a theory of mind will be redundant of the theory of the brain. At worst, it will be misleading.

More than one issue come together here. The more one understands about motor control and the differences in the kinds of mechanisms that produce carefully sequenced – even *deliberate* – behavior as opposed to, say, automatic behavior, the more we may change our ways of thinking about free will, what it means to have a self, or even the phusei–thesei issue.

On the issue of free will, Lightfoot, for instance, acknowledges the problem as still one of mystery, but since "scientists can offer no principles predicting which ideas will be expressed under what circumstances" (1983: 209), it seems that Lightfoot does not see how (or, presumably, why) it should be incorporated into linguistic theory. See, however, Taylor (1989) for an interesting historiographic account of the relevance of the concepts of agency, voluntariness, and normativity in current linguistics theory.

4 I am indebted to Barbara Herrnstein Smith for having made Parkes (1984) and Krebs and Dawkins (1984) available to me and for having pointed out their usefulness in an ethological concept of language.

BIBLIOGRAPHY

Aarsleff, Hans (1967) *The Study of Language in England, 1780–1860*, Princeton: Princeton University Press.

―――― (1982) *From Locke to Saussure. Essays on the Study of Language and Intellectual History*, Minneapolis: University of Minnesota Press.

Adam, Lucien (1882) "La linguistique et la doctrine de l'évolution," *Revue de Linguistique et de Philologie Comparée* 15: 21–38.

―――― (1886) "De l'incorporation dans quelques langues américaines," *Revue de Linguistique et de Philologie Comparée* 19: 254–68.

Albright, Robert (1958) *The International Phonetic Alphabet: Its Backgrounds and Development*, Bloomington, Indiana: Research Center for Anthropology, Folklore, and Linguistics.

Anderson, Stephen (1985) *Phonology in the Twentieth Century. Theories of Rules and Theories of Representations*, Chicago: University of Chicago Press.

Andresen, Julie (1981) "Linguistic Metaphors in Charles de Brosses's *Traité* of 1876 and the History of Linguistics," *Linguisticae Investigationes* V, 1: 1–25.

―――― (1982) "Langage naturel et artifice linguistique," in *Condillac et les problèmes du langage*, ed. Jean Sgard, 175–88, Geneva: Slatkine.

―――― (1983) "Signs and Systems in Condillac and Saussure," *Semiotica* 44, 3/4: 259–81.

―――― (1984a) "*Arbitraire* and *Contingence* in the Semiotics of the Eighteenth Century," review of S. Auroux, *La sémiotique des Encyclopédistes*, *Semiotica* 49, 3/4: 361–80.

―――― (1984b) "Les langues amérindiennes, le comparatisme et les études franco-américaines." *Amerindia* 6: 107–125.

―――― (1985a) "Why Do We Do Linguistic Historiography?" *Semiotica* 56, 3/4: 357–70.

―――― (1985b) "Images des langues américaines au XVIIIe siècle," in *L'Homme des Lumières et la découverte de l'autre*, ed. P. Gossiaux and Daniel Droixhe, 135–45, Brussels: University of Brussels.

―――― (1985c) "Mainstream Linguistics and the Nineteenth Century," paper presented at the Annual Meeting of the Modern Language Association, Chicago.

———— (1987a) "Whitney and Bloomfield on American English," paper presented at the Annual Meeting of the Linguistic Society of America, San Francisco.

———— (1987b) "Historiographic Observations on a Current Issue in American Linguistics," in *Papers in the History of Linguistics*, ed. Hans Aarsleff, Hans-Josef Niederehe, and Louis Kelly, 647–56, Amsterdam: John Benjamins.

———— (1988a) "The Ideologues, Condillac and the Politics of Sign Theory," *Semiotica* 72, 3/4: 271–90.

———— (1988b) Review of Paul Friedrich *The Language Parallax, Language in Society* 17, 4: 600–4.

Applebee, Arthur N. (1974) *Tradition and Reform in the Teaching of English: A History*, National Council of Teachers of English.

Auroux, Sylvain (1979a) *La sémiotique des Encyclopédistes. Essai d'épistémologie historique des sciences du langage*, Paris: Payot.

———— (1979b) "La querelle des lois phonétiques," *Linguisticae Investigationes* 3, 1: 1–27.

———— (1983) "La première société de linguistique – Paris 1837?" *Historiographia Linguistica* X, 3: 241–65.

———— (1985) "Deux hypothèses sur l'origine de la conception saussurienne de la valeur linguistique," *Travaux de linguistique et de littérature* 23: 295–9.

———— (1986a) "Le sujet de la langue: la conception politique de la langue sous l'Ancien Régime et la Révolution," in *Les Idéologues, Sémiotique, théories et politiques linguistiques pendant la Révolution française*, ed. Winfried Busse and Juergen Trabant, 259–78, Amsterdam: John Benjamins.

———— (1986b) Review of G. Sampson *Schools of Linguistics, Bulletin d'information de la Société d'Histoire et d'Epistémologie des Sciences du Langage* 16: 22–4.

———— (1987) "The First Uses of the French Word 'Linguistique' (1812–1880)," in *Papers in the History of Linguistics*, ed. Hans Aarsleff, Louis Kelly, and Hans-Josef Niederehe, 447–59, Amsterdam: John Benjamins.

———— and A. Boes (1981) "Court de Gébelin (1725–1784) et le comparatisme. Deux textes inédits," *Histoire Epistémologie Langage* 3, 2: 21–67.

———— Claude Désirat, and T. Hordé (1982) "La question de l'histoire des langues et du comparatisme," *Histoire Epistémologie Langage* 4, 1: 73–81.

Baron, Dennis (1982) *Grammar and Good Taste. Reforming the American Language*, New Haven: Yale University Press.

Barton, Benjamin Smith (1797) *New Views on the Origin of the Tribes and Nations of America*, Philadelphia: by the author.

———— (1803) "Letter to Dr. Thomas Beddoes. Hints on the Etymology of certain English words, and on their affinity to words in the Languages of different European, Asiatic, and American (Indian) nations." Microprint, unnumbered. Also in *Transactions of the American Philosophical Society* for 1806.

Baugh, Albert C. (1940) "Thomas Jefferson, Linguistic Liberal," in *Studies for William A. Reed*, ed. Nathaniel E. Caffee and Thomas A. Kirby, 88–108, Baton Rouge: Louisiana State University Press.

────── and Thomas Cable (1978) *A History of the English Language*, 3rd edn, Englewood Cliffs: Prentice Hall.

Bayard, John (1910 [1780]) *Charter of the American Philosophical Society held at Philadelphia for Promoting Useful Knowledge* (Granted in 1780); *Laws and Rules of Administration and Order* (Adopted Feb. 2, 1769, amended April 15, 1910), Philadelphia: printed for the society.

Belyj, V.V. (1975) "P.S. Duponceau – the Father of American Philology: His Contribution to the Development of Americanistics," *Zeitschrift fuer Phonetik, Sprachwissenschaft und Kommunkationsforschung* 28: 41–9.

Benfey, Theodor (1869) *Geschichte der Sprachwissenschaft und orientalischen Philologie in Deutschland mit einem Rueckblick auf die frueheren Zeiten*, Munich: Cotta.

Bieder, Robert and Thomas Tax (1976) "From Ethnologists to Anthropologists: A Brief History of the American Ethnological Society," in *American Anthropology. The Early Years. 1974 Proceedings of the American Ethnological Society*, ed. John Murra, 11–22, St Paul: West.

Bloomfield, Leonard (1914) *An Introduction to the Study of Language*, new edition with an introduction by Joseph Kess, with foreword by E.F.K. Koerner, Amsterdam: John Benjamins (1983).

────── (1922) "Review of Sapir," *The Classical Weekly* 15: 142–43 (in Hockett 1970: 91–4).

────── (1923) "Review of Saussure," *The Modern Language Journal* 8: 317–19 (in Hockett 1970: 106–8).

────── (1925a) "Why a Linguistic Society?" *Language* 1: 1–5.

────── (1925b) "On the Sound-system of Central Algonquian," *Language* 1, 4: 130–56.

────── (1926) "A Set of Postulates for the Science of Language," *Language* 2, 3: 153–64.

────── (1927a) "On Recent Work in General Linguistics," *Modern Philology* 25: 211–30.

────── (1927b) "Literate and Illiterate Speech," *American Speech* 2, 10: 432–9.

────── (1928) "A Note on Sound-change," *Language* 4: 99–100.

────── (1933) *Language*, New York: Holt, Rinehart & Winston.

Bloomfield, Maurice (1884) "On the Probability of the Existence of Phonetic Laws," *American Journal of Philology* 5, 18: 178–85.

────── (1925) "Philology," *Johns Hopkins Alumni Magazine* 14: 4–10.

Boas, Franz (1902) "Rudolf Virchow's Anthropological Work," *Science* 16: 441–5 (in Stocking 1974).

────── (1911) "Introduction," in *Handbook of American Indian Languages, Part I*, 5–83, Washington: Government Printing Office.

────── (1974a [1906]) "The Outlook for the American Negro," in Stocking 1974: 310–16.

────── (1974b [1906]) "Changing the Racial Attitudes of White Americans," in Stocking 1974: 316–18.

———— (1974c [1909]) "Race Problems in America," in Stocking 1974: 318–30.

Bolling, George (1929) "Linguistics and Philology," *Language* 5, 1: 27–32.

Bourdieu, Pierre (1977) "The Economics of Linguistic Exchanges," *Social Sciences Information* 16, 6: 645–88.

———— (1982) *Ce que parler veut dire. L'économie des échanges linguistiques*, Paris: Fayard.

———— (1984 [1979]) *Distinction. A Social Critique of the Judgement of Taste*, Cambridge, MA: Harvard University Press.

Bréal, Michel (1893) "On the Canons of the Etymological Investigation," *Transactions of the American Philological Association* 24: 17–28.

Bright, William, ed. (1966) *Sociolinguistics. Proceedings of the UCLA Sociolinguistics Conference, 1964*, The Hague: Mouton.

Brinton, Daniel (1885) "Translation of Wilhelm von Humboldt's 'On the Verb in American Languages,'" *Proceedings of the American Philosophical Society* 22, 4: 332–54.

———— (1888) "Report of the Committee appointed to examine the scientific value of *Volapük*," *Proceedings of the American Philosophical Society* 25: 3–17.

———— (1890) *Essays of an Americanist*, Philadelphia: Porter & Coates.

———— (1891) *The American Race: A Linguistic Classification and Ethnographic Description of the Native Tribes of North and South America*, New York: N.D.C. Hodges.

———— (1894) "Address by the President. The 'Nation' as an Element in Anthropology," in *Memoirs of the International Congress of Anthropology, held at Chicago in 1893*, ed. C. Staniland Wake, 19–34, Chicago: The Schulte Publishing Company.

Bruce, Philip (1920) *History of the University of Virginia 1819–1919*, vol. II *The Lengthened Shadow of One Man*, New York: Macmillan.

Bruce, Robert (1987) *The Launching of Modern American Science 1846–1876*, Ithaca: Cornell University Press.

Burnet, James (Lord Monboddo) (1970 [1774]) *On the Origin and Progress of Language* vol. I, Edinburgh and New York: Garland Facsimile Publishing.

Cameron, Deborah (1985) *Feminism and Linguistic Theory*, New York: St Martin's.

Campbell, Lyle (1988) Review of *Language in the Americas* by Joseph Greenberg (1987, Stanford University Press), *Language* 64, 3: 591–615.

Cass, Lewis (1826) "Indians of North America," *North American Review* 22: 53–93.

Charency, Hyacinthe de (1902) "Etudes algiques," *Journal de la Société des Américanistes de Paris* 4, 1: 8–54.

Chaumonot, P.J.M. (1831 [164?]) "Grammaire de la langue huronne," in J.K. Wilkie, *Grammar of the Huron Language, Transactions of the Literary and Historical Society of Quebec* 2: 94–198, Quebec.

Chomsky, Noam (1965) *Aspects of the Theory of Syntax*, Cambridge, MA: MIT Press.

———— (1966) *Cartesian Linguistics*, New York: Harper & Row.

Christy, Craig (1983) *Uniformitarianism in Linguistics*, Amsterdam: John Benjamins.

Cowgill, Warren (1986) "Einleitung," *Indogermanische Grammatik I*, ed. W. Cowgill and M. Mayrhofer, Heidelberg: Winter.

Darnell, Regna (1967) "Daniel Garrison Brinton: An Intellectual Biography," MA thesis, Philadelphia: University of Pennsylvania.

——— (1970a) "The Development of American Anthropology 1879–1920: From the Bureau of American Ethnology to Franz Boas," University of Pennsylvania, PhD dissertation. Ann Arbor: University Microfilms.

——— (1970b) "The Emergence of Academic Anthropology at the University of Pennsylvania," *Journal of the History of the Behavioral Sciences* 6: 80–92.

——— (1971) "The Professionalization of American Anthropology: A Case Study in the Sociology of Knowledge," *Social Science Information* 10, 1–3: 83–103.

——— (1984) "The Sapir Years at the Canadian National Museum in Ottawa," in *Edward Sapir. Appraisals of his Life and Work*, ed. E.F.K. Koerner, 159–78, Amsterdam: John Benjamins.

Désirat, Claude and Hordé, T. (1982) "Introduction," *Histoire, Epistémologie, Langage* 4, 1: 15–20.

Dillard, J.L. (1975) *All-American English*, New York: Random House.

Drake, Glendon (1977) *The Role of Prescriptivism in American Linguistics, 1820–1970*, Amsterdam: John Benjamins.

Duponceau, Peter Stephen (1818) "English Phonology," *Transactions of the American Philosophical Society*, n.s. I: 228–64.

——— (1819) "Report of the Historical and Literary Committee to the American Philosophical Society," *Transactions of the Historical and Literary Committee of the American Philosophical Society* 1: xi–xvi.

——— (1838) *Mémoire su le système grammatical des langues de quelques nations indiennes de l'Amérique du nord*, Paris: A. Pihan de la Forest.

Eble, Connie (1987) "Louise Pound and American English," paper read at the Southeastern Conference on Linguistics.

Eliot, John (1666) *The Indian Grammar Begun; or an Essay to Bring the Indian Language into Rules*. Cambridge, MA. (Repr. in *Collections of the Massachusetts Historical Society Series* 2, 9: 243–312. Boston, 1832.)

Emerson, Ralph Waldo (1985 [1836]) *Nature, as Natural History and as Human History*, introduction by Jaroslav Pelikan, Boston: Beacon Press.

——— (1911 [1883]) *The Complete Works of Ralph Waldo Emerson*, vol. X: *Lectures and Biographical Sketches*, Boston and New York: Houghton Mifflin.

Fay, Edwin (1895) "The Invariability of Phonetic Law," *Transactions of the American Philological Association* 26: lxiii–lxvi.

Finegan, Edward (1980) *Attitudes Toward English Usage. The History of the War of Words*, New York: Teacher's College Press, Teachers College, Columbia University.

Foucault, Michel (1966) *Les Mots et les choses. Une archéologie des science humaines*, Paris: Gallimard.

Franklin, Benjamin (1848 [1789]) *The Works of Dr. Benjamin Franklin: Consisting of Essays, Humorous, Moral, and Literary: With his Life, Written by Himself*, Hartford: S. Andrus and Son.

Franklin, Phyllis (1978) "English Studies in America: Reflections on the Development of a Discipline," *American Quarterly* 30, 1: 21–38.

—— (1984) "English Studies: The World of Scholarship in 1883," *Publications of the Modern Language Association* 99,3: 356–70.

Friedrich, Paul (1986) *The Language Parallax. Linguistic Relativism and Poetic Indeterminacy*, Austin: University of Texas Press.

Friend, Joseph (1967) *The Development of American Lexicography 1798–1864*, The Hague: Mouton.

Gallatin, Albert (1836) "A Synopsis of the Indian Tribes of North America," *Transactions and Collections of the American Antiquarian Society* 2: 1–422.

—— (1843) "Inaugural Address to the New-York Historical Society," New York: printed for the society.

Gamkrelidze, Tamaz and V.V. Ivanov (1980) "On the Reconstruction of the Proto-Indo-European Stops. Glottalized Stops in Indo-European," in *Typology Relationship and Time*, ed. and trans. Vitalij Sheveroshkin and T.L. Markey, Ann Arbor: Karoma.

Gildersleeve, Basil (1880) "Editorial Note," *American Journal of Philology* 1, 1: 1–3.

Goddard, Pliny Earle (1914) "The Present Condition of our Knowledge of North American Languages," *American Anthropologist*, n.s. 16: 555–601.

Golla, Victor, ed. (1984) *The Sapir-Kroeber Correspondence (1905–1925)*, Berkeley: Survey of Californian and Other Indian Languages.

Greenberg, Joseph (1987) *Language in the Americas*, Palo Alto: Stanford University Press.

Greene, Joan (1985) "Civilize the Indian: Government Policies, Quakers, and Cherokee Education," *Journal of Cherokee Studies* 10, 2: 192–204.

Grimm, Jacob and Wilhelm Grimm (1854) *Deutsches Woeterbuch*, Leipzig: S. Hirzel.

Guice, Stephen (1987) "A Chapter in the Early History of American Linguistics," paper read at the Annual Meeting of the Modern Language Association, San Francisco.

Haas, Mary (1967) "Roger Williams' Sound Shift: A Study in Algonkian [sic]," in *To Honor Roman Jakobson: Essays on the Occasion of his Seventieth Birthday*, vol. 1: 816–32, The Hague: Mouton.

—— (1969a) "'Exclusive' and 'Inclusive': A Look at Early Usage," *International Journal of American Linguistics* 35, 1: 1–6.

—— (1969b) "Grammar or Lexicon? The American Indian side of the Question from Duponceau to Powell," *International Journal of American Linguistics* 35: 239–55.

—— (1978) "Boas, Sapir, and Bloomfield: Their Contribution to American Indian Linguistics," in *Language, Culture, and History. Essays by Mary R. Haas*, selected and introduced by Answar S. Dil, 194–206, Stanford: Stanford University Press.

Haiman, John, ed. (1985) *Iconicity in Syntax*, with "Introduction", 1–7, Amsterdam/Philadelphia: John Benjamins.

Hall, Robert A., Jr, ed. (1987) *Leonard Bloomfield: Appraisals of his Life and Work*, special edition of *Historiographia Linguistica* 14, 1/2.

Hanzel, Victor (1969) *Missionary Linguistics in New France. A Study of Seventeenth- and Eighteenth-Century Descriptions of American Indian Languages*, The Hague: Mouton.

Harris, Roy (1980) *The Language-Makers*, Ithaca: Cornell University Press.

———— (1987) *Reading Saussure*, La Salle, IL: Open Court.

Harrison, James (1884) "Negro English," *Anglia Zeitschrift fuer Englische Philologie* 7: 232–79.

Hart, J.M. (1884) "The College Course in English Literature, How it may be Improved," *Proceedings of the Modern Language Association of America*, December 29, 30, 1884: x–xiii, Baltimore: MLA.

Hauer, Stanley (1983) "Thomas Jefferson and the Anglo-Saxon Language," *Publications of the Modern Language Association* 98, 5: 879–98.

Heath Shirley (1977) "A National Language Academy? Debate in the New Nation," *Linguistics. An International Review* 189: 9–43.

———— (1982) "American English: Quest for a Model," in *The Other Tongue. English across Cultures*, ed. Braj Kachru, 237–49, Urbana: University of Illinois Press.

Heckewelder, John (1881 [1819]) *An Account of the History, Manners, and Customs of the Indian Nations, who once inhabited Pennsylvania and the Neighbouring States*, Philadelphia: Abraham Small.

Hempl, George (1896) "Grease and Greasy," *Dialect Notes* 1: 438–44.

Herbst, Jurgen (1965) *The German Historical School in American Scholarship. A Study in the Transfer of Culture*, Ithaca: Cornell University Press.

Herder, Johann G. (1959 [1770]) *Ueber den Ursprung der Sprache*, Berlin: Akademie-Verlag.

Hockett, Charles, ed. (1970) *A Leonard Bloomfield Anthology*, Bloomington: Indiana University Press.

———— (1980) "Preserving the Heritage," in *First Person Singular*, ed. Boyd David and R. O'Cain, 99–107, Amsterdam: John Benjamins.

———— (1987) "Letters from Bloomfield to Michelson and Sapir," *Historiographia Linguistica* XIV, 1/2: 39–60.

Hoenigswald, Henry (1963) "On the History of the Comparative Method," *Anthropological Linguistics* 5, 1: 1–11.

———— (1966) "A Proposal for the Study of Folk-Linguistics," in Bright 1966: 16–26.

———— (1974) "Fallacies in the History of Linguistics: Notes on the Appraisal of the Nineteenth Century," in *Studies in the History of Linguistics. Traditions and Paradigms*, ed. Dell Hymes, 346–58, Bloomington: Indiana University Press.

Howard, Leon (1930) "Towards a Historical Aspect of American Speech Consciousness," *American Speech* 5, 4: 301–5.

Hymes, Dell (1974) "Introduction, Traditions and Paradigms", in *Studies in the History of Linguistics*, ed. D. Hymes, 1–38, Bloomington: Indiana University Press.

——— (1980) "In Five-Year Patterns," in *First Person Singular. Papers from the Conference on an Oral Archive for the History of American Linguistics*, ed. Boyd David and Raymond O'Cain, 203–13, Amsterdam: John Benjamins.

——— (1983) *Essays in the History of Linguistics Anthropology*, Studies in the Theory and History of Linguistics, vol. 25, Amsterdam: John Benjamins.

——— and John Fought (1981 [1975]) "American Structuralism," *Current Trends in Linguistics. Historiography of Linguistics. XIII*, ed. T. Seboek, 903–1176, The Hague: Mouton. (Repr. as *American Structuralism*, The Hague: Mouton, 1981.)

Jakobson, Roman (1944) "Franz Boas' Approach to Language," *International Journal of American Linguistics* 10, 4: 188–95.

——— (1959) "Boas' View of Grammatical Meaning," in *The Anthropology of Franz Boas. Essays on the Centennial of his Birth*, ed. Walter Goldschmidt, *American Anthropologist* 61, 5: 2, *Memoir* 89: 139–45.

——— (1965) "Quest for the Essence of Language," *Diogenes* 51: 21–37. (Repr. in *Selected Writings* II: 345–59, The Hague: Mouton, 1971.)

——— (1971) "The World Response to Whitney's Principles of Linguistic Science," in *Whitney on Language*, ed. Michael Silverstein, xxv–xlv, Cambridge, MA: MIT Press.

——— (1979) "The Twentieth Century in European and American Linguistics: Movements and Continuity," in *The European Background of American Linguistics. Papers on the Third Golden Anniversary Symposium of the Linguistics Society of America*, ed. H. Hoenigswald, 161–73, Dordrecht: Foris.

Jefferson, Thomas (1950) *Basic Writings of Thomas Jefferson*, ed. Philip Foner, Garden City, NY: Halcyon House.

Joseph, John (1987a) "Bloomfield's Saussureanism," paper given at the Annual Meeting of the Linguistics Society of America, San Francisco.

——— (1987b) *Eloquence and Power. The Rise of Language Standards and Standard Languages*, New York: Basil Blackwell.

Kemp, J. Alan, ed. (1981 [1863]) *Standard Alphabet for Reducing Unwritten Languages and Foreign Graphic Systems to a Uniform Orthography in European Letters*, Amsterdam: John Benjamins.

King, Duane (1977) "Who Really Discovered the Cherokee–Iroquois Linguistic Relationship," *Journal of Cherokee Studies* 2, 4: 401–4.

Kluckhohn, Clyde and Olaf Prufer (1959) "Influences During the Formative Years," in *The Anthropology of Franz Boas. Essays on the Centennial of his Birth*, ed. by Walter Goldschmidt. *American Anthropologist* 61, 5: 2, *Memoir* 89: 4–28.

Koerner, E.F.K. (1973) *Ferdinand de Saussure. Origin and Development of his Linguistic Though in Western Studies of Language*, Braunschweig: Vieweg.

——— (1977) "1876 as a Turning Point in the History of Linguistics," *Journal of Indo-European Studies* 4, 4: 333–53.

——— (1979) "L'importance de William Dwight Whitney pour les jeunes linguistes de Leipzig et pour F. De Saussure," in *Festschrift for Oswald Szemerényi*, ed. Bela Brogyanyi, 437–54, Amsterdam: John Benjamins.

—— (1982) "On the Historical Roots of the Philology/Linguistics Controversy," in *Papers from the Fifth International Conference on Historical Linguistics*, ed. Anders Ahlqvist, 404–13, Amsterdam: John Benjamins.

—— ed. (1984) *Edward Sapir. Appraisals of his Life and Work*, Amsterdam: John Benjamins.

—— (1986a) "Aux sources de la sociolinguistique," *Linguisticae Investigationes* 10, 2: 381–401.

—— (1986b) "Preface," *Historiographia Linguistica* 13, 1: i–iv.

Kramarae, Cheris and Paula Triechler (1985) *A Feminist Dictionary*, Boston: Pandora Press.

Krapp, George (1924) "The Test of English," *American Mercury* 1, 1: 94–8.

Krebs, John and Richard Dawkins (1984) "Animal Signals: Mind-Reading and Manipulation." in *Behavioural Ecology: An Evolutionary Approach*, 2nd edn, ed. J.R. Krebs and N.B. Davies, 380–402, Sunderland, MA: Sinauer Associates.

Kuhn, Thomas (1962) *The Structure of Scientific Revolutions*, Chicago: University of Chicago Press.

Labov, William (1972) *Sociolinguistic Patterns*, Philadelphia: University of Pennsylvania Press.

Ladefoged, Peter and Morris Halle (1988) "Some Major Features of the International Phonetic Alphabet," *Language* 64, 3: 577–82.

Laird, Charlton (1946) "Etymology, Anglo-Saxon, and Noah Webster," *American Speech* 21, 1: 3–15.

—— (1966) "Diversions of *The Diversions of Purley* in the New World," *Rendezvous: Idaho State University Journal of Arts and Letters* 1: 1–11.

Language Files. Materials for an Introduction to Language (1987) Compilers of the 4th edn: Carolyn McManis, Deborah Stollenwerk, Zhang Zheng-Sheng, Reynoldsburg, Ohio: Advocate.

Lanman, Charles, ed. (1897) *A Report of that Session of the First American Congress of Philologists, which was devoted to the memory of the late Professor William Dwight Whitney, of Yale University; held at Philadelphia, Dec. 28, 1894.* Boston: Ginn and Company (= *Journal of the American Oriental Society* 19). Also printed separately as *The Whitney Memorial Meeting.* Boston: Ginn & Co.

Leechman, Douglas and Robert Hall, Jr (1955) "American Indian Pidgin English: Attestations and Grammatical Peculiarities," *American Speech* 30, 3: 163–71.

Lehmann, Winfred (1986) "The Changing Picture of Indo-European," paper presented at University of North Carolina, Chapel Hill.

Lenneberg, Eric (1967) *Biological Foundations of Language*, New York: John Wiley.

Leopold, Joan (1984) "Duponceau, Humboldt et Pott: la place structurale des concepts de 'polysynthèse' et d'"incorporation,'" *Amerindia* 6: 65–77.

Lepsius, Karl Richard (1855) *Das allgemeine linguistische Alphabet*, Berlin: Hertz.

—— (1863) *Standard Alphabet for Reducing Unwritten Languages and Foreign Graphic Systems to a Uniform Orthography in European Letters*, 2nd edn, London: William & Norgate.

Lieber, Francis, ed. (1829–33) *Encyclopedia Americana*, 13 vols, Philadelphia: Carey & Lea.

—— (1860) "Plan of thought of the American Languages," in *Archives of Aboriginal Knowledge*, vol. II, ed. by H.R. Schoolcraft, Philadelphia: Lippincott.

—— (1880 [1837; 1850]) *Miscellaneous Writings*, vol. I: *Reminiscences, Addresses, and Essays*, Philadelphia and London: J.B. Lippincott.

Lightfoot, David (1983) *The Language Lottery: Toward a Biology of Grammars*, Cambridge, MA: MIT Press.

Lowie, Robert (1924) "The Origin and Spread of Cultures," *American Mercury* 1, 4: 463–5.

MacCurdy, George (1921–2) "American Linguistics in 1852," *International Journal of American Linguistics* 2: 74–5.

Malefijt, Annemarie de Waal (1977) *Images of Man. A History of Anthropological Thought*, New York: Knopf.

Malone, Kemp (1925) "A Linguistic Patriot," *American Speech* 1: 26–31.

Marsh, George P. (1860) *Lectures on the English Language*, New York: Charles Scribner.

Meillet, Antoine and Marcel Cohen (1924) *Les Langues du monde*, Paris: E. Champion.

Mencken, Henry L. (1919) *The American Language. A Preliminary Inquiry into the Development of English in the United States*, New York: Knopf.

—— (1924) "Editorial," *American Mercury* 1, 1: 27–30.

—— (1963 [1921, 1923, 1936, 1945]) *The American Language, An Inquiry into the Development of English in the United States*, 4th edn and two supplements abridged, with annotations and new material by Raven I. McDavid Jr, New York: Knopf.

Michelson, Karen (1981) "A Philological Investigation into Seventeenth-Century Mohawk," *International Journal of American Linguistics* 47, 2: 91–102.

Miller, Michael (1983) "A Jacksonian View of American English," *Revue française d'études américaines* 18: 397–403.

Miner, Kenneth (1974) "John Eliot of Massachusetts and the Beginnings of American linguistics," *Historiographia Linguistica* 1, 2: 169–83.

Monteith, Carmeleta (1984) "Literacy Among the Cherokee in the Early Nineteenth Century," *Journal of Cherokee Studies* 9, 2: 56–75.

Morgan, Lewis Henry (1877) *Ancient Society. Researches in the Lines of Human Progress from Savagery through Barbarism to Civilization*, New York: H. Holt.

Moss, Richard (1984) *Noah Webster*, Boston: Twayne.

Mueller-Vollmer, Kurt (1974) "Wilhelm von Humboldt und der Anfang der amerikanischen Sprachwissenschaft: Die Briefe an John Pickering," in *Universalismus und Wissenschaft im Werk und Wirken der Brueder Humboldt*, ed. Klaus Hammacher, 259–334, Frankfurt: Klostermann.

Murray, Stephen (1981) "The Canadian 'Winter' of Edward Sapir," *Historiographia Linguistica* 8: 63–8.

———— (1985) "A Pre-Boasian Sapir?" *Historiographia Linguistica* 12: 267-9.

———— (1986) "Edward Sapir's Coursework in Linguistics and Anthropology," *Historiographia Linguistica* 13, 1: 125-9.

Newmeyer, Frederick (1986 [1980]) *Linguistic Theory in America. The First Twenty-Five Years of Transformational Generative Grammar*, 2nd edn, New York: Academic Press.

———— (1986) *The Politics of Linguistics*, Chicago: University of Chicago Press.

Ogden, Charles and I.A. Richards (1930 [1923]) *The Meaning of Meaning. A Study of The Influence of Language upon Thought and of The Science of Symbolism*, 3rd edn, New York: Harcourt, Brace & Company.

Paine, Charles (1987) "Noah Webster, that Old American Standard," unpublished term paper, Duke University.

Parker, Geoffrey (1984) "Evolutionarily Stable Strategies," in *Behavioural Ecology: An Evolutionary Approach*, 2nd edn, ed. J.R. Krebs and N.B. Davies, 30-61, Sunderland, MA: Sinauer Associates.

Parker, William Riley (1967) "Where Do English Departments Come From?" *College English* 28, 5: 339-51.

Pedersen, Holger (1931) *Linguistic Science in the Nineteenth Century*, trans. by J. Spargo, Cambridge, MA: Harvard University Press. (Re-issued with main title, *The Discovery of Language*, Bloomington: Indiana University Press, 1962.)

Perry, Thomas, ed. (1882) *The Life and Letters of Francis Lieber*, Boston: James R. Osgood.

Pickering, John (1816) *A Vocabulary or Collection of Words and Phrases which have been supposed to be Peculiar to the United States of America*, to which is printed *An Essay on the Present State of the English Language in the United States*, together with Noah Webster's "A Letter to the Honorable John Pickering" (1817), New York: Burt Franklin Reprints.

———— (1819) Art. X and XI. "Review of Heckewelder (1819) and Duponceau (1819)," *North American Review* 9: 155-78; 179-87.

———— (1820a) Art. VII. "Discourse on the Religion of the Indian Tribes of North America; delivered before the New York Historical Society, December 20, 1819. By Samuel Farmer Jarvis," *North American Review* 11, n.s. II: 103-13.

———— (1820b) *An Essay on a Uniform Orthography for the Indian Languages of North America*, as published in the Memoirs of the American Academy of Arts and Sciences, Cambridge: Cambridge University Press; Hilliard & Metcalf.

———— (1822) Art. XI. "Review of *Uebersicht aller bekannten Sprachen und ihrer Dialekte*. By Friedrich Adelung," *North American Review* 14: 128-44.

———— (1830) "Americanism," *Encyclopedia Americana* I: 210-11.

———— (1830-1) "Indians" and "Indian Languages of America." *Encyclopedia Americana*, vol. VI: 569-75 and 581-600, Philadelphia: Carey & Lea.

———— (1834) *Ueber die indianischen Sprachen Amerikas*, aus dem Englischen des Nordamerikaners Herrn John Pickering, uebersetzt und mit Anmerkungen begleitet von Talvj, Leipzig: Friedr. Christ. Wilh. Vogel.

—— (1849a [1842]) "Presidential Address," *Journal of the American Oriental Society* 1: 1–60; with Appendix 61–78.

—— (1849b [1844]) "Necrology for Peter S. Duponceau, LL.D," *Journal of the American Oriental Society* 1: 161–70.

Pickering, Mary Orne (1887) *Life of John Pickering*, Boston: printed for private distribution.

Pound, Louise (1949) *Selected Writings of Louise Pound*, with foreword by Arthur Kennedy, Lincoln: University of Nebraska Press.

—— (1952) "The American Dialect Society. A Historical Sketch," *Publications of the American Dialect Society* 17: 3–28.

Powell, John W. (1877) *Introduction to the Study of Indian Languages, with Words, Phrases, and Sentences to be Collected*, Washington: Government Printing Office.

—— (1880) *Introduction to the Study of Indian Languages, with Words Phrases and Sentences to be Collected*, 2nd edn with charts, Washington: Government Printing Office.

—— (1891) *Indian Linguistic Families of America North of Mexico*, BAEAR 7, for 1885–6: 7–139.

Pyles, Thomas (1952) *Words and Ways of American English*, New York: Random.

Read, Allen Walker (1934) "The Philological Society of New York, 1788," *American Speech* 9, 3: 131–6.

—— (1938) "Suggestions for an Academy in England in the Latter Half of the Eighteenth Century," *Modern Philology* 36: 145–56.

—— (1939a) "The Speech of Negroes in Colonial America," *The Journal of Negro History* 24, 3: 247–58.

—— (139b) "Edward Everett's Attitude Towards American English," *New England Quarterly* 12, 1: 112–29.

—— (1966) "The Spread of German Linguistic Learning in New England during the Lifetime of Noah Webster," *American Speech* 41, 3: 163–81.

Rivet, Paul (1925) "Les Australiens en Amérique," *Bulletin de la Société Linguistique de Paris* 26: 23–63.

Robins, Robert (1987) "Duponceau and Early Nineteenth-Century Linguistics," in *Papers in the History of Linguistics*, ed. H. Aarsleff, Louis Kelly, and Hans-Joseph Niederehe, 435–46, Amsterdam: John Benjamins.

Rocher, Rosane (1979) "The Past up to the Introduction of Neogrammarian Thought: Whitney and Europe," in *The European Background of American Linguistics. Papers of the Third Golden Anniversary Symposium of the Linguistics Society of America*, ed. Henry Hoenigswald, 5–22, Dordrecht: Foris.

Rollins, Richard (1980) *The Long Journey of Noah Webster*, Pittsburgh: University of Pennsylvania Press.

Rousseau, Jean (1981) "R. Rask (1787–1832) et la transcription des langues amérindiennes – une lettre inédite à J. Pickering," *Histoire epistémologie langage* 3, 2: 69–83.

Rousseau, Jean-Jacques (1968 [1781]) *Essai sur l'origine des langues*, texte établi par Charles Porset, Ducros: Bordeaux.

Sagard-Théodat, G. (1865 [1636]) *Le Grand voyage du pays des Hurons* . . . *avec un Dictionnaire de la langue huronne*, Paris: Librairie Tross.

Sampson, Geoffrey (1980) *Schools of Linguistics*, Stanford University Press.

—— (1987) Review of D. Rumelhart, J. McClelland, *et al.*, *Parallel Distributed Processing: Explorations in the microstructures of cognition*, *Language* 63, 4: 871–86.

Sapir, Edward (1913a) "Wiyot and Yorok, Algonkin languages of California," *American Anthropologist* 15: 617–46.

—— (1913b) "Southern Paiute and Nahuatl. A Study in Uto-Aztekan," *Journal de la Société des Américanistes de Paris* 10, 2: 379–425.

—— (1914) "Southern Paiute and Nahuatl. A Study in Uto-Aztekan, Part II," *Journal de la Société des Américanistes de Paris* 11, 2: 443–88.

—— (1916) *Time Perspective in Aboriginal American Culture, a Study in Method*, Canada Department of Mines Geological Survey, Memoir 90, Ottawa: Government Printing Bureau.

—— (1917) "Linguistic Publications of the Bureau of American Ethnology, A General Review," *International Journal of American Linguistics* 1: 76–81.

—— (1921) *Language*, New York: Harcourt, Brace, & World.

—— (1924) "The Grammarian and His Language," *American Mercury* 1, 2: 149–55.

—— (1925a) "Sound Patterns in Language," *Language* 1: 37–51.

—— (1925b) Review of A. Meillet and M. Cohen, *Les Langues du monde*, *Modern Language Notes* 40: 373–8.

—— (1929) "The Status of Linguistics as a Science," *Language* 5: 207–14 (in Sapir 1949).

—— (1931) "The Concept of Phonetic Law as Tested in Primitive Languages by Leonard Bloomfield," in *Methods in Social Science*, ed. S.A. Rice, 297–306, Chicago: University of Chicago Press. (Repr. in Sapir 1949.)

—— (1949) *Selected Writing in Language, Culture, and Personality*, ed. David Mandelbaum, Berkeley: University of California Press.

—— (1984 [1907]) "Herder's *Ursprung der Sprache*," *Historiographia Linguistica* 11, 3: 355–88. (Repr. of: *Modern Philology* 5: 109–42.)

Saussure, F. de (1922 [1916]) *Cours de linguistique générale*, 2nd edn, ed. Charles Bally and Albert Sechehaye, Paris: Payot.

Schleicher, August (1983 [1850]) *Die Sprachen Europas in systematischer Uebersicht: Linguistische Untersuchungen*, new edition, with an introductory article by Konrad Koerner, Amsterdam: John Benjamins.

Schoolcraft, Henry (1962 [1826–7]) *The Literary Voyager or Muzzeniequn*, ed. with an introduction by Philip Mason, Westport, CT: Greenwood Press.

—— (1860) *Archives of Aboriginal Knowledge. Containing all the Original Papers laid before Congress respecting the History, Antiquities, Language, Ethnology, Pictography, Rites, Superstitions, and Mythology, of the Indian Tribes of the United States*, 6 vols, Philadelphia: Lippincott.

Silverstein, Michael, ed. (1971) *Whitney on Language, Selected Writings of*

William Dwight Whitney, with introduction, vii–xxiii, and an introductory essay by Roman Jakobson, Cambridge, MA: MIT Press.

Simon, Herbert (1962) "The Architecture of Complexity," *Proceedings of the American Philosophical Society* 106, 6: 467–82.

Simpson, David (1986) *The Politics of American English, 1776–1850*, New York: Oxford University Press.

Smith, Barbara Herrnstein (1988) *Contingencies of Value. Alternative Perspectives for Critical Theory*, Cambridge, MA: Harvard University Press.

Smith, Murphy (1983) "Peter Stephen Duponceau and his Study of Languages: A Historical Account," *Proceedings of the American Philosophical Society* 127, 3: 143–79.

Smout, Kary (forthcoming) "Apolitical Linguistics?" *American Speech*.

Spiller, Robert, ed. (1967) *The American Literary Revolution 1783–1837*, New York: University Press.

Stocking, George W., Jr (1974) *The Shaping of American Anthropology 1883–1911. A Franz Boas Reader*, New York: Basic Books.

Studdert-Kennedy, Michael, ed. (1983) *The Psychobiology of Language*, Cambridge, MA: MIT Press.

Swiggers, Pierre (1982) "De Girard à Saussure: Sur l'histoire du terme 'valeur' en linguistique," *Travaux de linguistique de littérature* 20, 1: 325–31.

—— (1984a) *Les Conceptions linguistiques des Encyclopédistes*, Heidelberg: Julius Groos.

—— (1984b) "Les Langues amérindiennes à la société de linguistique de Paris (1863–1982)," *Amerindia* 6: 383–404.

Tannen, Deborah (1987) "Repetition in Conversation: Toward a Poetics of Talk," *Language* 63, 3: 574–605.

Tarbell, Frank (1886) "Phonetic Law," *Transactions of the American Philological Association* 17: 5–16.

Taylor, Talbot (1989) "The Linguistic Sign and Free Will," in *Ideologies of Linguistics*, ed. T. Taylor and J. Joseph, London: Routledge.

Thwaites, R.G. (1987 [1636]) *Jesuit Relations and Allied Documents*, vol. 10, 117–23, Cleveland: Burrows Brothers.

Toumi, Sybille (1984) "Les Congrès des Américanistes: Quelques remarques," *Amerindia* 6: 367–81.

Toy, Crawford H. (1880) Review of Mallery *Introduction to the Study of Sign-Language among the North American Indians as illustrating the Gesture-Speech of Mankind*, *American Journal of Philology* 1, 2: 206–8.

Traugott, Elizabeth Closs (1985) "On Regularity in Semantic Change," *Journal of Literary Semantics* 14, 3: 155–73.

Trumbull, J. Hammond (1869–70a) "On the best Method of Studying the North American Languages," *Transactions of the American Philological Association* 1: 55–79.

—— (1869–70b) "On some Mistaken Notions of Algonkin Grammar, and on Mistranslations of Words from Eliot's Bible," *Transactions of the American Philological Association* 1: 105–23.

Uhlenbeck, E.M. (1979) "Linguistics in America 1924–1974. A Detached View," in *The European Background of American Linguistics. Papers of the*

Third Golden Anniversary Symposium of the Linguistics Society of America, ed. Henry Hoenigswald, 121–44, Dordrecht: Foris.

Vine, Brent (1988) Review of *Indoevropejskij jazyk i indoevropejcy* (1984) by Tamaz Gamrelidge and V.V. Ivanov, *Language* 64, 2: 396–402.

Warfel, Harry (1936) *Noah Webster: Schoolmaster to America*, New York: Macmillan.

Webster, Noah (1806) *Compendious Dictionary*, Hartford: Sidney's Press for Hudson & Goodwin; New Haven: Increase Cooke & Co.

—— (1817) "A Letter to the Honorable John Pickering," New York: Burt Franklin Reprints. Original letter appeared in the *North American Review* 5: 82–98.

—— (1828) *The American Dictionary of the English Language*, New York: S. Converse.

Weiss, Albert (1925) "Linguistics and Psychology," *Language* 1: 52–7.

Whitney, William Dwight (1861) "On Lepsius's Standard Alphabet," *Journal of the American Oriental Society* 7: 299–332 (in Silverstein 1971: 215–48).

—— (1869–70) "On the Present Condition of the Question as to the Origin of Language," *Transactions of the American Philological Association* 1: 84–94.

—— (1872) "On Material and Form in Language," *Transactions of the American Philological Association* 3: 77–96.

—— (1875) "Are Languages Institutions?" *Contemporary Review* 25: 713–32.

—— (1877) "The Principle of Economy as a Phonetic Force," *Transactions of the American Philological Association* 8: 123–34 (in Silverstein 1971).

—— (1880) "Logical Consistency in Views of Language," *American Journal of Philology* 1: 327–43.

—— (1887 [1867]) *Language and the Study of Language. Twelve Lectures on the Principles of Linguistic Science*, 5th edn, New York: Charles Scribner's. (*Die Sprachwissenschaft: W.D. Whitney's Vorlesungen ueber die Principien der vergleichenden Sprachforschung*, trans. Julius Jolly, Munich: Th. Ackermann, 1874.)

—— ed. (1889–91) *Century Dictionary and Cyclopedia*, 10 vols, New York: The Century Company.

—— (1892 [1877]) *Essentials of English Grammar for the Use of Schools*, Boston: Ginn.

—— (1894) "Examples of Sporadic and Partial Phonetic Change in English," *Indogermanische Forschungen* 4: 32–6.

—— (1896 [1875]) *The Life and Growth of Language. An Outline of Linguistic Science*, New York: D. Appleton. (*Leben und Wachstum der Sprache*, trans. August Leskein, Leipzig, F.A. Brockhaus, 1876.)

—— (1951 [1789]) *Dissertations on the English Language*, with an introduction by Harry Warfel, Gainesville, FL: Scholars Facsimiles and Reprints.

—— (1971 [1875]) "Phusei or Thesei – Natural or Conventional?" *Transactions of the American Philological Association for 1874*: 95–116 (in Silverstein 1971: 111–32).

Willard, Sidney (1817) Art. V. "A Letter to the Honourable John Pickering on the Subject of his Vocabulary," *North American Review* 5: 82–98.

Williams, Roger (1973 [1643]) *A Key into the Language of America*, edited with a critical Introduction, Notes and a Commentary by John J. Teunissen and Evelyn J. Hinz, Detroit: Wayne State University Press.

Wissler, Clark (1942) "The American Indian and the American Philosophical Society," *Proceedings of the American Philosophical Society*, 86: 189–204.

Wolfart, H. Christoph (1982) "Historical Linguistics and Metaphilology," in *Papers from the 5th International Conference on Historical Linguistics*, ed. Anders Ahlqvist, 394–403, Amsterdam: John Benjamins.

INDEX OF NAMES

INDEX OF SUBJECTS